PURGING
your HOUSE,
PRUNING your
FAMILY TREE

PURGING your HOUSE, PRUNING your FAMILY TREE

PERRY STONE

Charisma
HOUSE
A STRANG COMPANY

Most STRANG COMMUNICATIONS BOOK GROUP products are available at special quantity discounts for bulk purchase for sales promotions, premiums, fund-raising, and educational needs. For details, write Strang Communications Book Group, 600 Rinehart Road, Lake Mary, Florida 32746, or telephone (407) 333-0600.

PURGING YOUR HOUSE, PRUNING YOUR FAMILY TREE by Perry Stone
Published by Charisma House
A Strang Company
600 Rinehart Road
Lake Mary, Florida 32746
www.strangbookgroup.com

Cover design by Justin Evans
Design Director: Bill Johnson

Visit the author's website at www.voe.org.

Library of Congress Cataloging-in-Publication Data
Stone, Perry F.
  Purging your house, pruning your family tree / Perry Stone. -- 1st ed.
     p. cm.
  Includes bibliographical references.
  ISBN 978-1-61638-186-8
  1. Families--Religious life. 2. Blessing and cursing. 3. Spiritual warfare. 4. Christian life--Church of God authors. I. Title.
  BV4526.3.S76 2011
  235'.4--dc22
                          2010039946

E-book ISBN: 978-1-61638-265-0

First Edition

11 12 13 14 15 — 987654321
Printed in the United States of America

Contents

Introduction

Do the following questions express what you have felt—or asked—in the past?

- Does a *weeping willow* describe your family tree?
- Do you secretly wish you had been born to a different family?
- Did you pick up some *bad DNA* from someone in your lineage?
- Would you like to put on a new set of *genes* and make a new you?
- Is there a warfare going on that you won't talk about?
- What are the keys to a happy home and marriage?

If so, keep reading! There are two important ways for you to alter your present personal situations and prepare for a great emotional and spiritual future—by purging your house and pruning your family tree. Purging your house involves removing spiritual, emotional, and mental hindrances from the three houses that I will discuss in this book. Pruning your family tree involves a process I call redemptive alterations that positively impact your future when the Word of God defeats the sin habits and overcomes the carnal nature through regeneration.

Jonathan Edwards

Jonathan Edwards was married in 1727. He was one of the most noted and respected early preachers in the early American colonies. His classic message, "Sinners in the Hands of an Angry God," was so convicting that the unrepentant sitting under his preaching would cry out in anguish, dropping to the floor. Yet many are unaware that in Edwards's private life, he was a very loving, compassionate man who spent quality personal time with his family.

Edwards was blessed with eleven children. When he was at home, Edwards had a special chair that he alone sat in. In the evenings, he would sit down with his children for one hour each day. The smaller ones would sit in his lap, and the older ones would spend quality time conversing with their dad. Edwards took time to pray a special blessing over each child.

To prove that Edwards's prayers and blessings were effective, in 1900 A. E. Winship tracked down fourteen hundred descendants of Jonathan Edwards. In his published study *Jukes-Edwards: A Study in Education and Heredity*, Winship revealed that the one marriage of Edwards produced an amazing lineage, including 285 college graduates on the Edwards family tree. The Edwards lineage produced:

- Three hundred preachers
- Thirteen noted authors
- Thirteen college presidents
- Sixty-five college professors
- One hundred lawyers and a dean of a law school
- Thirty judges
- Fifty-six physicians and a dean of a medical school
- Eighty holders of public office
- Three United States senators
- One vice president of the United States
- One comptroller of the United States Treasury[1]

The spiritual seeds of faith, hope, and love planted into the hearts of the Edwards's children blossomed into a family tree, producing numerous generations of spiritual fruit. Is it possible that today's families can begin planting a family tree that nourishes a generational seed that will become a legacy of righteousness? Edwards's family tree proved that this generational blessing is possible.

There are other well-known individuals who not only were successful businessmen who birthed economically profitable corporations, but even today, seven of these names are known as representative of active and successful companies. They include:

- John D. Rockefeller (Standard Oil industrialist who began earning $3.50 a week and dominated the oil industry for fifty years)
- H. J. Heinz (H. J. Heinz Company, world-class American food company)
- H. P. Crowell (founder of the Quaker Oats Company)
- J. L. Kraft (founder of Kraft Foods, Inc.)
- M. W. Baldwin (founder of M. W. Baldwin & Company, builders of locomotives)
- F. W. Woolworth (founder of F. W. Woolworth and Company, one of the original American five-and-dime stores)
- William Wrigley (known as "the father of chewing gum" and founder of William Wrigley Jr. Company)
- M. S. Hershey (founder of Hershey Chocolate Corporation)
- William Colgate (founder of Colgate and Company, makers of Colgate toothpaste)

These successful business owners all had one thing in common: they were all professing Christians who were givers to charity or tithers to the Lord's work. John D. Rockefeller began tithing to the work of God when earning $3.50 a week. I have toured the Hershey chocolate factory in Hershey, Pennsylvania, and was pleasantly surprised to discover that the founder, Mr. Hershey, was a dedicated Christian who heavily supported orphans and continually raised his level of giving to support the kingdom of God. The spiritual principles these men understood are proven by time and based upon the inspired words of God.

What if, on the other hand, a man chooses to live a life of selfishness and greed or makes decisions contrary to righteous judgment? In a book by Bob Proctor titled *You Were Born Rich*, he wrote:

> In 1923, at the Edgewater Beach Hotel in Chicago, eight of the world's wealthiest financiers met. These eight men controlled more money than the United States' government at that time. They included:
>
> - The president of the largest independent steel company
> - The president of the largest gas company
> - The greatest wheat speculator
> - The president of the New York Stock Exchange
> - A member of the president's cabinet
> - The greatest "bear" on Wall Street
> - The head of the world's greatest monopoly
> - The president of the Bank of International Settlement
>
> Certainly, one would have to admit that a group of the world's most successful men was gathered in that place, at least, men who had found the secret of "earning money." Now let's see where these men were twenty-five years later:
>
> - The president of the largest independent steel company lived on borrowed money for five years before he died bankrupt.
> - The president of North America's largest gas company, Howard Hopson, went insane.
> - The greatest wheat speculator, Arthur Cutton, died abroad, insolvent.
> - The president of the New York Stock Exchange, Richard Whitney, was sent to Sing Sing Penitentiary.
> - A member of the president's cabinet, Albert Fall, was pardoned from prison so he could die at home.
> - The greatest "bear" on Wall Street, Jesse Livermore, died by suicide.
> - The head of the greatest monopoly, Ivar Krueger, killed himself.

- The president of the Bank of International Settlement, Leon Fraser, also died by suicide.[2]

Many of these wealthy individuals were financially impacted by the 1929 stock market crash, which ignited a time in North America called the *Great Depression*—an economic and job crisis that continued for about fourteen years. Many of the wealthiest business owners in America were negatively impacted and suffered great financial losses.

It is not only financial crisis that can "bankrupt" an individual. At times a person's background and upbringing handcuff him or her to a mental prison of failure. Generations of mental or sexual abuse, or a lineage of alcoholism and drug abuse, can cause an individual to visualize himself or herself as just another victim in the graveyard of dying dreams—dreams of spiritual, physical, and emotional freedom from their past.

Created to Dream

No one wants to be viewed as a failure. You were created to dream and given gifts to make the dream happen. However, unplanned disruptions build roadblocks on the road to destiny. In the world in which we live today, there are many indicators to show that dissatisfaction and disillusionment are on the rise in the lives of many Americans. You may feel as though you are one of the "frozen chosen" stuck in the ice on the road to nowhere, but there are many others who feel just like you.

External factors contribute to some of the dissatisfaction. We are facing a declining world economy, jobs are scarce, and most people face more expenses than their incomes can cover. However, not all of the reasons for an individual's negative feelings and attitudes come from external causes. Internal root problems can hinder you from success in your life. When more than 50 percent of marriages end in divorce and millions of Americans cannot sleep without being medicated, we should find out where the root problem is.

In this book you will find principles that can help you to understand what the roots to your circumstances are. The important insights and illumination in this book from God's Word can alter the circumstances of your life and bring a change that will positively impact you and your family. There is a way for you to purge your house from negative family or generational roots, and there are steps that you can take to prune your family tree of lifeless, non-fruit-bearing branches. If you will read this book, believe what you read, and begin to practice these biblical principles, this revelation can change your situation.

If you answer yes to the following questions, then this book is for you:

- Do you dislike the detours on the road to your destiny and long to find a clear direction?
- Are you ready to get rid of the negative family attributes you see in your family? Are you looking for ways to change them?
- Do you desire freedom from addictions, bad habits, stinking thinking, and other hindrances?

Then, enough for this introduction! Let's begin by taking a close look at how Satan selects his victims and launches his attack against us. Once we understand his tactics and learn to recognize the devastation he brings into our lives, we will be ready to get into the Word of the Lord together and begin the process of purging our homes and pruning our family trees.

Chapter 1

HOW SATAN SELECTS HIS VICTIMS

Then they brought him to Him. And when he saw Him, immediately the spirit convulsed him, and he fell on the ground and wallowed, foaming at the mouth. So He asked his father, "How long has this been happening to him?" And he said, "From childhood. And often he has thrown him both into the fire and into the water to destroy him. But if You can do anything, have compassion on us and help us." Jesus said to him, "If you can believe, all things are possible to him who believes."

| MARK 9:20–23 |

REMEMBER *THE WALTONS*? It was a popular weekly television series when I was a teenager. The setting was in the mountains of Virginia in the 1930s. A very large family with many children lived in one house, farming the land, eating large meals each night, and working hard for their father's small lumber business. There was a day when this show typified real-life America, back in the days when Dad worked, Mom raised the kids, and the children were well disciplined, respected their elders, and worked hard from a very early age on the farm. My own father had eleven siblings—two who died young and seven who still survive. I've always teased Dad that they didn't have a large family; they had a TRIBE!

Things have changed. Mom and Dad both work to make ends meet; the children are placed in day care and school during the week; are entertained with television, movies, and the Internet; and family members travel on separate paths, preventing quality family time. Then there is the ever-present problem of teen rebellion that moves through the home just like the spreading leprosy in the ancient homes in Israel.

If a family consists of two children, it is likely that one is compliant and the other is defiant—or one is cooperative and the other rather inoperative. One child can be disciplined by a mere look and respond by bowing his or her head and walking away with tears beginning to flow from his or her eyes. However, the other immediately initiates a discussion that leads to a debate and ends in an argument. Most parents with numerous children understand the oddity that often one child tends to encounter more struggles, to battle more addictions, or to rebel.

As parents, we deal with many forms of satanic attacks during our lifetimes. Most can be overcome through wise decisions and prayer. However, rebellious children bring continual, never-ending stress and concern to loving parents. We must not only pray for rebellious children to experience the Lord, but we must also pray for God to protect those children from themselves or from the danger of their own foolish decisions.

Have you ever wondered why one child is often the target of the adversary?

Spirits Attacking Children

On one occasion during Christ's ministry, He brought deliverance to an epileptic boy whom the spirits had been physically attacking since early childhood (Mark 9:21). On another occasion, he freed a woman's young daughter who had been possessed by an evil spirit (Matt. 15:22). These two incidents indicate that certain types of spirits will attempt to invade the lives of children at a very early age.

Throughout history, the adversary has set his focus on infants and children, especially during major prophetic seasons when God was raising up a deliverer for His people or for His nation. The pharaoh of Egypt assigned the Egyptian midwives, and later, all the Egyptian people, to cast every newborn Hebrew son into the Nile River (Exod. 1:16, 22). This decree of death on the sons forced the mother of Moses to hide the infant in a small handmade ark in the Nile River. Centuries later, Herod heard that a king of the Jews had been born in Bethlehem. Out of fear, he commanded Roman soldiers to slay all infants under two years of age (Matt. 2:16). Through God's protection, both Moses and Jesus escaped from these decrees of death. As grown men, Moses led the Hebrew nation out of Egypt, and Jesus brought the possibility of redemption to the world.

America's children have been faced with their own decree of death since abortion was legalized in 1973. The enemy has blinded the eyes of doctors, politicians, and yes, even expectant mothers who participate in the premature death of the unborn. Contained in the Scriptures' End Time prophecies is a major prophetic promise directed at youth— the sons and daughters—that will take place prior to the return of the Messiah. It is found in both the Old and New Testaments.

> And it shall come to pass in the last days, says God,
> That I will pour out of My Spirit on all flesh;
> Your sons and your daughters shall prophesy,
> Your young men shall see visions,
> Your old men shall dream dreams.
> And on My menservants and on My maidservants
> I will pour out My Spirit in those days;
> And they shall prophesy.
> —ACTS 2:17–18; see also JOEL 2:28–29

A unique outpouring of the Holy Spirit is promised to the youth prior to the return of Christ! This outpouring will be initiated by the sons and daughters. This younger generation will also witness an increase of spiritual visions and dreams, revealing the plans of God and exposing the strategies of the adversary. With such a dynamic promise, is it any wonder that the youth of our time are experiencing the most subtle and sly attacks of the adversary?

By hindering young people's relationship with God, the enemy blocks their ears from hearing God's Word. By binding them with addictions to drugs or alcohol, he prevents them from feeling the peaceful and joyful presence of the Holy Spirit. By keeping them in rebellion, demonic forces prevent them from experiencing the love their parents have for them. Satan is conducting a *mass bondage program* to defeat the next generation because he does not know who may be the next deliverer—the next Moses, Joshua, Daniel, Deborah, Rachel, Rebekah—or the next great leader to bring the nation out of its lukewarm, spiritual lethargy.

Satan—Getting Inside the House

Adults who are struggling today were children only yesterday. Many who battle addictions and bondages first encountered the snares of the enemy as children. Many women who today are engaged in prostitution were raped or molested as children or teens. Pornographic addictions that breed sexual abuse and perversion usually begin at preteen or in the early teen years. Many of the men and women in prison are there for using or selling illegal drugs. Many began their addictions in their teenage years, never knowing where their addictions would eventually lead. Many male homosexuals began experimenting with homosexual acts at a very early age. Some were actually molested as children by older men, and others entered into the lifestyle in their teen years.

The enemy selects his victims when they are but children. The enemy is fully aware of the importance of early teaching, and he plans strategies against our seed when they are still young children. At an early age children are very emotionally sensitive and mentally impressionable. This is why we are instructed: "Train up a child in the way he should go, and when he is old he will not depart from it" (Prov. 22:6). The seeds of the gospel must be planted into the tender soil of the hearts of children before time, circumstances, and pressures from the world form a callus on their hearts.

Holes in the Soul

I once heard a great pastor from Fayetteville, North Carolina, teach a message at a conference that explained how Satan attempts to choose his future victims while they are very young. He explained how cruel words, sexual abuse, anger, and other physical and emotional weapons create a hole in the emotions of a person. As the neglect, abuse, and sexual sins continue, more holes are punched in the emotions, and the previous holes become bigger and bigger. Eventually a person feels so unclean inside, so unworthy and rejected, that he or she seeks affirmation through prostitution, a gay lifestyle, or even through drugs. That person believes, wrongfully so, that drugs are needed to dull his or her emotions and thus feels better when he or she is high. The problem is this: when that person comes down from a false high, the holes in the soul are still there. Thus addiction becomes his or her companion, and the drug becomes the monkey on the back that cannot be defeated.

Soon these hurting individuals become attracted to other individuals who are experiencing the same form of pain. They team up with other wounded people who are drinking alcohol, taking illegal drugs, or are sexually active in an illicit manner. They get drunk or high, and then they give themselves over to another person, thinking that it will *fill the void*. When the party is over and the sun rises in the morning, the friends are gone, and they awake with the same holes in their hearts.

Some go as far as marrying someone just like themselves—"because he or she understands me." Other young girls form a connection with the first boy who gives her attention or who masquerades love for sexual favors. Soon she is pregnant, and the boy has gone AWOL. A hole of rejection is created. The problem is compounded because two people with holes in their emotions can never make each other whole or complete.

The holes in our souls must be sealed off before wholeness can occur. The more holes in our souls, the more prayer and seeking God it takes to seal up the leaky emotions. The good news is that repenting of our sins and placing our faith in Christ bring not only deliverance from our bondages but also wholeness to our inner soul!

The Atoning Work of Christ

In Scripture, the word *atonement* is used eighty times, and it means "to appease, dismiss, or reconcile." In the atoning work of Christ, there is a threefold atoning work:

1. The work of Christ brings salvation to man through His blood (1 Pet. 1:18–19).

2. The work of Christ brings healing through His stripes (Isa. 53:5; 1 Pet. 2:24).

3. The work of Christ brings emotional healing through the act of Christ carrying your grief and sorrows (Isa. 53:4).

We see this threefold work of the Messiah in Isaiah 53:

1. The atonement for sin: "He was wounded for our transgressions" (v. 5).

2. The promise of physical healing: "By His stripes we are healed" (v. 5).

3. The hope of emotional healing: "Surely He has borne our griefs and carried our sorrows.... The chastisement for our peace was upon Him" (vv. 4–5).

Grief and sorrow are the result of painful events that occur in our lives. Death brings grief, and loss brings sorrow. However, the heavenly Father placed upon Christ our grief, pains, and sorrows.

We must come to the point where we understand this and by faith transfer our grief, sorrow, and rejection to the heavenly High Priest, who is touched with the feeling of our weaknesses.

Four Things to Do

I once heard a pastor from North Carolina explain the four things a person must do to bring deliverance and release to his or her spirit.

1. *Face it.* Do not deny your feelings, and don't blame others for your negative emotions. Face it as a man or woman

who loves God. You will never change what you permit and never face what you deny.

2. *Trace it.* After you face it, then you must trace it. Get to the root of your conflict. Was it pride on your part? Did you reject godly advice? Was it the enemy attempting to create a rift? Did you misunderstand someone's comment? Realize what the root was, not just the surface circumstance.

3. *Erase it.* By asking forgiveness—at times you may even write a letter or face a person directly to ask forgiveness— you are, in reality, erasing the offense. God will blot it from any record in heaven and will help to cleanse it out of your spirit. The enemy may attempt to bring back a memory for a season, but the Holy Spirit will remind you that *you need not remember a sin that God has forgotten!*

4. *Replace it.* Old images can be replaced with new pictures. Make fresh memories. Build new relationships. Get on with your life as you leave behind your past.

Thousands of men and women have followed this simple and yet powerful pattern and have experienced freedom and deliverance through faith in Christ. You may have been marked as a target for the adversary from the time you were a child or a teenager. However, you were also marked for a redemptive covenant that will redeem you out of the prison house of the enemy! Change your outlook from a victim mentality to a victory mentality when you enter a covenant of salvation and freedom through Christ! The prison doors have been opened, but you must walk through the doors.

Chapter 2

DON'T BRING ACCURSED THINGS INTO YOUR HOME

And you, by all means abstain from the accursed things, lest you become accursed when you take of the accursed things, and make the camp of Israel a curse, and trouble it.

| JOSHUA 6:18 |

SEVERAL YEARS AGO my neighbor was watching our weekly telecast, *Manna-fest*, as I was explaining that placing certain objects from other religions in your home that may have been used in idol worship could open the door to a spirit entering your house. Later he came to my office and related a bizarre story.

He was living in a new house, but strange supernatural manifestations were occurring. At times he and his wife had felt a strange, somewhat evil presence coming from a certain room. On several occasions, out of the corner of her eyes, his wife caught the imagery of a shadowy figure, like a vapor, moving swiftly across the floor in this same room where they felt this negative energy. They had not said anything about this to their children, but their concern peaked when their daughter began to express certain fearful and negative feelings she sensed and said she had seen a dark shadow in the same area. He knew something was wrong.

As this concerned man, his wife, and I began searching for answers, I asked him if there was any object in his home that could attract a spirit. He immediately told me about a piece of furniture, several hundreds of years old, that was an altar used in a particular Asian religion. He purchased it because of its beauty and age. I explained to him how this altar was more than an antique; it had actually been used during a religious ceremony to pray to an idol god. I told him that all idolatry attracts some form of evil spirits.

I explained the amazing incident during Christ's ministry, recorded in Mark 5, of when a man possessed with two thousand evil spirits was delivered. The evil spirits requested permission to enter a large herd of swine feeding on the mountainside (v. 12). This confused me, since Jews do not raise pigs or eat pork and consider the pig unclean (Lev. 11:7). Later, during a tour of Israel, I learned that there was a temple to Zeus on the mountain near the tombs. We know that Satan has always desired worship (Matt. 4:8–9), and these swine were being raised so they could be slaughtered on a sacrificial altar of this Greek idol god. The evil spirits understood that these swine would be worshiped and knew that if they possessed these pigs, they would also be a part of this idol worship. The evil spirits did not know that the swine would run down the mountain and drown in the sea (Mark 5:13)!

Although an altar is made of stone, ceramic, or wood and cannot see or hear, evil spirits linked to idolatry are still attracted to such objects since the kingdom of darkness centers on counterfeit worship. I told my neighbor to remove the altar from his home and see if the atmosphere in the room changed. He removed the object, and months later he told me that once the altar was removed, the strange presence and shadowy figure completely ceased. A peaceful atmosphere prevailed in the home.

The Jericho Curse

Scripture relates the story of one man in ancient Israel who discovered that bringing accursed objects into your dwelling place not only can affect your spiritual victory but also can eventually cost you your life!

The Hebrews were preparing to conquer their first city after forty years of going in circles in the wilderness. The conquest took place between the Feasts of Passover and Firstfruits. The Feast of Firstfruits is unique because it honors God's blessings on the land. The first ripened barley was to be marked and presented to God during this feast, thus allowing the remaining harvest field to be blessed by God.

Jericho was the first of approximately thirty-one Canaanite cities that Joshua and the Hebrew nation were to conquer. Thus, Jericho was a firstfruits city. All of the spoils gathered from this conquest were to go into the treasury of the tabernacle of the Lord as a firstfruits offering.

> And you, by all means abstain from the accursed things, lest you become accursed when you take of the accursed things, and make the camp of Israel a curse, and trouble it. But all the silver and gold, and vessels of bronze and iron, are consecrated to the LORD; they shall come into the treasury of the LORD.
>
> —JOSHUA 6:18–19

The firstfruits belong to the Lord, and if they are withheld, not only are they cursed, but also disobedience brings a curse, just as it brought a curse on the entire camp of Israel. The word *accursed* is *cherem* and alludes to a doomed object or something marked for destruction. If the firstfruits are withheld, then the object being held back becomes a curse and not a blessing. During the conquest of Jericho, Achan, a man from the tribe of Judah, secretly seized some gold bars and a beautiful Babylonian garment and hid them in his tent. Sounds like an innocent act, right? Perhaps he needed a financial blessing and saw an opportunity to bring some needed prosperity to his family. After all, don't soldiers enjoy the spoils of war? The problem was that God had already commanded the Hebrews not to take *any* items for themselves. All objects in the city belonged to the treasurer of the Lord.

Afterward when the Hebrew troops engaged in the second conflict at a much smaller city named Ai, several Israelites were slain, and Israel experienced defeat. In frustration, Joshua reminded God that He had not kept His word that Israel would defeat all her enemies (Deut. 11:25).

God commanded Joshua to get up and listen (Josh. 7:10). God revealed the hidden reason for Israel's defeat; someone had disobeyed God's orders and was hiding the accursed things among their possessions. Only when the sin of Achan was exposed and the cursed things (buried in his tent) were removed from the house was Israel victorious over her remaining enemies. (See Joshua 7:24–26; 8:1–2.)

The Accursed Things in Your House

It may seem strange to some, but it is possible to have certain objects or items in your house that create an accursed atmosphere. For example, at times individuals may bring an object home that was used in another religion as an idol or used during idol worship. Other things like pornography may open a door to certain types of spirits. Sometimes an object may carry a curse that was placed on it.

The drum from India

One example comes from one of our missionaries who has traveled to India and has witnessed thousands of souls coming to Christ. Earlier in his ministry, a convert to Christ gave him a drum as a gift. The drum was old and had animal skin stretched on the top and bottom. He was unaware, until later, that this drum had been used in the past during Hindu worship ceremonies. My friend brought the drum home for his young son and set it in a corner of the house.

One evening he and his wife were preparing their tax returns in the kitchen when they began hearing a strange scratching noise periodically coming from the other room. Eventually they discovered that it was coming from inside the drum. At first he thought a large insect had managed to get into the drum, but this was impossible because skin enclosed it tightly on both ends. He then felt it may have been used in some kind of religious ceremony and therefore may have some type of a spirit attached to it. He took the drum outside and cut the leather holding the animal skin on. He said, "Suddenly I heard a screeching sound so loud that it sounded like a person inside the drum. The animal cover flew off, and I ran!" He destroyed the drum.[1]

The robe from Egypt

Years ago I too experienced a rather bizarre situation. While touring Egypt, I had purchased a long flowing white robe. After returning home and wearing the robe, I began experiencing strange pains around my chest. For months, whenever I put this robe on, the pains would strike me. I began searching for more information about this particular robe and discovered it was actually a prayer robe worn by religious leaders of another, non-Christian religion. I removed the robe from my house, and the pain completely ceased.

The cane from Haiti

The country of Haiti is known for being a center of voodoo worship. In parts of Haiti, the voodoo worship is mixed with a strange form of Catholic traditions. For example, in some voodoo temples you will also see paintings of Mary and Christ.

I was ministering years ago in Florida and noticed a man attending the meeting who was walking with a strange-looking cane. It was made of wood and had the image of a face on the top. I asked him where he got the cane, and he said, "I was ministering in Haiti, and a man making this cane told me I would need it one day, and that the face was the face of the God I was serving. I purchased it and brought it home." Then he said this: "The man was right. I fell after returning home and have been using this cane ever since."

I immediately knew that the face carved on that cane by a stranger in Haiti was not the face of God or of Christ. The fact that he fell after returning made me suspicious. I told him that the cane may have been made by a voodoo worshiper and that he should get rid of it. Then the Lord would heal him. That moment I prayed for him, and the Lord instantly healed his back. He was jumping and rejoicing. He gave me the cane. I wasn't interested in falling down and needing this cane, so I got rid of it.

I realize that these stories will sound odd and strange to many people. However, spiritual warfare is not waged in the mind or imagination; it is very real. Paul said it well when he wrote:

> For we are not wrestling with flesh and blood [contending only with physical opponents], but against the despotisms, against the powers, against [the master spirits who are] the world rulers of this present darkness, against the spirit forces of wickedness in the heavenly (supernatural) sphere.
>
> —Ephesians 6:12, AMP

In the spirit realm, the Holy Spirit moves toward us when we pray, worship, or read the Scriptures. Angels are commissioned to minister to the righteous and are moved toward us by the words we say (Dan. 6:22). They are also involved at times in bringing answers to our prayers (Luke 1:11–13). In ancient Israel, altars were built to mark the spot where covenants were made between the people and God (Gen. 8:20; 12:7; 26:25). On special occasions, God commissioned an angel to meet a patriarch at the altar (Gen. 22:9–11). If the angelic world is moved toward us by prayer, praise, and worship and can identify the exact locations of ancient altars and blood sacrifices, then the kingdom of darkness is also moved by our words and attitudes and can be attracted to certain objects we bring into our lives or homes.

Things That Can Open a Door to the Adversary

Most Christians, especially those living in North America, are not bringing idols into their homes, and they certainly would not willfully allow these deaf and dumb stone idols to be shelved in their houses, especially when they are aware of the negative spiritual atmosphere and spirits they can attract. However, it is the more common objects and things that surround us that may be opening a door to some form of a spirit or a spiritual attack.

Pornography

Men are sexually stimulated through sight. This is why most pornography is geared toward men and not women. When I was a child, pornographic magazines were hidden under the store counter or had brown covers to hide the images. Eventually they were placed on open counters in convenience stores (how convenient). Later a system developed where a person could pay to have adult movies in their home, but today pornography has progressed from behind the counter to the computer screen—free of charge. Millions of men are now addicted to pornographic websites.

For a man, the images are imbedded into the brain. I can practically guarantee you that any man, of any age, can tell you when he saw his first pornographic pictures, and he can still see that particular image in his mind. It is something that cannot be erased because of the imprint of the image on the brain. Pornography is such a deception for men, especially when they leave their wives for a more physically perfect woman.

It has been reported that porn magazines print photographs that have been airbrushed to remove all of the blemishes and defects of the woman photographed. Computer programs are used to darken a woman's skin or to alter the physical appearance of a person. As a result, men think they are looking at a *perfect 10* woman, and soon they begin to see the defects in their own wives. Without deliverance, they may walk out on their marriages as they search for that perfect 10.

Before you make such a stupid decision to wreck your family, just remember that if you have been married for many years, you have a proven commodity. Your wife picks up your stinking clothes, washes and folds them, cooks your meals, helps raise the children, and keeps the house clean. You may think you are God's gift to women now, but in the future your muscles will sag, your face will wrinkle, and your hair will turn gray or fall out. The young chick you are chasing will leave you for a younger man, and you will be stuck in a lonely apartment regretting your decision.

Pornography can release a "seducing spirit" (1 Tim. 4:1, KJV). The Greek word for "seducing" in this passage is *planos*, which means "to wander and to stray like a roving tramp." Seduction pulls a person away from the truth and causes that person to wander around in circles. This happened to Samson. He loved Philistine women and fell in love (or lust) with Delilah, who discovered that his Nazirite vow was the secret to his strength (Num. 6:2–13). When she cut his seven locks of hair, she severed his vow with God (Judg. 16:19). Samson was captured by the Philistines, his eyes were plucked out, and he was placed in the enemy's prison house, where he was yoked to a large grindstone like an animal, going 'round and 'round in circles continually (v. 21).

Pornography leads to bondage and opens doors to seducing spirits.

Occult games

In North America interest in the supernatural is gaining ground, especially among the youth in public schools. Interest usually begins by dabbling in occult games that are considered innocent forms of entertainment. When I was growing up, many public school teens were conducting séances, chanting and burning candles, or using incantations in an attempt to place a curse on their enemies. But the real world of the occult is not a game; it is very serious and can eventually open the door to demonic oppression, depression, or possession.

One of the popular games when I was young was the Ouija board. It was based on an ancient Egyptian principle of using oracles to call upon the gods. The board is rectangular and has certain words and letters on it. Two people ask the board a question as they place their hands on a triangular object with a round piece of glass in the center. Allegedly, a spirit will give you the answer by supernaturally sliding the triangular base across the board as the people playing the game read each letter the object pauses at.

Practicing such games is dangerous; they can—and will—introduce the players to *familiar spirits,* a very seductive type of demonic entity. A familiar spirit is a demonic spirit that is familiar with people, places, and circumstances. It can also attach itself to a family and remain for many generations. Because of the activity of familiar spirits, séances are very dangerous. A participating person may believe he or she is literally making contact with a departed loved one, when in reality, the séance leader is either a well-trained fake, or a familiar spirit is manifesting. I saw one such activity on television, where one man had consulted a psychic who allegedly talked with the dead. After the encounter, the man believed he had actually contacted his loved one because of the information the spirit knew that only the family member could have known.

In reality, a familiar spirit can know information about a person and even have limited knowledge of future events. When Christ was casting out evil spirits, they often recognized him as the Son of God (Mark 3:11). In one encounter, the spirits asked Christ, "Have You come here to torment us before the time?" (Matt. 8:29). These demons were fully aware of their future doom, as indicated when Christ was casting out the legion from the man of Gadera. As the spirits were departing, they begged Jesus "that He would not command them to go out into the abyss [deep, KJV]" (Luke 8:31). The word *deep* in the King James translation is the Greek word *abussos*, which is translated eight times in the Book of Revelation as "bottomless" in the phrase "bottomless pit" (Rev. 9:1–2, 11; 11:7; 17:8; 20:1, 3). This underground pit is the final destination of eternal confinement for the demonic powers. Note that the demons knew who Christ was, knew He was sent to destroy them, and knew about their final doom. Evil spirits are very deceptive, and familiar spirits work through séances and occult games. They can reveal information that has already been public and actually know about events planned in the spirit world.

Illegal drugs

The Book of Revelation lists the sins that will be prominent in the last days prior to Christ returning to the earth.

> But the rest of mankind, who were not killed by these plagues, did not repent of the works of their hands, that they should not worship demons, and idols of gold, silver, brass, stone, and wood, which can neither see nor hear nor walk. And they did not repent of their murders or their sorceries or their sexual immorality or their thefts.
> —REVELATION 9:20–21

According to these verses, there are five prominent sins in the time of the end:

Idol worship. Many of the world's leading religions permit the worship of idols and false gods. In the Hindu religion, almost anything and everything that can be seen with the human eye is accepted as a god. In India there is a rat temple, where hundreds of thousands of rats are worshiped, and the worshipers provide food for the rats. Everyone prays to see the white rat, which is the premier god of the temple.

Murder(s). Murder is the slaying of the innocent. It includes cold-blooded killing, voluntary manslaughter, and shedding innocent blood such as occurs when a doctor in a clinic takes the life of an infant in its mother's womb. About fifty million abortions have occurred just in America since *Roe v. Wade* in 1973.[2] In the Book of Revelation we are told that the world will be judged for shedding the blood of the martyrs (Rev. 6:10) and for killing the saints and prophets (Rev. 18:24).

Sexual immorality. By biblical definition, sexual immorality would include adultery (sex between two married persons not married to one another), fornication (sex between single individuals), and same-sex relationships. When having a sexual relationship with a person outside of your marriage, Scripture says the two are made one flesh. This not only is a sinful act, but it also creates a physical and emotional soul tie that brings both parties into a level of bondage and dependency, often leading to a terrible divorce and impacting the families of both individuals.

Thefts. We think of a thief as someone who steals from a local store or puts their hand in the petty cash and takes a few bucks for rising fuel costs. However, we are seeing high-ranking business executives steal thousands and millions of dollars from investors and shareholders without blinking an eye. As economic downturns occur, there is always a rise in thefts and robberies.

Sorceries. This is perhaps the strongest spirit of all the spirits who will control the people at the time of the end. We think of sorcery as being linked to the occult or witchcraft. The meaning of this word, however, is much deeper. The Greek word for "sorcery" is *pharmakeia* (Rev. 18:23). We derive our English word *pharmacy* from this word. It is used five times in the New Testament (Gal. 5:20; Rev. 9:21; 18:23; 21:8; 22:15). At times it is translated as "sorceries" and other times as "witchcraft."

According to *Vine's Expository Dictionary of New Testament Words*, the meaning of *sorcery* is: "An adjective signifying 'devoted to magical arts,' is used as a noun, a sorcerer, especially one who uses drugs, portions, spells and enchantments."[3] According to the apostle John, entire nations will be deceived by sorceries (Rev. 18:23).

In reality, this *pharmakeia* spirit is the spirit of illegal drugs and drug addiction! There is no doubt that the chief demonic spirit controlling North America is a spirit of sorcery, or a spirit of *pharmakeia*. Look at the numerous drugs that have been and are prominent in North America:

- Marijuana (pot)
- LSD
- Heroin
- Cocaine
- Crack cocaine
- Meth
- DXM in cough medicines

There are entire movements being organized in America to legalize marijuana for medical use, saying that it should be legalized because it is a positive herbal drug. Marijuana is not a new weed. It has been used for thousands of years, as far back as the Shamanistic rituals in India, China, and Asia. In the year 100, the Chinese writer Pen Ching said that if taken over a long time, marijuana makes one communicate with spirits. A Taoist priest said in the fifth century B.C. that marijuana was employed by necromancers to discover the future.[4] According to the Drug Abuse Warning Network (DAWN), in 2005 marijuana was involved in 242,200 emergency room visits.[5] Twenty percent of those surveyed who have used marijuana said they had been taken over by an outside force or will that is hostile or evil.[6] Marijuana always opens the door to other types of stronger and addictive drugs.

There are numerous stories I can share about drug abuse and evil spirits. As a teenager, one of our ministry friends, Kelvin McDaniel, was smoking mushrooms with a friend. They were sitting on the couch tripping out, when suddenly Kelvin saw a demonic spirit walk through the walls and mockingly say, "See, your mother's prayers aren't working." Kelvin screamed out, and so did his friend on the couch.

His friend said, "Did you see that little man and hear what he said?" They both saw and heard the same thing, and being raised in church, Kelvin knew they had both seen an evil spirit.

A close pastor friend was once at a party with fifteen other individuals. Suddenly he saw a strange creature step out of the television, and it began cursing him. He knew he was tripping out, but what really shook him was when several others in the room saw and heard the same thing at the exact same time. What really scared him was discovering that those who saw this spirit all had church backgrounds and had been raised in Christian homes! Tripping out and getting high may seem like innocent fun that helps you to escape from the hurts in your life, but the adversary never shows you the thousands of people who died because of an overdose, or those whose hearts quit and lungs collapsed, or those who pass out and die in their own vomit. This demon of addiction is the main spirit controlling the United States.

Alcohol

When I was growing up, we seldom if ever heard of a dedicated Christian who drank any form of strong drink. Most Christians, even from the more nominal backgrounds, considered the use of alcohol as a spiritual snare that would open the door to many dangers, including alcoholism. Today, using Christian liberty as their scapegoat, many Christians are now taking a little toddy for the body. They teach that drinking alcohol is fine as long as it is in moderation. I remind them that what they do today in moderation, their children will do tomorrow in excess. This is because the next generation is always more tolerant of sin and more liberal in their thinking than the previous generation.

I am reminded of a true story I once heard of a father who was awakened in the middle of the night by a policeman who asked him about his son and the type of car he drove. The policeman said the man's son, who had just turned eighteen, was killed in an auto accident and was drunk at the time. The father went into a rage and said, "I will destroy the man who gave my son that alcohol to drink!" After informing his wife, the heartbroken dad went to his liquor cabinet and found a note from his son. The lad had taken several bottles of liquor and wrote, "Dad, now that I'm eighteen, I'm sure you won't mind if I have a few drinks tonight with some friends." The father's liquor killed his own son. You may enjoy your glass of wine, and your children will move to the local bar and drink with friends. Your grandchildren may become alcoholics and eventually kill themselves or another person while driving drunk. It happens thousands of times each year. Do you want this on your conscience? As a Christian, there may be things I could do *but will not do* because I want to set a right example before my children and not be a stumbling block to others. You never have to convince an ex-alcoholic that drink is wrong!

Consider the following:

- In the United Sates, alcohol consumption leads to more than 100,000 deaths each year from alcohol-related injuries and illnesses.[7]

- Forty-one percent of traffic crashes, the leading cause of death for Americans through age thirty-four, are alcohol-related, according to NHTSA.[8]

- In 2001–2002, about 70 percent of young adults in the United States, or about 19 million people, consumed alcohol in the year preceding the survey.[9]

- Over 15 million Americans are dependent on alcohol. Five hundred thousand are between the ages of nine and twelve.[10]

- Americans spend over $90 billion total on alcohol each year.[11]

Consider this. In the Bible nothing good ever resulted from drinking strong, fermented drink. Noah was drunk, and Canaan did something so bad that he was placed under a curse by Noah (Gen. 9:24–25). When Lot's daughters got their father drunk, he committed incest, and the daughters bore two sons by their own father (Gen. 19:32–38). David attempted to get Uriah the husband of Bathsheba drunk to cover for his sin of adultery (2 Sam. 11:13). King Belshazzar drank wine from the sacred vessels of the Jewish temple, and the same night he was slain by the invading armies of the Persians (Dan. 5:23–30). When the temple priests began straying from God and drinking wine, they forgot God's laws and perverted judgment

(Isa. 28:7–8). God punished the priests with death if they drank strong drink when entering the tabernacle (Lev. 10:9).

There are literally millions of people who have an addictive personality. When they smoke the first cigarette, they end up smoking several packs a week. When they take their first alcoholic drink, they need a drink to get up and another to go to bed. When they smoke pot, they must continue the process or they become depressed.

The reality is, you cannot play with the spirit of *pharmakeia*, as this spirit is one of the strongest spirits, if not the strongest spirit, controlling much of North America. Your flesh nature wants to be fed fleshly sin because sinning feels good. Your spirit must be strong to resist the desires of the flesh man.

Sexual perversion

God created men and women with an attraction toward one another. He created sex not only for procreation but also to enjoy intimate moments in the bond of a marriage covenant. Today, with more than 50 percent of marriages ending in divorce, the relationship void is often filled with sexual activity outside of the normal act of marriage, including fornication and adultery. The Bible teaches that certain forms of sexual perversion can actually cause a spirit of confusion.

> Thou shalt not lie with mankind, as with womankind: it is abomination. Neither shalt thou lie with any beast to defile thyself therewith: neither shall any woman stand before a beast to lie down thereto: it is confusion.
>
> —LEVITICUS 18:22–23, KJV

> And if a man lie with his daughter in law, both of them shall surely be put to death: they have wrought confusion; their blood shall be upon them.
>
> —LEVITICUS 20:12, KJV

When a young man is molested by an older man, it brings confusion and can lead to same-sex relations as the boy himself becomes a man. The same is true when a young girl is sexually abused by her father or by a male relative. It brings mental confusion and can create an unnatural

27

attraction to the same sex that eventually leads men to be with men and women to be with women.

I have known several individuals who have been in the alternative gay lifestyle. When I heard their personal stories, it broke my heart. Three of the men I know were molested at an early age by men within the church they were attending. One was molested by the pastor. Several of the young women tell stories of their fathers abusing their mother, and even of their fathers having sexual relations with them as a child. These assaults on children and teenagers will create a spirit of confusion.

In the early church, there were individuals who had lived in such fleshly bondages before coming to Christ. Paul had warned:

> Do you not know that the unrighteous and the wrongdoers will not inherit or have any share in the kingdom of God? Do not be deceived (misled): neither the impure and immoral, nor idolaters, nor adulterers, nor those who participate in homosexuality, nor cheats (swindlers and thieves), nor greedy graspers, nor drunkards, nor foulmouthed revilers and slanderers, nor extortioners and robbers will inherit or have any share in the kingdom of God.
>
> —1 CORINTHIANS 6:9–10, AMP

Notice the next statement Paul made:

> And such some of you were [once]. But you were washed clean (purified by a complete atonement for sin and made free from the guilt of sin), and you were consecrated (set apart, hallowed), and you were justified [pronounced righteous, by trusting] in the name of the Lord Jesus Christ and in the [Holy] Spirit of our God.
>
> —1 CORINTHIANS 6:11, AMP

He said, "Such some of you were." The early church was filled with men and women who had been *delivered* from every form of sin, bondage, and unclean lifestyle. The power of Christ's blood not only forgives sins, but it can also break the yoke of bondage over a person's life.

Psychic hotlines

Years ago I heard of one woman who spent more than $30,000 in one month running up a phone bill while contacting a psychic hotline. There are several important statements I want to make concerning these profit-making scams.

First, why would you want to pay someone $4.95 a minute to hear that person tell you information you already know? You already know you are married, you have children, or you are living under stress at times. You know you need more money and want more affirmation and so forth. Yet some people will hang on to every word of an alleged psychic. Many of these phone operators have no psychic powers but will engage in a conversation and begin to tell people what they want to hear. Perhaps they say, "You are coming into a new job with a lot of money," or "You will meet a person who will become a major friend and help make your dreams come true." The caller never personally meets the voice on the other line, and therefore when the psychic misses it, there is no accountability—just a good commission check for holding the caller on the line for as long as possible.

Years ago I was preaching in Modesto, California, where, allegedly, there was a woman who had lost her psychic abilities after having a brain scan at a local hospital. She was suing the hospital for two million dollars. The sad thing is that she won her case! I would have loved to have been in the courtroom to ask her one question: "So you say you were a psychic and could reveal the future? Then how come you didn't know that the brain scan would take your ability?" Case closed!

One of America's most popular psychic hotlines was hosted and promoted by a well-known Hollywood celebrity. The advertisements would encourage people to call the number late at night to get a word that person needed to hear. Those psychics must have really been off their predictions, because the hotline filed for bankruptcy after going twenty million dollars in debt!

Besides avoiding those kinds of moneymaking scams, Christians in covenant with God are also forbidden to consult witches, sorcerers, and those operating through familiar spirits (Deut. 18:10–12). This includes consulting astrologers who believe your life cycles are patterned after the position of your star charts. Your life is not directed by the stars but by the Creator! The reason God forbids contact with familiar spirits is a simple one—the adversary is a liar and the father of lies (John 8:44). Any prediction made by a familiar spirit involves sorrow, death, suffering, and trouble. Jesus came to give you life and life more abundantly (John 10:10).

The Holy Spirit can show you things to come, and His revelation will always be accurate and always point you to Christ (John 16:13).

Giving Spirits Authority in Your Life

One of the strangest yet greatest eye-opening conversations I ever took part in happened in the mid 1980s. I was conducting a three-week revival in South Carolina. During the meeting I met a gentleman who had moved to this small town from a large western city. He was presently working for a major computer company and was well educated from a secular point of view. One evening after service I spent several hours listening to this fellow reveal what he had learned about spiritual warfare when he was a sinner.

He described being raised in a secular home, but eventually he became involved in a religion that was a mixture of New Age, Hinduism, and other beliefs. He and his wife attended a so-called church where a mixture of many strange teachings were presented to the people. At the time he had never heard biblical teachings on angels and demons. He was taught there were spirits of light and darkness. He revealed that individuals within the group would actually consult dark spirits to place curses on people who were competitors in business. On one occasion a man sent a spirit to make his wife die prematurely so he could marry another woman with whom he had fallen in love.

This man then said something I have never forgotten. He said that on several occasions he had actually seen evil spirits, and he continued to see them for a time even after his conversion. He said, "I know of no other way to describe them than they are various sizes, and some have an appearance of a large ugly ape or monkey." He continued, "When I lived in the large cities, these spirits were larger in size, like a huge gorilla. When I moved to the Bible Belt in South Carolina, they were much smaller, like a small chimp, or small enough to sit on a person's shoulder and speak into his or her ears." But it was what he said next that I will never forget.

I asked him why the spirits appeared larger in size in major cities and smaller in rural communities. He replied, "Perry, evil spirits feed off of sin in the same manner that people physically grow and receive their nourishment from food!" He continued, "In larger cities there is more sin, especially sexual perversion and drug abuse, and as people sin, these spirits gain more strength and authority. In the Bible Belt, there are more churches, Bible teaching, and people who have a higher moral standard than in most cities. Thus the spirits do not have the same level of sin to feed off of, and their size and authority are much smaller, since God's Word has authority over them."[12]

Had this conversation been with a wild Christian projecting an overactive imagination, I would have smiled and said, "That's interesting." But I knew this man was an intellectual, and his details were beyond what a vivid imagination could paint. When he said that spirits feed off of sin and grow in size and authority in the same way people who eat food will grow, I believe it was an important revelation that may explain why spirits are stronger over some nations than others. As the Bible states, our spiritual warfare is with "spiritual hosts of wickedness in the heavenly places" (Eph. 6:12).

For example, Daniel was a Hebrew captive in Babylon, and he spent twenty-one days in prayer and fasting, seeking God for understanding to a vision he had experienced. After twenty-one days, the angel of the Lord informed Daniel that he (the angel) was on his way to the earth the *first day* when Daniel's prayer was heard but was restrained by a powerful prince of Persia, who hindered the angel's access to Daniel for three full weeks (Dan. 10:1–13). Normally, an angel of the Lord had immediate access between heaven and the earth, but this angel was hindered by a much stronger spirit than we normally see in Scripture.

Daniel was not living in or practicing sin; however, the nation of Babylon where he was residing was filled with idolatry and wickedness. The Babylonian government had prepared a burning furnace to cast in those who refused to bow to their images (Dan. 3), and later, the Persian leaders ruling from Babylon passed laws to prevent individuals from praying, which sent an uncompromising Daniel into the lions' den (Dan. 6). This attack on the righteous is possibly what Paul alluded to when he taught, "For we do not wrestle against flesh and blood, but against principalities, against powers, against the rulers of the darkness of this age, against spiritual hosts of wickedness in the heavenly places" (Eph. 6:12).

Perhaps as you have prayed, God has heard your words, but your answer is being restrained by unseen forces in the heavenly atmosphere. Daniel refused to give up and eventually received his breakthrough from the Lord.

Changing the Atmosphere in Your Home

None of us wish to leave work, return from college, or visit our family and walk into a lions' den of anger, a fiery furnace of strife, or an atmosphere of tension. I suggest there are four methods that can help you make your home a dwelling place of peace and joy.

1. *Setting the boundaries in your house*

Boundaries are a set of limits that indicate what is permitted and what is not permitted. Some are set from a practical perspective and others for health reasons. My wife and I have two children; one is a son who is twenty, and the other, a daughter almost ten. When a child becomes a teenager, he or she will test these boundaries and often challenge the authority they have lived under. This is when tough love is necessary to hold your line and not compromise.

For example, we do not allow smoking within our house. My wife and I do not smoke, and we don't want our house smelling like something is burning inside, nor do we want a possible fire breaking out at night because of someone smoking in the bedroom. We do not allow any alcohol in our home, such as beer, wine, or strong liquor. We are teetotalers and do not want to participate in something that would encourage our children to follow our practice, which could eventually lead to alcoholic bondages. We do not have any pay channels that allow pornography to come across the television. These are boundaries that we have set, and if they are broken, they are broken against our will and without our knowledge. You must agree upon and set the boundaries to prevent entrance of unwanted junk into your dwelling place.

2. *Building an altar in your house*

We think of altars as being a special wooden altar in a local church or at the front of the sanctuary. In the Bible, altars were constructed of stone, brass, and even gold, as in the golden altar for incense.

By definition, an altar was a meeting place between God and man. The most important altar is the place we set aside to meet with God and encounter His presence.

I have a friend whose altar is a white cane-back chair once owned by a dedicated intercessor who spent hours sitting in that chair praying. On two occasions when visiting this friend, I have sat in the old chair praying and petitioning God for specific direction. Oddly, in both instances, I received clear instructions and inspiration needed to complete an assignment that had hitherto been unclear and uncertain.

In Scripture, altars were hot spots where patriarchs and men of God marked special visitations from angels and from the Almighty. At times of distress and need, they returned to the original place of visitation and presented offerings to God, requesting His intervention. Likewise, in our homes we should have a specific place set apart where we meet intimately with the Lord. In my early ministry I actually cleared out a spot in a closet, taking the words of Christ very literally: "But you, when you pray, go into your room, and when you have shut your door, pray to your Father who is in the secret place; and your Father who sees in secret will reward you openly" (Matt. 6:6). Today I have several places in my ministry offices and at home where I spend alone time with the

Lord. Identify a peaceful place—on your porch, in your office, or in a bedroom—where you can close the door and enter into prayer.

3. *Anointing your house*

The anointing of the Holy Spirit is an inward presence, a divine energy that dwells in the spirit (holy of holies) of a Spirit-filled believer. There is, however, an act of anointing that is performed by anointing with oil those who are sick and desiring healing (James 5:14–15). Anointed prayers are the most effective types of prayer to pray.

Anointing your house involves taking a small portion of olive oil, which represents the Holy Spirit's anointing, and applying it with your finger to the posts of your door, both outside and inside the home. While the oil itself does not have any intrinsic value, in Scripture the act of anointing was seen as a consecration of a person or thing to God. In the time of Moses oil was used to anoint the high priest, his sons, the furniture of the tabernacle, and was even mixed with the bread on the table of showbread, recorded in Exodus chapters 29, 30, and 40.

When the anointing oil was poured upon the heads of leaders, the Holy Spirit descended upon them, as recorded when Samuel anointed young David in the midst of his brothers (1 Sam. 16:13). Throughout the Bible the oil alludes to the anointing, and the anointing is what sets a person apart for the ministry and spiritual authority.

4. *Marking your house*

The Lord instructed the early Israelites to mark the gates of their homes with the Word of God. This would be difficult today and would certainly draw attention if we began painting scripture on the outside of our homes. In Bible times a sacred object called a *mezuzah* (meaning "doorpost") was designed. It is a small case that has a rolled parchment within it, on which are written scriptures. It is attached to the right side of the doorposts on the homes of Torah-observant Jews. It is based upon the following scripture:

> Hear, O Israel: The LORD our God, the LORD is one! You shall love the LORD your God with all your heart, with all your soul, and with

all your strength. And these words which I command you today shall be in your heart. You shall teach them diligently to your children, and shall talk of them when you sit in your house, when you walk by the way, when you lie down, and when you rise up. You shall bind them as a sign on your hand, and they shall be as frontlets between your eyes. You shall write them on the doorposts of your house and on your gates.

—DEUTERONOMY 6:4–9

In my book *Breaking the Jewish Code* I wrote:

How can a person "bind" God's Word on their hands and as frontlets between their eyes and write it on the gates and doorposts of their house? From these commandments, several Jewish customs emerged. The first was the creation of a *tefillin*, also called a *phylactery*. This is a small, square black box with a long flowing leather strap. The box contains four compartments with four scriptures: Deuteronomy 6:4–9; Deuteronomy 11:13–21; Exodus 13:1–10; and Exodus 13:11–16. These verses for the tefillin are written by a scribe on a small kosher parchment with a special black ink.

The tefillin have two boxes, each attached to the black leather straps. One is attached around the biceps about heart level and the other above the forehead, but not lower than the hairline. The straps are then wound around the fingers, palm, wrist, and arm. Two blessings are repeated as the tefillin is placed on the biceps and the forehead. In the time of Christ, the phylacteries were donned by Torah-observant Jews. Jesus, being Jewish, would have worn the phylactery. However, He rebuked certain Pharisees for enlarging the boxes to make themselves appear more spiritual than others and to be seen of men (Matt. 23:5). Most Jewish young men begin wearing the tefillin just prior to their thirteenth birthday.

The second article created from Deuteronomy 6:4–9 was the mezuzah. An actual kosher mezuzah has the words of the Shema (Deut. 6:4–9) and a passage from Deuteronomy 11:13–21 written by a trained scribe on a small parchment of a kosher animal (cow or sheep). The name of God is written on the backside of the parchment, and the tiny scroll is rolled up and placed in the mezuzah case.

The case is usually a decorated case made of ceramic, stone, copper, silver, glass, wood, or even pewter. The designs vary and are not spiritually significant, but the parchment itself holds the significance of the mezuzah. Most mezuzahs on the outer surface have the Hebrew letter *shin*, the twenty-first letter of the Hebrew alphabet, which represents the first letter in God's name, *Shaddai*. The name *Shaddai* is a name that serves as an acronym for "Guardian of the doorways of Israel." The box is designed to protect the parchment from the weather or other elements that could harm the ink.[13]

The Purpose for the Mezuzah

The word *mezuzah* is the Hebrew word for "doorposts." Some have suggested that the purpose for the mezuzah was to remind the Jewish people, on a continual basis, of the blood of the lamb, which, when applied on the doorposts in Egypt, prevented the destroying angel from entering the home and killing the firstborn. This theory, however, is an opinion and not based on the rabbinic understanding of the purpose of the mezuzah.

Some Jews, identified as mystics, tend to see the mezuzah as some form of a charm designed to ward off evil spirits, but this is certainly not the original intent. It is a reminder to those living in the home that the house has been dedicated to God and that those living therein should commit to walk in accordance with God's Word. It is viewed however, as an object, reminding God to protect the home. The Talmud teaches that a proper mezuzah *can* bring long life and protection to the household. A Talmudic story tells of a king who gave a diamond to a rabbi as a present, and the rabbi in return gave the king a mezuzah, which insulted the king. The rabbi commented to the king, "I will have to hire guards to protect my home because of the gift you gave me, but the gift I gave will protect your home."

Affixing a Mezuzah

Just as there are very strict laws instructing scribes on writing and preparing sacred parchments, there are strict guidelines on how to affix a mezuzah and the prayers that should be prayed.

First, the mezuzah should be attached on the right side of the door as you are entering a room. In Jewish homes, every door (except the bathroom door) has a mezuzah, unless the door has been boarded up. The mezuzah is placed about shoulder height, underneath the door's lintel. The Ashkenazi Jews place the mezuzah at a slight angle, with the top facing toward the room. The Sephardic custom is to place the mezuzah at a vertical angel.

It is also a custom to kiss the right hand and touch the mezuzah when entering the home. It reminds the person entering the house to keep God's Word: "…when you sit in your house, when you walk by the way, when you lie down, and when you rise up" (Deut. 11:19).

The Prayer

Before placing the mezuzah, a special prayer is prayed:

> Blessed are You, Adonai our God, ruler of the universe, who sanctifies us with holy commandments and commands us to fix a mezuzah.

As a personal note, each time I enter and exit my home, I pass by the mezuzah. It is a physical reminder that my home and family are dedicated to God. I am also reminded that I am a representative of the Lord in my calling and work and should endeavor to follow the requirements of His covenant. When I return in the evening, I see the mezuzah, reminding me that our home is a dwelling place for the Lord and that in all I do I must glorify Him, setting the example of faith in my family and teaching my children the Scriptures. Thus, for me, the purpose of the mezuzah is evident—a reminder of God's covenant with my family and my dwelling place.

Strengthen the Foundations

I personally placed four scriptures in protective cases in the four corners of two special buildings when they were being constructed: in our second ministry facility, which houses the office where I study, write, and pray, and in the foundation of our home. The four scriptures each relate to a particular promise from the Lord:

- A scripture for *angelic protection*—Psalm 34:7
- A scripture for *health and healing*—1 Peter 2:24
- A scripture for *family salvation*—Acts 16:31
- A scripture for *prosperity*—3 John 2

These verses were encased in concrete to ensure they will endure through time. This was not some expression of magical formulas or strange ritual; it was done to show the Almighty our faith in His Word to perform His promises in our lives. As it is written:

> Then said the Lord to me, You have seen well, for I am alert and active, watching over My word to perform it.
>
> —JEREMIAH 1:12, AMP

> Thou art my hiding place and my shield: I hope in thy word.
>
> —PSALM 119:114, KJV

The Word of God is not activated and operative in your life simply because you hold a Bible in your hand or have a Bible placed in every room of your house. The Word of God is inspired, and when it is taught, there is a divine energy released as the words are received into the human spirit. When you act upon your faith, God's creative power can be released into your situation.

Christ would continually command a person to do something prior to that person receiving a miracle. He told a man with a withered hand, "Stretch out your hand." And as the fellow made the effort, he experienced an instant healing (Matt. 12:10–13). Christ smeared mud over the eyes of a blind man and said, "Go, wash in the pool of Siloam," and as he was led to the waters of this famous pool, he washed and came away seeing (John 9:6–11). He commanded a paraplegic, "Rise, take up your bed and walk," and as the paralyzed man made the effort, he received strength and was healed (John 5:1–12). If any of these individuals had said, "I've been trying to stretch my hand out all my life, and nothing has happened," or "Why did you put this dumb mud in my eyes?" then that person would not have received his miracle. This truth can be seen when Christ was ministering in His hometown, where He could not do any mighty miracles because of their unbelief (Matt. 13:54–58).

Your spiritual foundation must be in your knowledge of what is written in the Scriptures. You cannot engage in spiritual warfare without the proper weapons. (See Ephesians 6:12–18.) You cannot receive an answer to prayer if you do not understand the law of faith and the types of prayers in the New Testament. Many individuals have sat in local churches and heard ministers preach messages that never gave them the covenant promises for healing, prosperity, and the infilling of the Holy Spirit. Perhaps this is why it is written, "My people are destroyed for lack of knowledge" (Hosea 4:6).

Not only must your knowledge be on what God can and will do for you, but you must also discover the methods the enemy uses to bring defeat into your life. At times this lack of knowledge, or spiritual ignorance, prevents you from properly purging your house and stopping the spiritual plagues that are building strongholds in your life. We must discover how to stop the plagues that are infesting your house!

Chapter 3

STOP THE PLAGUES IN YOUR HOME

And he who owns the house comes and tells the priest, saying, "It seems to me that there is some plague in the house," then the priest...shall examine the plague; and indeed if the plague is on the walls of the house with ingrained streaks, greenish or reddish, which appear to be deep in the wall...then the priest shall command that they take away the stones in which is the plague, and they shall cast them into an unclean place outside the city. And he shall cause the house to be scraped inside, all around, and the dust that they scrape off they shall pour out in an unclean place outside the city.

| LEVITICUS 14:35–37, 40–41 |

WHEN THE ISRAELITES took possession of the Promised Land, they were retaking the land once owned by their ancestor Abraham. Having lived in Egypt for more than four hundred years, the Hebrews returned to homes that were previously built and owned by idol-worshiping heathen tribes, commonly referred to as *Canaanites* (Gen. 15:21). After reentering the Promised Land, the Hebrews discovered three major hindrances that are a reflection of the three battles believers will encounter as they pursue the promises of God's blessings for their lives.

1. The walled cities (Num. 13:28)
2. The race of giants (Num. 13:33)
3. The seven opposing nations (Deut. 7:1)

Each of these hindrances that stood in the path of progress for Israel has an application today and represents hindrances that believers will experience as they journey on their road to experiencing God's fullness.

1. *There were walled cities.*

These walled cities represented strongholds. Ancient city walls were originally made from mud bricks, as was discovered by archeologists who excavated Jericho, also known as the *Tel es-Sultan*, in Israel.[1] Eventually the buildings were constructed from stones. The city gates were also framed from large stones with huge wooden doors, and watchmen guarded the gates from intruders and watched for approaching armies. As the Hebrews contemplated how they could take possession of the Promised Land, their question was, "How can we conquer these cities when we are unable to penetrate the gates and the walls?" They didn't realize that God would supernaturally allow the city walls to fall, as they did at Jericho (Josh. 6:5).

These walled cities are a picture of *spiritual barriers* that we encounter on our spiritual journey. There are four spiritual barriers believers encounter on our road to spiritual blessing. They are:

1. The traditions of men
2. Wrong thinking
3. Unforgiveness
4. Unbelief

Every denomination claims to base its doctrinal teachings on the Scriptures. In fact, the major Protestant denominations all have the same foundational teachings concerning Christ's virgin birth, His death and resurrection, and the fact that Christ is the Son of God. There are, however, various man-made traditions that each group has forged over their years of existence. Often these traditions became *the truth* instead of a tradition and were given more importance than the Word of God.

I was raised in an ultratraditional full-gospel church that in its early teaching taught it was a sin for a woman to cut her hair or wear any makeup or any type of jewelry, including a wedding band. I have taught that if a woman has a personal conviction on these matters, she should follow those convictions, since we are to work out our own salvation with fear and trembling (Phil. 2:12). However, some of our practical commitments were mere traditions based upon someone's private interpretation of certain scriptures. Often traditions are exalted higher than the Word of God itself. People were often prejudged by their outward appearance and not accepted by others if they didn't fit the traditional picture of what a Christian should look like. Man-made traditions not founded on solid biblical evidence will form a spiritual barrier.

In Jesus's time the Pharisees taught that demons could cling to a person's hands. This is why they rebuked the disciples for picking corn without washing their hands (Mark 7:2). I have often said that they were *nitpicking* at corn picking! There is not one scripture in the entire Old Testament that even implies that an evil spirit clings to the hands and that if you don't wash them before eating you may swallow a demon.

Jesus taught:

> There is nothing that enters a man from outside which can defile him; but the things which come out of him, those are the things that defile a man.
>
> —MARK 7:15

Christ rebuked the Pharisees for exalting the traditions of the elders above the commandments of God: "All too well you reject the commandment of God, that you may keep your tradition" (Mark 7:9). While some traditions are based on Scripture, unbiblical traditions will stop the authority of God's Word in your life:

> …making the word of God of no effect through your tradition which you have handed down. And many such things you do.
>
> —MARK 7:13

There are hundreds of thousands of Christians who sincerely love the Lord, yet they do not believe the nine gifts of the Holy Spirit listed in 1 Corinthians 12:7–10 are in operation today. They believe that healing ceased with the death of the last apostle, John. They are unbelieving believers because they say they believe the Bible, but some man-made theological tradition handed down in a denominational school has created a spiritual barrier, just as the walled cities were barriers to the Hebrew people. Instead of breaking through the barrier, it is easier to become passive and say, "Oh well, that's not my cup of tea."

2. *There were giants in the land.*

The second hindrance was a race of giants, large men who were eight feet tall to as high as thirteen feet tall (1 Sam. 17:4). These giants were real, and they were frightening. Josephus the Jewish historian wrote about the giants when he said, "There were till then left the race of giants, who had bodies so large, and countenances so entirely different from other men, that they were surprising to the sight, and terrible to the hearing."[2]

Giants existed before and after the flood of Noah. In Noah's time, the race of giants caused the imagination of men to be evil continually. (See Genesis 6:1–5.) The giants in the Promised Land created fear because they impacted the imagination, creating fear. When ten of the twelve spies brought back a report to Moses, they all agreed the land was blessed, but ten said the giants were so large that the Hebrews would look like grasshoppers beside them (Num. 13:33). These ten spies never interviewed a giant who said, "Hey, you little Hebrew grasshopper, I'm going to stomp you into the ground!" The grasshopper image was in their imagination—they had seen *themselves* small and insignificant. Two men, Joshua and Caleb, had another spirit (Num. 14:24), and forty years later, Caleb, at age eighty-five, ran three giants off a mountain in Hebron (Josh. 15:13–14). That's pretty good intimidation from an eighty-five-year-old grasshopper!

Giants played with the imagination of the people. Your imagination frames images in your mind, and those images then stir emotions. For example, pornography forms imaginations, and the emotions stir desires in the flesh. The image of a coming tornado seizes the imagination with an image of a person's home in ruins, thus opening the emotion of fear. When a doctor enters a room with an X-ray and tells your loved one he or she has cancer, the mind begins to form the image of a person lying in a hospital room, slowly dying. These mental images are like giant road-blocks on the road to blessings.

While many mental pictures are accurate, some are based upon wrong information. Fear is often based on assumptions and possibilities and not on what will actually occur. When I say *Iraq*, some see defeat and others see victory. When I say *Israel*, some visualize danger or internal fighting, while others, including myself, visualize thirty-two Holy Land tours with thousands of pilgrims having the time of their life. When I say the word *Muslim*, some will see the twin towers falling and the war on terror. Others will see a group of nomadic people living in tents in the deserts of the Middle East. Your images are often based upon correct or incorrect information sent to the mainframe of your mind.

Knowledge and understanding can prevent wild imaginations from taking control of your mind and creating mental giants in your life. Years ago my entire family was flying back from Nashville, Tennessee, on our ministry's Cessna 421 plane. I had appeared on a major Christian network, and we were only thirty minutes from home. Between Nashville and Chattanooga, we flew into clouds, and the wind began tossing the plane around. Suddenly, rain began pounding against the plane, and lightning danced through the clouds. This was the first time I had experienced all three at once—wind, rain, and lightning. To be honest, I felt a cold blanket of fear settle inside the entire plane. At that moment my little four-year-old girl looked at her mom and said, "Mommy, don't be afraid, because I'm here with you. It will be OK." Instantly she fell asleep in her mother's arms. I thought, "She doesn't know how dangerous this is. That's why she can sleep!"

After landing safely, I asked the pilot why he took a risk and flew into a storm. He looked at me and laughed. He said, "That lightning was more than an hour away from us. The light carries in the clouds and makes it look like it is next to the plane. The wind was normal, and the rain was no big deal. We can fly through rain." He let me know (which I already knew) that he would never put himself or me at risk. My fear was based upon my imagination and lack of knowledge. My little girl had more faith than I did. She was like Jesus, sleeping during the storm

(Matt. 8:24). In my mind the storm had been a giant, when, in fact, it was just a grasshopper!

3. *There were seven opposing nations.*

As Israel entered the Promised Land, they were told to defeat and overtake the land where the heathen pagan tribes were living among them.

> When the LORD your God brings you into the land which you go to possess, and has cast out many nations before you, the Hittites and the Girgashites and the Amorites and the Canaanites and the Perizzites and the Hivites and the Jebusites, seven nations greater and mightier than you, and when the LORD your God delivers them over to you, you shall conquer them and utterly destroy them. You shall make no covenant with them nor show mercy to them.
>
> —DEUTERONOMY 7:1–2

These seven tribal nations are:

1. The Hittites
2. The Girgashites
3. The Amorites
4. The Canaanites
5. The Perizzites
6. The Hivites
7. The Jebusites

These seven tribal nations dwelt in the Promised Land for hundreds of years prior to Israel's exodus from Egypt. They built cities, worshiped idols, and controlled many of the primitive roads within the Promised Land. God warned the Hebrews of dire consequences if they did not deal with these opposing nations.

> But if you do not drive out the inhabitants of the land from before you, then it shall be that those whom you let remain shall be irritants in your eyes and thorns in your sides, and they shall harass you in the land where you dwell.
>
> —NUMBERS 33:55

If these seven nations, which I have nicknamed "the seven ites," were not conquered, then their gods would become a snare to the Hebrews (Judg. 2:3). These seven tribes would affect the people's eyes and their sides. From a practical application, your spiritual eyes are used to discern, and your side is your hip area. You cannot run any race if you have a limp in the hip. Many believers are vexed by the people with whom they associate. Often Christians are required to work with or be around individuals who have no respect for the Scriptures and actually persecute them for their beliefs. Hanging with the wrong crowd will stunt your spiritual discernment and affect your walk with God!

The walled cities, giants, and seven ites are all strongholds in the Promised Land. There is a danger in suggesting to folks that if they come to Christ, all their problems will cease. Ministers often emphasize the blessings of a salvation covenant, including the financial aspect, that will follow a Christian. However, some new Christians become disillusioned when persecution, spiritual battles, and problems continue in their lives following their conversion. Weak believers are often unprepared for the strongholds in the promised land and unaware of the fact that battles often precede blessings.

Seizing These Strongholds

Since giants, walled cities, and seven nations form strongholds, read what Paul wrote concerning dealing with mental strongholds:

> For the weapons of our warfare are not carnal but mighty in God for pulling down strongholds, casting down arguments and every high thing that exalts itself against the knowledge of God, bringing every thought into captivity to the obedience of Christ.
>
> —2 CORINTHIANS 10:4–5

The enemy exerts pressure in your mind to suppress your knowledge of God. One form of knowledge is that which is stored in the memory bank of your mind. The Lord often uses your memories in a positive manner to remind you of His goodness and ability. When David requested from King Saul the permission to fight Goliath, David reminded Saul of two recent victories David had experienced—when he killed a bear and a lion (1 Sam. 17:34–35). In his later life David recalled how God supernaturally provided wealth, food, water, and clothing for Israel in the wilderness (Ps. 78), and he knew these same provisions were available for those in covenant with God.

Each of us has both good and bad memories. Bad events and your past life of sin must never control your future. When Paul was the famed Saul of Tarsus, he persecuted the saints and consented to the death of Stephen (Acts 8:1). After his conversion, some churches were concerned that Paul was faking his conversion to secretly infiltrate deeper into the church, collecting names for future arrests. Paul understood their concern and once wrote that we must forget those things that are behind and reach for the things that are before (Phil. 3:13). Bad memories must be buried in the grave of the past and never be resurrected. However, good memories can be recalled to remind us of when God came through for us—when He answered a prayer, performed a miracle, or blessed us in an unexpected manner.

This memory recall is used by the Holy Spirit when a person who is out of fellowship with God sits in a local congregation and experiences the convicting power of the Holy Spirit. An old song, a verse from the Bible, an older saint in the congregation, or a certain message will trigger the memories from that person's childhood, which will rise again and remind him or her, as they reminded the prodigal son, of the blessings in the Father's house (Luke 15:17–18).

Scripture is clear that God desires for us to have a mind that is clear from the clutter that creates barriers and prevents the peace of God from preserving our minds. Paul wrote:

> For God has not given us a spirit of fear, but of power and of love and of a sound mind.
>
> —2 TIMOTHY 1:7

The Greek word for the phrase "sound mind" indicates a mind that is self-controlled and disciplined. A disciplined mind will guard the eyes, ears, and heart, allowing certain thoughts and feelings to enter the soul and spirit and preventing others. God gives us power and love to create a sound mind. The Greek word for "power" in this verse is *dunamis*, which scholars say alludes to inward power and ability. When believers receive the gift of the Holy Spirit, they receive power (*dunamis*—Acts 1:8). The same word is used when the woman with the issue of blood touched Christ's garment, and virtue (*dunamis*) went out of His body into the woman and cured her (Mark 5:30). The inner working of God's power resists the spirit of fear! Perfect love is the key to overcoming fear.

> There is no fear in love; but perfect love casts out fear, because fear involves torment. But he who fears has not been made perfect in love.
>
> —1 JOHN 4:18

Perfect love is complete love (Greek—*agape*), love that understands that you and the Almighty are in covenant and you are a daughter or a son of the heavenly Father. If He cares for the small sparrow and watches the lilies of a field as they grow, then you are far superior to all other creatures He created, and He will care for you!

There are three Greek words for "love" in the New Testament:

1. *Agape*—a word used to speak of the type of love God has for Christ and requires of us to have

2. *Phileo*—a word used to allude to tender affection; used of the love Christ had for His disciples

3. *Philanthropia*—a word that denoted the love for a fellow man; humanitarian love[3]

When crisis comes and you question, "Why me, God? You don't care for me. You are against me. You have forsaken me," then love is not perfected. When crisis comes and you can say, "I don't know why, but God is not surprised. He is with me despite this. He will not forsake me. God is preparing a test so I can have a testimony," then your love relationship has been perfected in the knowledge of your Father.

We are also promised a transformed mind.

And do not be conformed to this world, but be transformed by the renewing of your mind, that you may prove what is that good and acceptable and perfect will of God.
—ROMANS 12:2

The word *transformed* is the Greek word *metamorphoo*, which means "to change and transform one state to another." The root word is *morphe* and stresses an inward change.[4] Christ was transfigured in front of His disciples, and His countenance was glowing with God's glory (Matt. 17:1–2). Literally, His countenance was altered from one form to another. We are transformed by the renewing of our mind. A third blessing is a renewed mind.

And be renewed in the spirit of your mind.
—EPHESIANS 4:23

The word *renew* is "to make back new again: not as it was but different from what it was." It does not mean to destroy your attitude but to impart within your mind a new attitude. It does not stop you from thinking, but it gives you new thoughts. Whatever is occurring in you will affect those living around you. Any spiritual conflict in your mind will flow over into the atmosphere of your house. Thus the soulish realm (the mind) is the center of the spiritual conflict. The mind controls the body, and the mind can either believe or doubt when it comes to receiving blessing in a person's spirit. All information—good and bad—is filtered through the mind!

Back to the Streaks

What would cause these colored streaks to form on the outer walls of the house, creating uncleanness and a plague in the home? When Israel departed from Egypt, the people stripped the Egyptians of their valuable gold and silver jewelry (Exod. 12:35–36). The seven pagan nations living in the Promised Land had heard how the Hebrew God had destroyed the Egyptian army, and great fear seized their hearts. When two Hebrew spies secretly entered the home of Rahab, a harlot living in Jericho, she stated that all men in Jericho had heard of the amazing feats of the Hebrew God forty years earlier and how two giants, Sihon and Og, were slain. She reported that the hearts of all the men in Jericho fainted after hearing these reports (Josh. 2:10–11)!

Out of fear, the tribal inhabitants, called the *Canaanites*, would hide their money and their idols in the walls of their homes. There were no bank vaults to secure your wealth, and coins were often buried in dirt floors. Idols were often hidden behind the plaster walls. The purpose for hiding the money and sacred objects was the hope that if the people were expelled from their homes in the future, they could return and reclaim their hidden wealth or their god.

The heathens were unaware that the land was actually a promised possession to Abraham and his descendants (Gen. 12:7). For several hundred years the Hebrews had dwelt in Goshen in Egypt. But once they were able to enter the land with Joshua, they were prepared to retake their promised possessions. God said that the Hebrews would live in homes that they did not build (Deut. 6:10–11). However, there were things *hidden* in the homes that needed to be exposed and dealt with. Thus strange-colored streaks suddenly appeared on the plaster walls inside the houses. Once these streaks were visible, the priest was called in to perform a five-phase examination of the house. (See Leviticus 13 and 14.) At that moment the house was emptied, and the priest announced that the home was unclean as he continued his examination. In his examination:

- He examined the physical evidence appearing on the walls.
- He waited seven days to see if the streaks had spread.
- He scraped the house to remove the fungus of the plague.
- He watched, and if it returned again, it was called *the fretting leprosy.*
- If it was fretting, the owner must tear down the house and rebuild it again.

It is important to note that if the streaks were lower than the walls, then they were coming from the foundation of the house. The foundation was often where valuables were hidden (money and jewelry or idols). If the leprosy overtook the house, they had to tear out the old foundation and rebuild a new foundation, constructing a new home. The danger was that the leprosy inside the house could spread to the individuals personally, eventually affecting the health of the homeowners. Mold in any home can create health problems and serious sickness.

The Wrong Foundation

In the early days of Israel, the foundation of most homes consisted of stones and dirt floors. The stones were covered with a plaster, and in the more expensive homes beautiful mosaic tiles carpeted the floors of main rooms. Smaller compartments could be dug under the floor and in the walls as hiding places.

There is a significant spiritual application. Anyone can *own* a house, but it is the people living in the physical structure who create the *atmosphere* within a home. For more than thirty-five years, every Christmas I would travel to Davis, West Virginia, to join my parents, siblings, and my Italian grandparents, John and Lucy Bava, for the Christmas holidays. The three-bedroom house was overflowing with family. The kitchen became a twenty-four-hour restaurant, and we laughed, played games, and made unforgettable memories. My grandparents had been married for sixty-six years when Granddad passed away. After he passed, I took Grandmother back to the house. I saw her sitting alone, rocking in Granddad's easy chair as she cried. She said, "This house doesn't feel the same anymore. It was your granddad's presence that made this a home." The home of John and Lucy Bava was built entirely on a spiritual foundation of faith, passed on to their two daughters, Janet and Juanita (my mother), and eventually transferred to the four children of Juanita and Fred Stone: Diana, me, Phillip, and Melanie (my younger sister)!

The spiritual foundation for our families must be laid out at an early age. Children are instructed by parents, siblings, close relatives, and friends. The foundation must be built with solid truth and teaching—as firm as the stones laid in the ancient floors. Too many foundations, instead of being cement, are dirt with little mites and bugs running around—the proverbial little foxes spoiling the vines (Song of Sol. 2:15).

The Walls in the House

The walls of each home were also constructed with large stones dug up from the surrounding area. I have toured the ruins of ancient cities from Christ's time, including Capernaum, Chorazin, and Bethsaida (Matt. 11:21–23), and have stood among the remains and ruins of many of the homes and shops from the Roman period. The homes were constructed from the stones and basalt rocks. Especially in the Golan Heights of northern Israel, all of the ancient buildings were made of black-gray basalt stones—a volcanic rock that covers the area just above the Sea of Galilee.

The walls were built for security—to protect the inhabitants and their possessions and prevent unwanted people or animals from entering. In Scripture, the walls of Jericho fell on the seventh day, after the Hebrews had marched around daily for seven days (Josh. 6:20). Years ago my Israeli tour guide, Gideon Shor, pointed to a large jar split in half that was discovered and embedded within the clay bricks of Jericho. The archeologists found the small bones of what appeared to be an infant within the jar that had been encased within the walls. Perhaps this is why Jericho was the only Canaanite city that was destroyed when the walls fell. God knew what the Canaanites had placed within the walls, and God hates the hands of those who shed innocent blood (Prov. 6:17).

The enemies of Israel were able to penetrate the walls of Jerusalem, which were once considered impregnable (Lam. 4:12). Christ taught that Jerusalem would be destroyed because of generations of religious leaders who permitted the shedding of the innocent blood of the righteous (Matt. 23:35–38). What was hidden in the walls could bring disfavor and spiritual judgment against the owner of the house or city!

We Are Called "Lively Stones"

Just as the foundation, walls, and entrance gates of each home were built from large, strong stones, the church is built upon the solid foundation of Christ (called the "chief cornerstone" in 1 Peter 2:6), written about by the prophets and apostles. As the church began to grow throughout the Book of Acts, Peter revealed that we are "lively stones."

Ye also, as lively stones, are built up a spiritual house, an holy priesthood, to offer up spiritual sacrifices, acceptable to God by Jesus Christ.

—1 PETER 2:5, KJV

Just what is a lively stone? When Christ was being worshiped in Jerusalem, the ultrareligious Pharisees were offended that small children were caught up in the emotion of the moment and that Christ's followers were waving palm branches and preparing the way for the Messiah to enter the temple. When these religious stiff-necks came to Christ demanding that He silence the multitude, Scripture tells us:

But He answered and said to them, "I tell you that if these should keep silent, the stones would immediately cry out."

—LUKE 19:40

Were these stones that could cry out the literal white limestone rocks surrounding the mountains of Jerusalem? Or was this an allusion to a certain group of people whom He would raise up? The answer is in Matthew 3:9:

And do not think to say to yourselves, "We have Abraham as our father." For I say to you that God is able to raise up children to Abraham from these stones.

These stones were the young followers of Christ and the common people who received His ministry. In Christ's day the established religion had turned into a stiff, formal ritual filled with man-made routines and lifeless motions. The first-century believers, and believers in the church today who are true worshipers, are the living, or lively, stones that are crying out in praise and worship!

The Spreading Leprosy on the Walls

If a Hebrew family living in a house suddenly saw green and yellow streaks appear on the inside walls of the house, it indicated that a form of leprosy was breaking out. If the plague was not immediately dealt with, the leprosy could spread throughout the house. The leprosy would also affect the health and well-being of those dwelling within its walls.

In Scripture, because leprosy made a person unclean and caused a separation from the temple and from the family, it is a picture of the results of sin. The effects are similar. Leprosy begins small but grows fast, just as sin often begins small but spreads fast. If left unchecked, leprosy will eventually destroy a person, just as sin left to fester in a human soul will eventually destroy a person.

In ancient Israel, when a person was diagnosed with leprosy, that person was forcibly separated from those who were clean and was placed in a leper colony to eventually die, separated from loved ones. Sin can certainly cause a separation from those you love.

Often an idol hidden in the house would produce streaks of leprosy. In like manner, any hidden sin that continually binds a person to its stronghold will create a spiritual fungus in our spiritual house, which includes our minds, bodies, and families, and in our churches.

The Procedure for Purging the House

Once the leprosy was identified, the priest would order a special procedure for purging the house and removing the dangerous plague. The first inspection involved detailed examinations of both the foundation and the walls. The priest would remove the dust from the stones. The dust could reveal the origin of the leprosy.

It is significant that God formed man from the dust of the ground (Gen. 2:7). After man sinned, the main culprit, the serpent, was cursed and told he would eat dust (Gen. 3:14). Serpents have a forked tongue and use the tip of their tongues to sense odors and the direction they are coming from. The closer to the serpent an object walks, the more dust is stirred up. Reptiles are continually sticking out their tongues and *reading* what is surrounding them. A snake's tongue is often called *a stinger,* although it doesn't sting. Our tongues, however, can emit words to create life or death, and negative words are called "darts" and "arrows"—evil words that can crush, sting, and bring pain to a person (Ps. 64:3; Prov. 18:21). A person who is hypocritical and says one thing but does another is said to have a forked tongue.

The spiritual application is amazing. Man's flesh came from the dust of the earth. Dust represents man's carnal nature. The carnal man, called the *natural man* (1 Cor. 2:14), continually clashes with the spiritual man. Since the body comes from dust, and the carnal nature is a picture of dust, the serpent eats the dust, or feeds off the flesh nature of men and women. The more dust (carnal nature) that is stirred up, the easier it is for the serpent (the adversary—Rev. 20:2) to read the situation, smell the stink being created, and move toward the situation! Just as the plague can be found in the dust of the house, so the enemy can gain access by feeding from the dust of our carnal nature!

Once the streaks were spotted, the priest would then remove any stones in the house where the streak was visible. If controlling and disciplining our mind and our flesh do not change our situation, then this procedure of the priest removing the stones where the streak was found also has a practical spiritual application.

As pointed out earlier, stones in the Bible can represent people. At times it becomes necessary to separate from certain *types of people* who are detrimental to your spiritual life. Christian teenagers are very often pulled into a life of alcohol, drugs, and illicit behavior because of the people who surround them. At times you must remove the stones in your house, or sever relationships with people who are bringing leprosy into your life. If the stones (bad influences in your life) are not removed, then the third process of the priest holds an application for you.

If the leprosy was a fretting leprosy, it indicated that the house was controlled and dominated by the plague. It was impossible for a family to live in the house under these dreadful conditions. The mold would make a person very sick and could eventually cause lung disease and death. The priest knew it was necessary for the house to be taken apart and rebuilt with new materials.

Individuals under the bondage of alcohol, drugs, or certain vices may find it necessary to leave home and enter a season of rehabilitation, where they detoxify their bodies and separate themselves from the negative influences that are wrecking their minds and bodies. Some individuals receive instant and complete deliverance when they enter a powerful redemptive covenant with Christ. However, others need the support of a group that understands the bondage and will help the new Christian defeat the giant and tear down the stronghold. It will then be possible to rebuild a new life and a new beginning! Perhaps you need a complete spiritual makeover!

Reviewing the Procedures

1. *Remove the leprosy* by laying aside any weights or sins that are weighing down your walk with God. This removal process begins with the *desire to change* from what you presently are to what God planned for you to be. This desire begins with repentance, which means not only to regret your deeds and actions and be sorry for your sins, but also to turn and go in a new direction.

2. *Rebuild a fresh foundation* by replacing your old thoughts with new thoughts centered on the inspired Word of God. Each new truth you learn and put into practice in your daily walk with the Lord is a *new stone* laid on the foundation of your life. You continually grow in the grace and knowledge of Christ, which creates a strong spiritual house.

3. *Restore the house* with new materials: new friends, new relations, and new directions. God loves new things. The Bible speaks of God doing a new thing (Isa. 43:19)! God also said that we would have a new heart and a new spirit (Ezek. 36:26), become a new creation (2 Cor. 5:17), speak with new tongues (Mark 16:17), and live on a new earth in the New Jerusalem (Rev. 21:1–2)! Don't be afraid of losing old friends—God will give you a new family, the family of God.

When an individual enters the redemptive covenant through the atoning work of Christ, then "if any man be in Christ, he is a new creature: old things are passed away; behold, all things are become new"

(2 Cor. 5:17, KJV). At that moment you receive your name inscribed in the heavenly registry, the Lamb's Book of Life (Rev. 21:27). You become a child of God through spiritual adoption (Rom. 8:15) and are privileged to address the Almighty as "Abba," an Aramaic name found in Romans 8:15 meaning "Father!" Through entering a born-again experience by faith, you now receive a new spiritual family of brothers and sisters, identified as the "family of God" (Eph. 3:14–15). Your old house becomes a newly renovated dwelling filled with righteousness, peace, and joy in the Holy Spirit (Rom. 14:17). The Almighty has given each person a will to choose what is right, good, and best for him or her. By choosing a lifetime covenant with God, you receive blessings in this life and eternal life in the life to come!

Chapter 4

PATTERNS FOR PURGING YOUR HOME

Do you not know that you are the temple of God and that the Spirit of God dwells in you? If anyone defiles the temple of God, God will destroy him. For the temple of God is holy, which temple you are.

| 1 CORINTHIANS 3:16–17 |

THE ILLUSTRATION IS told of a man who had such compassion for animals and reptiles of all types that he once came upon a seriously injured snake and took the dangerous reptile into his home to nurse the creature back to health. He became comfortable with placing his hand into the cage, leaving food and water. One day, to his shock, the serpent coiled back and bit the hand that was feeding it. The man jerked back his hand and yelled, "Why did you do that? I cared for you, and you bit me!"

The serpent replied, "You knew when you brought me into your house that I was a snake, so why are you so surprised?"

The moral of the story is—watch out for what you allow in your house!

The Sanctity of the House of God

Two magnificent houses of God, or temples, once sat high on Mount Moriah in Jerusalem. The first temple was constructed by King Solomon. The second temple was a reconstruction of the ruins of Solomon's temple, which had been destroyed during a Babylonian invasion. Under Nehemiah's leadership after the Jews returned from Babylonian captivity, the toppled stone walls, burned gates, and rubbish were removed and repaired to prepare a house of worship for the Almighty. Prior to Christ's birth, a Judean Gentile king named Herod expanded the Temple Mount platform, enlarging the southern section of the sacred mountain.

Both Jewish laws and the revelation from the Almighty that was given to Israel were extremely strict regarding the construction, care, and treatment of His sacred house in Jerusalem.

Consider the sanctity of the construction of the temple. The Hebrew people were not permitted to carve or chisel in stone any form of an image of man or beast in, on, or around the sacred compound. The huge columns and archways were engraved with designs of flowers, fruit, and geometric patterns but not with any human face or animal. Even the two gold cherubim on the ark of the covenant, beaten from pure gold, were left faceless to prevent the priests and people from being tempted to worship the metallic angels on the mercy seat. When foreigners carried coins to give to the temple treasurer, moneychangers exchanged them for special temple coins. Many of the coins in the Roman period were minted with faces of emperors, gods and goddesses, or animals. Idol gods were impressed on some of the coins, and these were not permitted to be carried onto the holy mountain, lest a form of idolatry be allowed.

There was also a special level of holiness and sanctification required of the Levites and the high priest. According to Leviticus 21:17–24, any priest entering the priesthood could not have any form of physical defect or blemish on his body. According to Jewish history and tradition, there were 104 defects that would permanently disqualify a priest and 22 others that would temporarily cause him to be disqualified. These physical restrictions have an amazing application for the believer today.

Seven Physical Restrictions	Application for Today
He could not be *blind*.	We must have spiritual *vision*.
He could not be *lame*.	We must have a steady and *straight walk* with God.
He could not have a *flat nose*.	We must use our *senses* to discern right from wrong.
He could not be *hunchbacked*.	We must not have *twisted thinking*.
He could not be *dwarfed*.	We must experience *spiritual growth*.

Seven Physical Restrictions	Application for Today
He could not have *scabs*.	We must remain *pure* and clean inwardly.
He could not be a *eunuch*.	We must be able to *reproduce* spiritual fruit.

Before entering the temple, all priests were to submerge in a mik'vot, a large hollowed-out chamber with steps carved out of natural limestone, filled with rain or spring water. Today it would be similar to a baptistery in a local church. All priests, and all the men entering the temple, would disrobe, step down into the water that came up to between the waist and the shoulders, and lower themselves under the water. A man was assigned to stand above them, placing his foot on their heads to ensure they went fully under the water, covering all parts of their bodies. This was an act of sanctification and a ritual cleansing that every man had to perform before entering the holy house of God in Jerusalem.

The priests also donned white robes, representing purity and righteousness, when ministering at the temple (Rev. 19:8). The priests' spiritual duties were numerous, but their main focus was preparing the many sacrifices offered by the people on a daily basis and receiving the offerings of the Israelites into the temple treasury.

Three Levels in Approaching God

In ancient Israel, there were three types of people who approached God. The first were the Israelites, which consisted of common Hebrew families scattered throughout the entire land of Israel from Dan to Beersheba. The second group was the Levites. Unlike the other sons of Jacob, the sons of Levi were not granted any land among the tribal inheritance (Num. 18:23). This was due to the fact that the Levites were to be full-time ministers in the temple and were to live in and around the area of God's house, which was eventually built in Jerusalem. The third and most important person who approached God was the high priest. The first high priest appointed by God was Moses's brother, Aaron, who ministered at the tabernacle in the wilderness (Num. 17:1–13). The priesthood was hereditary and was handed down from father to son for many generations. The temple and the Jewish priesthood ceased in Israel after the destruction of the temple and Jerusalem in the year 70.

Each group—the Israelites, the Levites, and the high priest—was permitted into specific areas when engaging in worshiping God and offering sacrifices. The temple was divided into three specific areas: the outer court, the inner court, and the holy of holies. The common people were only permitted to worship in the outer court. The Levites were granted access to both the outer and the inner courts of the house of God. The high priest, however, was permitted unlimited access to all three levels—the outer court, the inner court, and the holy of holies.

The Torah, the first five books of the Bible written by Moses in the wilderness, became the divine instructions providing moral, judicial, and spiritual guidelines for all Israelites to follow. God demanded stricter requirements from the high priest than from the Levites, and He required more specific guidelines and regulations for the Levites than for the common people. The reason for this demand of holiness, or separation in the ministry, had to do with the various levels of glory and divine presence that rested in each level.

The Spiritual Application

When we as human beings hunger to draw nearer to God, we soon discover that the closer we move to the light of heaven (which is identified by the phrase "the glory of the Lord"), the more flaws we are apt to see in our own lives and character. This is why we are to "lay aside every weight, and the sin which so easily ensnares us" as we run the race of faith (Heb. 12:1). As we move closer to Him, we increase the level of supernatural light that brings illumination to our souls.

For example, there were three levels of approach and three dimensions of light present at the temple. When the Israelites were in the outer court, the only light they experienced was the light of the sun. This natural light enabled them to see what was in front, beside, and behind them. Individuals today who are living short of the wonderful presence of God are abiding in the natural world and operating by their natural senses. The Bible teaches that the natural man, who is carnal, cannot receive the things of the Spirit of God, for they are foolishness to him and can only be spiritually discerned (1 Cor. 2:14). It is more comfortable to live in the sunlight, where you can see your surroundings with your natural eyes and know that you are in control within your own comfort zone, than to move into a spiritual dimension with God where you must walk by faith and not by sight (2 Cor. 5:7). Many Christians are living in this natural level. They are moved and shaken by what they see and feel and are not established by their personal faith.

The Levites, however, had to move beyond the outer court sunlight to an inner court, where the light of the menorah (a golden lampstand) was burning. A Levite (priest) was selected each morning to offer the incense in the inner court, also called *the holy place* (Luke 1:8–10). The only light in this second chamber was the seven-branched candlestick called the *menorah*. Once the priest stepped behind the large curtain, called *the veil*, separating the holy place from the outer court, this golden lamp-stand cast a golden aura around the room. The first pressing of oil from crushed olives, collected from the olive trees on the Mount of Olives, provided the oil for the light of the menorah.

Moving from the outer court into the inner court, the priest experienced a sudden shock to his eyes, similar to that of a person who steps from outside on a sunny day into a restaurant or building where the light is dim. Eventually the dull surroundings become clearer as the eyes become adjusted to the light, and a person is able to see more clearly. The menorah provided light from oil, and the seven-branched light lit the sacred chamber where the table of showbread and the golden altar rested. This was the chamber where the priest would offer incense each morning, believing the smoke from the incense held the words (prayers) of God's people. The offering of the incense would be impossible without the oil and the light emitting from the candlestick.

Once a year, on the Day of Atonement, the high priest would pass through the great veil separating the holy place from the most sacred area of the temple, the holy of holies (Exod. 30:10; Lev. 23:27). According to most sources, there was no natural light emitting from the holy of holies, especially in Solomon's time. This would mean that unless the curtain (veil) was drawn back, the only light making visible the ark of the covenant was the glory of God, the same light that lit the camp of Israel for forty years in the wilderness (Num. 14:14).

These three levels of light reveal an important truth. Most believers live continually in the realm of the natural, rubbing elbows with nonbelievers eight hours a day and dealing with the cares of life. Once the sun sets, there is no light, and they are in darkness. Eventually, living in the flesh will produce darkness, and people will stumble over snares and fall into traps.

We must have the light from the menorah, which represents the Spirit of God working in the church and in our lives (Rev. 1:20). As we move closer to God through prayer, fasting, and intimacy with God, we then walk in the light as He in the light—the light of His presence, moving from the natural to the supernatural.

As believers progress in their intimacy with God, they will eventually find themselves in the holy of holies, where they receive supernatural illumination and revelation directly from the Lord Himself!

In my own life I have discovered that the most effective messages came after spending hours in prayer and meditation before God. I have written more than forty songs, including many that have been recorded. The most moving songs came under the inspiration of the Holy Spirit. The same is true with the books and resource materials made available through our ministry. When a believer spends time on Earth seeking the God who dwells in heaven, then heaven and Earth will kiss, and the believer will be caught in the middle of the smack!

You Are a Walking Temple

Christ knew that the temple in Jerusalem would be destroyed within a generation (Matt. 24:1–2). He also realized that the divine presence of God would be transferred from a man-made building in Jerusalem to the physical bodies and spirits of believers who walked in the new covenant. Each believer is a walking temple. Instead of meeting God in one designated location, we take Him with us everywhere we go. Just as the ancient tabernacle of Moses and the temples of Solomon and Herod (as some call the rebuilt temple) were sacred structures with a distinct design consisting of three sacred courts and chambers, so too the human body is a tripartite temple. The Bible reveals that we consist of a body, a soul, and a spirit (1 Thess. 5:23). The physical body is a reflection of the temple's outer court, the soul reflects the temple's inner court, and the human spirit represents the sacred chamber called the holy of holies.

In the earthly temple, men could see the outer court, just as the human body is visible to all human eyes. The soul is housed within the body and cannot be seen to the natural eye, just as the temple's inner court was hidden behind the temple veil or two large doors in the early Jewish temples. The soul is the seat of our thinking, reasoning, and illumination and is a reflection of the seven-branched candlestick whose light illuminated the inner court. The holy of holies was hidden from public view and was the most sacred and holy part of the temple. Just so, the human spirit is a reflection of the holy of holies, the place where God's presence dwelt. All spiritual blessings begin in the spirit and work their way outward into our lives.

The Manna, the Law, and the Rod

In the third chamber, the holy of holies, was the sacred ark of the covenant. According to Paul, there were three important items stored within the golden box: a golden pot of manna, the tables of the Law, and the rod of Aaron (Heb. 9:4). The manna was the bread sent from heaven that the Israelites ate during their forty years in the wilderness (Num. 11:6–9). The rod of Aaron was a dead tree limb that blossomed, producing almonds and leaves, a visible sign to Israel that Aaron was God's appointed priest (Num. 17:7–9). The tablets of the Law were the commandments carved on stone and laid inside the golden ark of the covenant by Moses (Deut. 10:5).

The ark is a perfect picture of Christ Himself. When we receive Christ, we can also receive the manna, the Law, and the rod. The manna was the bread from heaven (Exod. 16:4), and Jesus was the bread come down from heaven, or the heavenly manna (John 6:32–35). This represents the gift of salvation, which is imparted when we receive Christ in our spirit as our redeemer. Once we are saved, we then pursue the tablets of the Law, or the Word of God, to abide in us (John 15:7). The Law represents our sanctification, which follows our gift of salvation. Just as the Law was designed to separate the people from their heathen counterparts, the Word of God separates us from the desires of the flesh and marks us as a holy people. When we progress from salvation to sanctification, we can also experience the pattern of the rod of Aaron, which represents the power of the Holy Spirit.

When Moses was challenged as to who would be the true priests in Israel, he asked for the twelve tribes to take their chief leaders' rods and lay the twelve rods in front of the tabernacle door. Of the twelve, Aaron's rod was the only one that produced almonds and blossomed. Notice that the true priesthood produced visible fruit. There are many rods or ideas of how the Holy Spirit works in a believer's life. Some churches teach that you receive the Holy Spirit at conversion, while others teach that you receive the gift of the Spirit upon receiving sanctification. Others believe the gift comes when you are baptized in water. Classical Pentecostals teach that the initial manifestation comes when a person speaks with other tongues. The most important evidence of the Holy Spirit in a believer is when, just like Aaron's rod, the believer produces spiritual fruit in his or her life that demonstrates a true change and Christlike character! As Christ said:

> You will know them by their fruits. Do men gather grapes from thornbushes or figs from thistles? Even so, every good tree bears good fruit, but a bad tree bears bad fruit. A good tree cannot bear bad fruit, nor can a bad tree bear good fruit. Every tree that does not bear good fruit is cut down and thrown into the fire. Therefore by their fruits you will know them.
>
> —MATTHEW 7:16–20

Just as the manna, rod, and Law remained in the ark in the time of Moses, so salvation, sanctification, and the Holy Spirit baptism are spiritual blessings that remain in the life of a believer when we have the ark, which is Christ, abiding in us!

There Are Three Temples on Earth

There are presently three temples that God has established on Earth. Each provides a different function and purpose in this life. We understand that:

1. Your *body* is the temple of God.

2. Your *home* where you live is a miniature temple of God.

3. Your *local church* is type of a temple or a house of God.

The three physical structures ordained by God on Earth in ancient times were the tabernacle of Moses in the wilderness, the magnificent temple built by Solomon, and the temple that existed in the time of Christ. The tabernacle was constructed out of animal skins. Solomon's temple was built from cut stones and cedars. Like all buildings made by men's hands, the natural elements of sun, rain, and wind eventually wore upon the natural materials, and the temple needed occasional repairing. After long periods of time, junk could pile up in the sacred compound if the cleaning and purging processes were neglected.

Just as the three early dwelling places of God required cleansing, renewing, and removing of any excessive junk from the premises, the three present dwelling places for the Lord today need to be renewed, repaired, and cleansed on a continual basis.

1. *Your body must be purged of filthiness of the flesh and spirit.*

Scripture says, "Therefore, having these promises, beloved, let us cleanse ourselves from all filthiness of the flesh and spirit, perfecting holiness in the fear of God" (2 Cor. 7:1). Many individuals are in bondage to a particular habit, mental stronghold, or negative attitude such as unforgiveness, fear, or unbelief. Believers often pray, "Lord, help me to get rid of this or that." It is interesting that the above passage does not say, "Ask God to cleanse you." It says, "*Let us cleanse ourselves.*" This language is similar to the statement the author of Hebrews wrote, when he said, "Let us lay aside every weight, and the sin which so easily ensnares us" (Heb. 12:1). Peter spoke of "laying aside all malice, all guile, hypocrisy, envy, and all evil speaking" (1 Pet. 2:1).

How can we cleanse ourselves? This does not imply that we, in our own ability, can deliver ourselves from the evil inclination. If we alone were able, there would have been no need for Christ as the redeemer. It takes the power of God moving within a person to break the yokes and bondages that tie us to addictions (Isa. 10:27; Acts 10:38). Once the yoke is destroyed, it is up to the individual to keep the doors closed, preventing further intrusion from outside forces that would revive the particular addiction or bondage.

We cleanse ourselves by willfully choosing to lay aside any weights and sins that would hold us down from effectively running our race. There are certain unclean habits that affect the physical body, eventually causing disease and suffering. The physical temple must go through a purging process to remove distractive and dangerous habits and uncleanness. This is done by our willpower and choosing to receive God's breakthrough anointing into our situation.

2. *Your home must be purged of idols and objects that attract spirits.*

As we will point out later, your physical dwelling place, whether a trailer, apartment, or home, must maintain an atmosphere of peace, joy, and righteousness. Part of the process of purging your house includes removing anything and everything from the premises of your physical dwelling that would open the door to negative thoughts, mental strongholds, or evil spirits.

Just as your body, mind, and spirit must occasionally be cleansed or experience daily renewals, there are times your physical dwelling must also be sanctified or set apart from objects that would create a negative atmosphere (more on this in a later chapter).

3. *Your church must be purged from faultfinding, unforgiveness, and strife.*

The third dwelling place for God is among those who unite in worship at local congregations. In the early church, the believers practiced the Lord's Supper on a daily basis, going from house to house. (I talk more about this in my book *The Meal That Heals*.) According to Paul, a person is to perform self-examination prior to receiving the Lord's Supper (1 Cor. 11:28). This inward judging of the motives in our hearts and spirits is for the purpose of discovering any form of unforgiveness, malice, strife, bitterness, or other inner weights that corrupt the human spirit and block the connection between the Father and us. James taught, "Confess your faults one to another, and pray one for another, that ye may be healed" (James 5:16, KJV). Believers are required to forgive one another so that we too may be forgiven by the Father in heaven (Matt. 6:14).

When a minister conducts the Lord's Supper, he should emphasize the importance of examining yourself (1 Cor. 11:28) and, by confession and repentance, removing anything that would be a spiritual hindrance from your spirit. Local churches should have special seasons in their congregations during which they emphasize repentance and forgiveness of sins. Prior to the Jewish New Year (*Rosh Hashanah*), Jewish people have a yearly season called *Teshuvah*, in which they perform self-examination and release forgiveness toward others. Ministers often emphasize the importance of asking God to forgive us, but local congregations need seasons where the members ask forgiveness of one another and of those with whom there has been an offense.

What If You Refuse?

What would happen if you permitted all of the negative junk and spiritual dark matter to remain in the temple of your mind and spirit? What if you neglected to remove the trash from your body, your home, or your church?

Without complete deliverance from the power of sin, your life will eventually be tied to bondages and spiritual yokes. A yoke connects you to something over which you have no control. What you are linked to becomes master over you. Paul warned that believers must not be unequally yoked together with unbelievers (2 Cor. 6:14). A person who is attempting to serve God and yet also serves his or her own flesh will be torn in two opposing directions. Paul wrote that we should "stand fast therefore in the liberty wherewith Christ hath made us free, and be not entangled again with the yoke of bondage" (Gal. 5:1, KJV).

If a person's home is not cleansed from idols or items that motivate a life of sin, it can actually open a door to evil or unclean spirits. While a Christian who is actively serving Christ cannot be possessed by a demonic spirit, believers can be influenced and even oppressed by spirits. We read where Satan entered the heart of Judas (Luke 22:3), and Christ rebuked Peter for his statements that were inspired by Satan (Matt. 16:23). Satan filled the hearts of two church members, Ananias and Sapphira, to lie to the Holy Spirit (Acts 5:3). Certain types of thinking are like magnets that attract evil inclinations, opening the door to possible attacks by unclean spirits.

If a local church allows strife to enter the congregation, then the church will be filled with confusion and will be spiritually hindered. James wrote, "For where envying and strife is, there is confusion and every evil work" (James 3:16, KJV). Many divisions in local churches would have been prevented if an offended person had forgiven the offender.

In ancient times there was a need to cleanse the temple in Jerusalem. It is critically important that you do the same self-examination in your body, home, and church. It is the only way you can close the door on the adversary, who will enter the house through even the slightest crack in the door. One small crack can eventually open the door to major attacks from the adversary and enable him to introduce numerous spiritual plagues into your dwelling place.

Purging your house can prevent the adversary from attaching certain types of bondages to your body, soul, and spirit. I am reminded of an illustration related by Dr. E. L. Terry. In ancient times it was common to yoke a large ox to a long, round beam that was attached to a grinding stone. As the ox would walk the same circle continually for hours, the grain would be separated. As the precious hard grain would pile up, the ox could stop and begin eating from the pile of grain—thus the owner would place a muzzle over the mouth of the ox to prevent it from eating the grain.

Paul wrote to Timothy that he should give double honor to an elder who was worthy and "not muzzle the oz that treadeth out the corn" (1 Tim. 5:17–18, KJV). Dr. Terry noted that the neck of an ox was very thick, and when an ox would eat additional grain, this four-footed beast's neck would expand, and the yoke might not properly fit. At times the ox could break a portion of the yoke by continually eating. The imagery for a believer is that when a person is bound by addictions and spiritual problems, he or she must continually eat from the Word of God and devour the precious seed of the Word, which will eventually build the believer's faith and cause the yoke to be destroyed through the anointing of the Holy Spirit (Isa. 10:27; Acts 10:38). If you are ready for a change, the Lord is ready to move into your body, your family situation, and your local church to bring forth a new dwelling, controlled by His presence!

Chapter 5

THE AUTHORITY OF THE BLOOD OF CHRIST

And they overcame him by the blood of the Lamb and by the word of their testimony, and they did not love their lives to the death.

| REVELATION 12:11 |

IN THE EARLY 1990s, I, along with a pastor and a missionary, was invited to Peru to minister. We were welcomed into the house of a man who was a wealthy architect and had recently become connected with a local Peruvian congregation. He was unable to speak English, and none of us spoke Spanish, but I could easily recognize it when it was spoken. I went to bed, and as I was lying on my stomach, suddenly I felt the pressure of a fully grown man lying on my back, with each part of his body pressing against me. He felt as though he weighed two hundred pounds or more. Suddenly I heard this being speak Spanish in my ear. There was one weird fact: no man was in the room, and this was not a literal person or human—it was some type of a demonic presence that had manifested in the room!

I immediately rebuked the spirit in Christ's name and felt it lift. I turned over in the bed, not knowing what to do next. The Holy Spirit impressed me to stand up and confess the authority of Christ's blood over the wall, doors, and windows of the bedroom. I did this boldly, saying, "I confess the protective power of Christ's blood on this wall...then that wall...and I command the evil spirits not to enter this room again as long as I am sleeping here!" Then I lay down and went to sleep. We stayed at the house three days and then returned to the States. Months later I learned that the owner of the house had been involved in the gay lifestyle and that many men had stayed in his home continually. I believe the spirit I encountered was familiar with certain local men and was making itself manifest to us during our stay. It was certainly very stupid to make a move on me, since I am married to a very beautiful woman and have never had—nor ever will have—a physical or emotional attraction to the same sex! This situation, however, taught me that the blood of Christ is applied through faith and confession.

While growing up, I occasionally heard godly men or women speak about pleading the blood of Christ over their children for protection from the powers of Satan. Some Bible teachers point out that the idea of *pleading the blood* is better referred to as *confessing the blood* over a situation.

For a moment, consider the supernatural spiritual authority that was vested in the numerous Old Testament offerings. The Torah spoke of rams, lambs, bullocks, pigeons, and turtledoves as offerings to be sacrificed and burned on the brass altar at the tabernacle and, later, the temple in Jerusalem. The blood of a lamb was placed on the outer posts of the doors of all Hebrew families in Egypt on the night of Passover, preventing the angel of death from entering the house (Exod. 12). Hundreds of years later, David laid an animal sacrifice on an altar at the future temple platform in Jerusalem, and an angel stopped a plague that had cost the lives of seventy thousand men (1 Chron. 21:14–28). In Exodus 29:39 God instructed the priests to offer a lamb in the morning and another in the evening—a picture, I believe, of the need to begin your morning with the Lord to ensure a good day and to conclude your evening with the Lord to provide needed rest.

When a person receives the redemption covenant called *salvation* (Luke 1:77) and is born again (John 3:3) and redeemed (1 Pet. 1:18), that person enters into the covenant through the blood of Christ (v. 19). When a sinner is convicted by the Holy Spirit and repents and asks Christ into his or her life, that individual does not see or experience an angel of the Lord bringing the literal blood of Christ to repaint the heart and doorway. However, a real, very literal transformation occurs when you confess the Lord Jesus with your mouth. This confession causes Christ to remove the guilt of sin and replace it with the peace of God (Rom. 8:1). Christ, who is our High Priest in the heavenly temple (Heb. 9:23–28), bears in His hands, feet, and sides the scars of His work of redemption for you (John 20:25–27). The removal of the presence of sin is very real and literal. However, the blood is applied through the confession of your faith. Many old-timers understood this and would resist the authority of the adversary by speaking in faith the name of Christ and confessing the blood of Christ over their children, homes, and families.

Three Cleansing Substances

There is a parallel between the substances biblical priests used to cleanse a house from a plague of leprosy and how believers are to cleanse their own temples. Leviticus 14:51–52 reveals three substances that were used in the process:

1. Blood
2. Running water
3. Hyssop and scarlet

The importance of blood

I must emphasize that blood was the only substance used in both covenants to redeem men. Paul wrote that without the shedding of blood there was no remission (forgiveness) of sins (Heb. 9:22). Under the old covenant, there were numerous types of sacrifices offered at the tabernacle and the temple. Some involved oil, wine, grain, and other earthly substances. The most important, however, were the offerings of specific animals listed in the Torah. During the Hebrew Exodus, the Hebrews were told to place the blood of the lamb on outside posts of the door. This blood was applied using the branch of a hyssop plant.

> And you shall take a bunch of hyssop, and dip it in the blood that is in the basin, and strike the lintel and the two doorposts with the blood that is in the basin. And none of you shall go out of the door of his house until morning.
> —Exodus 12:22

> And a clean person shall take hyssop, and dip it in the water, and sprinkle it upon the tent, and upon all the vessels, and upon the persons that were there, and upon him that touched a bone, or one slain, or one dead, or a grave.
>
> —NUMBERS 19:18, KJV

> Purge me with hyssop, and I shall be clean;
> Wash me, and I shall be whiter than snow.
>
> —PSALM 51:7

The hyssop plant was used to apply the blood to the posts in Egypt and was dipped in the blood and sprinkled on the top, left, and right sides of the outer doorpost. It was also used in ritual purification ceremonies when the water of purification was prepared and then sprinkled upon a person who was ceremonially unclean after touching a dead carcass of a human or animal. The hyssop plant was used in the ancient times as an herbal medicine; it can also be made into an herbal tea.

The spiritual application is important. All of our spiritual blessings are obtained through the precious blood of Christ! The shed blood of Christ served as the final sacrifice for all mankind. The Bible indicates that if the rulers of this world had known that the death of Christ would defeat them, they never would have crucified Christ (1 Cor. 2:8).

The use of running water

Still water becomes stagnant and can retain germs and bacteria. Running water is necessary when washing your hands in order to remove any existing bacteria. Years ago, when delivering children, doctors would use a bowl of warm water to wash their hands. They were unaware that germs were being passed into the mother's body, causing sickness and, in some instances, infection leading to death. Only when the hands of the physicians or midwife were washed with running water did the mortality rate in mothers and infants drop.[1]

God continually instructed the priests to use running water (Lev. 14:5–6, 50–52). After we have received redemption through Christ's blood, we are commanded to be baptized (Acts 2:38). Baptism is performed by submerging the person under water. Contemporary churches have a baptistery to perform this important sacrament. When I was a teenage minister, very few churches where I preached had baptisteries. The baptisms were performed in a local river or occasionally in a large lake of water on a believer's farm. I recall that on one occasion while preaching in a small rural church, there were some new converts who needed to be baptized. We broke the ice on a nearby lake and baptized them as our teeth chattered and our bodies shook—yet no one became sick!

Some older Christians preferred a river because of the principle of running water. To them the water was a picture of washing their sins away into the waters of the Jordan. The priests needed running water to perform the purification of the house, and all believers are to repent and be baptized in water for the remission of sins and as an outward evidence of our commitment to Christ.

The Bible also speaks of the washing of the water of the Word.

> Husbands, love your wives, just as Christ also loved the church and gave Himself for her, that He might sanctify and cleanse her with the washing of water by the word, that He might present her to Himself a glorious church, not having spot or wrinkle or any such thing, but that she should be holy and without blemish.
>
> —EPHESIANS 5:25–27

> Not by works of righteousness which we have done, but according to His mercy He saved us, through the washing of regeneration and renewing of the Holy Spirit.
>
> —TITUS 3:5

At times when your mind feels cluttered, spend time listening to gospel music, reading the Word aloud, or quoting scriptures that apply to your situation. You will soon sense a cleansing feeling wash over you. This is the water of the Word refreshing you inwardly.

The use of hyssop and scarlet

Throughout Scripture, the color scarlet was a picture of our redemption. A scarlet thread was tied around the hand of the baby twin, Zerah, to show that he was firstborn (Gen. 38:30). Scarlet was used in the fabric of Moses's tabernacle (Exod. 25:4). It was also thrown into the midst of the burning fire at a red heifer sacrifice (Num. 19:6). Even the harlot Rahab was commanded to place a scarlet thread in her window as a sign that she had a covenant with the Lord (Josh. 2:18–21).

The most interesting use of the scarlet thread dates back to the ancient temple on the Day of Atonement. On this day the high priest would take two identical goats and place a scarlet thread on the neck of one goat and a second thread on the horn of the other goat. A third thread was nailed to the door of the temple. When the goat bearing the sins of Israel was thrust off a cliff in the wilderness, it is said that the scarlet thread nailed to the temple door supernaturally turned white, signifying that the sins had been forgiven.[2] Rabbis believe this is why Isaiah wrote:

> "Come now, and let us reason together,"
> Says the LORD,
> "Though your sins are like scarlet,
> They shall be as white as snow;
> Though they are red like crimson,
> They shall be as wool."
>
> —ISAIAH 1:18

At Calvary, the soldiers who were mocking Christ placed a scarlet robe over His shoulders. Scarlet robes were worn by kings, and the soldiers mocking Him called Him "King of the Jews" (Matt. 27:28). The scarlet identifies the covenant.

Summary

The items used to cleanse the houses in Scripture from a plague of leprosy have a spiritual application for the cleansing and purging of our lives as believers:

1. *The blood of Christ cleanses us and redeems the house to God.* Under the old covenant, sacrificial blood was used to purify the Israelites, priests, and the high priest; the outer court, inner court, and the holy of holies; and all of the sacred furniture used for approaching God. All things

were purified with blood, and without blood no remission of sins occurred.

2. *The washing of the water of the Word renews our thinking.* Under Moses's law, a red heifer was burnt and the ashes were collected in a clean place. When a person became ceremonially unclean, a small amount of ashes from the red heifer were sprinkled in water. When the water was poured on the unclean, it initiated a ritual purification (Num. 19).

    The Word of God is compared to cleansing water. We read, "Husbands, love your wives, just as Christ also loved the church and gave Himself for her, that He might sanctify and cleanse her with the washing of water by the word" (Eph. 5:25–26).

3. *The scarlet thread is a picture of the covenant relationship we have with God.* The scarlet blood of Christ is applied to our sin-stricken souls, and as a result, we are redeemed and set free.

The Blood in the Time of the Temple

The central theme of the Bible's first five books (the Torah) is the various sacrifices. It was necessary that an innocent animal be offered and its blood spread over the altar for the sins and transgressions of the people. Without the shedding of blood, there was no remission of sins (Heb. 9:22). There was a specific routine that was established by the divine Law related to the temple sacrifices.

First, only the priests (high priest and Levites) could administer the blood offerings. Once the animal was slain, the blood was caught in gold and silver vessels and sprinkled at the base of the altar. On the Day of Atonement, it was sprinkled upon the corners of the sacred furniture. The blood was also poured out around the base of the altar (Lev. 3:2) and before the veil seven times (Lev. 4:6). On Yom Kippur, the blood was placed on the golden lid of the mercy seat on the ark of the covenant

(Lev. 16:15). It is also significant that the blood was used to sanctify a leper who had been healed (Lev. 14:7) and on a house that had been cleansed from leprosy (v. 51). At the ancient Jewish temple, any remaining blood that was not used was to be poured out on the ground at the base of the brass altar. God was so serious about the blood that human blood and animal blood were not to be mixed.

Years ago I was invited to tour the Western Wall tunnels prior to their being opened to tourists. I was shown an area where steps had been carved into the foundation of the hill of Moriah. I was told that in the Roman period, when the temple existed in Jerusalem, there was an escape route underground that a priest would enter from the top of the mount if he cut his finger while slaying a sacrifice. The priest was required to remain in a special chamber until the cut was healed. The point is that his human blood and the sacrificial blood of the animal could not be mixed, or the power of the offering was void.

Today, individuals are mixing portions of biblical truth with their own ideas, theories, and traditions, thus making the redemptive power of the covenant null and void. Your spiritual life is not changed by bowing your head when a person prays, signing a membership card after standing at the front of a church, or by simply confessing that you are a good person on a journey and will make "good choices for a positive outcome." This mix of a few seeds of the gospel and New Age, positive confessions will not defeat the enemy or break a yoke. Confessing the Word of God and confessing your faith in the blood of Christ are the tools that can smash a yoke of bondage!

The power of the blood sacrifices

After the Flood, Noah laid out a sacrifice, and God entered a covenant for all generations, promising that never again would He allow the earth to be destroyed by floodwaters (Gen. 8:20–21). The blood of the Passover lamb in Egypt prevented the death angel from entering the homes of the Hebrew families (Exod. 12:13). When David placed a sacrificial offering on the altar in Jerusalem, the angel of the Lord stopped a deadly plague from striking any more men in the city (1 Chron. 21:1–30). As long as Job made a continual blood offering on behalf of his sons and daughters, the blood provided a supernatural protective hedge around Job, his family, and his possessions (Job 1:5–6).

If the blood from a small lamb, ram, goat, or a large bull could bring the attention of angels and the Almighty to forgive, hide sins, and protect from destruction, imagine the inherent spiritual authority that is provided to humanity through the shed blood of Christ!

The final and ultimate sacrifice

There are numerous reasons revealed in Scripture as to why the blood of Christ has such spiritual authority to redeem, forgive, and bring a healing covenant for humanity. First, consider Christ's conception. Matthew reveals that Christ was conceived by the Holy Spirit and was not born through the normal birth process of a husband and wife. Mary was a virgin when she conceived Christ. The seed that was placed in the womb of Mary was the seed of God's Word, and this seed "was made flesh" (John 1:14, KJV). This miracle of conception is important when understanding that the nature of Christ's blood was different from that of a child born under sin through the normal birth process. Christ was born without the same sin nature that all the rest of mankind is born with.

His birthplace was Bethlehem, a small town about eight miles from Jerusalem. It was in Bethlehem that all the lambs used in the morning and evening offerings at the temple were born and raised. Christ was born in Bethlehem, a town also known as the "city of David" (Luke 2:4). It should come as no surprise to us that Christ was born in a stable (a place where animals are placed) and laid in a manger (a feeding stone for animals), for He was born to become the final and ultimate sacrifice for man. Christ's blood can make a person into a new creation (2 Cor. 5:17). It can form a hedge of protection around the believer (Rev. 12:11) and give access to eternal life—promised only to those who receive His sacrificial offering for the remission of sins!

Chapter 6

PRUNE YOUR FAMILY TREE

For there is hope for a tree,
If it is cut down, that it will sprout again,
And that its tender shoots will not cease.
Though its root may grow old in the earth,
And its stump may die in the ground,
Yet at the scent of water it will bud
And bring forth branches like a plant.

JOB 14:7–9

HE FOUND HIMSELF living on the streets in New York as a runaway at age fifteen. His older brother had robbed a convenience store and was sent to prison for several years. Another sibling spent much of his life incarcerated, continually battling drug addiction. When asked to describe his family tree, he said, "There is only one tree that fits my family: the weeping willow!" Every person has a genealogy, often called a *family tree*. Some are proud of the legacy and the fruit generations of family members have produced. To others, however, the leaves are withered, the branches are dead, and the tree is fruitless. There are family members a person doesn't want to talk about and personal incidents that are hidden and never discussed. Exposing the past would lead to embarrassment and humiliation.

To produce a proud lineage and spiritual fruit, you may need to prune your family tree! There are about twenty-nine different trees mentioned in the Bible. These various trees are often linked to different biblical stories and at times are a mirror of the strength or weaknesses of particular individuals in the stories. At time a particular tree's characteristics are used for spiritual applications. The oak tree was often linked to the early patriarchs—Abraham, Isaac, and Jacob—or, in Genesis 35:8 (KJV), to Deborah. The oak is strong and majestic and survives long—an imagery of the early patriarchs who built a strong foundational legacy and lived long lives.

The cedar of Lebanon was used in the construction of Solomon's temple. The psalmist compared the righteous to palm trees (Ps. 92:12). A palm tree's roots are planted deep and can survive strong winds and storms. When a drought strikes, a palm tree's roots will search for water.

The willow has always been a tree that is a picture of sorrow. It often grows along riverbanks in parts of the world. When the captive Jews were taken captive to Babylon, they hung their harps in the willow trees, and when they were asked to sing a Hebrew song, they refused to sing the Lord's song in a strange land (Ps. 137:2–4). The bramble is a tree whose branches have thorns, and a person can easily be cut if they do not handle the bramble branches properly (Luke 6:44).

In the New Testament it was a sign of summer when the fig tree began to bring forth fruit (Matt. 24:32). The mustard tree produces one of the world's smallest seeds and is referred to as a picture of simple faith—faith as the grain of a mustard seed (Luke 17:6). There is also a tree that is identified as wormwood in Deuteronomy 29:18. The word *wormwood* means "bitter."

In the Bible, the characteristics, actions, or personality of people can represent certain trees.

- The oak represents the strength and determination of Abraham.
- The cedar represents Solomon, the builder of the first temple.
- The palm tree can allude to David, who continually survived life's storms.
- The willow was a tree of sorrow that represents the captive nation in Babylon.

- The bramble is a picture of the house of Saul.
- The fig represents the pure, simple faith of the first-century church.
- The mustard seed grows into a great tree, and this is a picture of Timothy's family.
- Wormwood is bitter, and this was the condition of Naomi when she returned to Bethlehem.

Four Parts of a Family Tree

Every tree consists of four different parts, all working together to produce a healthy tree:

1. The roots
2. The trunk with the bark
3. The leaves and branches
4. The fruit

Every family tree also has these four important parts:

1. The roots are the early foundation and beginning of a family.
2. The trunk is the strength of the family tree.
3. The leaves are the beauty and the protective covering of the family unit.
4. The fruit are the spiritual results and blessings that follow the family.

Since trees are compared to people and spiritual applications are made throughout the Bible to these various types of trees, then the same dangers that can harm or destroy a tree are the same dangers we must guard against in our lives as we build our own families.

Storms destroy the branches.

Sudden and unexpected storms will place pressure on the branches, and eventually they can snap. Once a branch has been destroyed, it will no longer produce fruit. Dead branches are eventually removed from the tree and usually burned in a fire. Likewise, sudden storms—such as children in rebellion, family conflicts, severe financial crisis, and division between husbands and wives—can lead to a severing of the family unit through separation or divorce.

Drought destroys the leaves.

Drought comes in a time of lack of rain or a severe famine. Trees must have water in order to survive and produce fruit. When there is a lack of water, the leaves wither and the fruit is lacking. When the fall months arrive, the normally beautiful leaves that splash the mountains with a rainbow of red, orange, and yellow become a dull brown and black. From a biblical perspective, water is a picture of the Holy Spirit.

The Bible says, "With joy you will draw water from the wells of salvation" (Isa. 12:3). Isaiah said:

> For I will pour water on him who is thirsty,
> And floods on the dry ground;
> I will pour My Spirit on your descendants,
> And My blessing on your offspring.
> —ISAIAH 44:3

Christ alluded to the Holy Spirit when He told believers, "He who believes in Me, as the Scripture has said, out of his heart will flow rivers of living water" (John 7:38). The presence of the Holy Spirit always brings a refreshing to our spirits in the same manner as rain brings new life to trees and vegetation.

Cold weather destroys the fruit.

You have witnessed it many times; a sudden cold snap strikes the orange groves in Florida, destroying the fuit and wiping out millions of dollars of profit for the growers. Just as cold weather can destroy the fruit on a tree, when our hearts become spiritually cold and callous, we will no longer produce the fruits of righteousness, peace, and joy in the Holy Spirit (Rom. 14:17). There are nine fruit of the Spirit mentioned in Galatians 5:22–23. This spiritual fruit must mature in a heart that is warmed by the fire of God's Word and the glowing embers of the Holy Spirit. Fruit cannot successfully grow in extreme cold, and neither can spiritual results manifest in a spiritually cold heart.

Floods destroy trees.

When a major river overflows and torrents of water rise over their boundaries, even strong trees with deep roots are removed from their places and rolled like toothpicks across the violent waters. In Scripture, floods are both literal and spiritual. As a metaphor, floods can also allude to sudden trouble that comes like a raging storm into our lives. Such an example is Job. One day he was a rich prince, and the following day he was a pauper. The enemy came against Job like a sudden flood (Isa. 59:19), killing his ten children, stealing his livestock, and destroying his health (Job chapters 1 and 2; John 10:10). Job's grief was so severe that he refused to speak for seven days (Job 2:13). The very foundation of all Job had worked for was stripped from him within twenty-four hours. This is the picture of a sudden flood!

Families have been suddenly, economically wiped out through natural fires, floods, earthquakes, hurricanes, and tornados. The unexpected death of the breadwinner devastates a family. When a sudden car accident takes the life of a child, the parents are grief stricken. This type of sudden trouble stuns the mind, weakens the heart, and crushes the spirit of a person. Some floods cannot be detected or controlled. At other times, discerning believers can discern the signs and prepare in advance for the dark waters of trouble, building a bulwark of faith and prayer to prevent the planned destruction from the adversary.

Insects destroy the inside (root).

We have all heard of termites—those tiny insects that make a banquet out of the wood in your house. Certain types of insects destroy trees. Joel spoke of this when he wrote:

That which the palmerworm hath left hath the locust eaten; and that which the locust hath left hath the cankerworm eaten; and that which the cankerworm hath left hath the caterpiller eaten.

—JOEL 1:4, KJV

The palmerworm in Hebrew is *gazam* and alludes to the worm state of the insect when it is without wings. *Locust* is the word *arbeh*, identifying the stage where the destructive insect is in its first skin. The word is used of a little one without legs or wings. This is the second stage of growth. The third stage is a cankerworm, identified in the Hebrew text as *yekeq*. This is when the insect has cast off its little wings but is still unable to fly. The word *caterpillar* is *chaciyl*, and this is a fully mature insect with wings that can fly, able to eat anything in sight.

I recall a dear minister friend, Dr. E. L. Terry, explaining these four insects and how they symbolize the fourfold destruction that can occur to a tree. The insects begin by *gnawing,* then *swarming,* followed by *devouring,* and then *consuming.* Dr. Terry described how one insect attacks the fruit on the tree, while another goes after the leaves on the tree. One will gnaw away at the outward bark, while still another will bury itself in the ground and eat at the root. If the root of a tree is ever destroyed, the tree will die.

A good tree that is planted in good soil and well watered will eventually produce good fruit. In the past I complained about individuals who did not seem to understand what I was preaching or who questioned my sincerity in ministry and were always throwing stones at me. Then I recalled, as a child, standing under two trees in my backyard. One was an old, dried-up tree near the point of being made firewood, and next to it stood an apple tree, loaded in its season with apples. I began throwing rocks at the tree with the fruit, trying to knock an apple off a branch. As I did that, I thought, "People never throw sticks and stones at dead trees—only at trees with fruit!" If you are being picked on, then it may be an indication that there is fruit in your life.

Growing a Family Tree

Large family Bibles were popular in the early nineteenth century. In the front of each Bible were colorfully designed pages with blank lines and a heading: "Family Tree." A family member would interview older, living relatives and record information on several generations of family members, including names, birth dates, and marital history, recording the information in the opening pages of a Bible designed to be passed to succeeding generations. Every *family tree* was initially planted generations ago when our ancestors came on ships from foreign nations; that is, unless you are a descendent of a Native American Indian whose family was living in America long before America was a republic.

A family in America begins with your first ancestors from the mother's and father's sides. On my mother's side, my ancestors were Italian, and on Dad's side, they were a mixture of Cherokee Indian and Scotch-Irish. For many in North America, their original roots were from Europe or, for the black race, from Africa. These early ancestors form the roots of the tree.

The second generation forms the trunk of the tree as the children marry and begin to procreate a second generation of seed. As the third generation begins producing offspring, the family tree now has numerous branches—of aunts, uncles, cousins, and in-laws. By the time of the fourth generation, the children born are likely to inherit houses, lands, and businesses that were birthed through the hard work of the previous generations.

As an example, Abraham and his barren wife, Sarah, traveled to the deserts of Canaan digging new wells to water his flock and taking possession of land that was promised to him by the Almighty. His son, Isaac, was the second generation and began building upon his father's legacy by adding on to the flocks and land. Isaac's son Jacob was the third generation, and he was blessed with twelve sons, who became the children of Israel.

Curses on the Family Tree

They have been perhaps the most famous family in America politics, and yet they have experienced more unusual tragedies than perhaps any other noted family in the world. Even members of the family have occasionally questioned whether they were under some sort of curse. I am speaking of the Kennedy family.

> The Kennedy clan is embedded in American political culture of the past half century like no other family. They arrived at that power base through cold calculation and blunt instruments of their immense wealth but also because of honorable service to the nation.[1]

Joseph Kennedy Sr. was the third-generation Kennedy to live in Boston. He was born on September 6, 1888. The lives of the four sons of Joseph Kennedy Sr. reveal the circumstances of why some people suggest there is a curse on the family. Below are the names of the four sons:

- Joseph Kennedy Jr., born July 25, 1915
- John F. Kennedy, born May 29, 1917
- Robert F. Kennedy, born November 20, 1925
- Edward M. Kennedy, born February 22, 1932

All four sons of Joseph Kennedy Sr. experienced tragedy in their lives. The oldest son, Joseph Jr., was killed in a military plane crash in 1944. John Kennedy was elected president of the United States in 1960 and was assassinated in Dallas, Texas, on November 22, 1963. The third son of Joseph Kennedy, Robert Kennedy, was moving forward in the 1968 primaries to be selected by the Democratic Party as their candidate for president of the United States. His life was taken shortly after midnight on June 5, 1968, in the Ambassador Hotel Embassy Ballroom in Los Angeles, California. He was shot by a twenty-four-year-old Palestinian immigrant named Sirhan Sirhan.

According to a diary of Sirhan Sirhan, he wrote that Kennedy must die before June 5, 1968.[2] Since Kennedy was supportive of Israel, it has been suggested that the assassin wanted to kill Kennedy on the anniversary of the Six-Day War between the Arabs and Israel, which had occurred one year earlier. Following the war, Israel annexed part of Jordan, the West Bank, and East Jerusalem under their control.

The fourth and youngest son of Joseph Kennedy was Edward (Ted) Kennedy. Many people believed that eventually Ted would run for the office of US president, but a strange event that occurred one evening in July 1969 would hinder those possibilities.

On July 18, 1969, Edward Kennedy was attending a party on the small island of Chappaquiddick, a small island near Martha's Vineyard. Also in attendance were six women who had worked for Robert Kennedy, nicknamed *the boiler room girls*, including a girl named Mary Jo Kopechne, who had been secretary to Ted's assassinated brother, Robert Kennedy.

According to Ted's testimony, he announced he was leaving the party, and Mary Jo asked if he would take her back to her hotel. He agreed, and both were in Ted's car when Kennedy said he made a wrong turn onto Dyke Road and accidentally drove off the side of the bridge. Amazingly Ted was able to swim to safety, but Mary Jo drowned in the car. The incident created a scandal, especially when Kennedy pled guilty to leaving the scene of an accident after causing injury and the judged dismissed any jail time. There was also suspicion that Mary Jo and Kennedy had more than a close friendship.

It was after the death of Robert Kennedy in 1968 that Michael Kennedy said, "It was as if fate turned against us. There was now a pattern that could not be ignored."[3]

The Tragedy Continues

Joe Kennedy's first son, Joe Jr., was killed at age twenty-nine while on a secret bombing mission when his plane exploded over the English Channel. He died without having anyone to carry on his name.

The second son, John F. Kennedy, had three sons. On August 23, 1956, a daughter was stillborn while John and Jackie were living in Newport, Rhode Island. While the Kennedys were living in the White House, another son, Patrick Kennedy, died on August 9, 1963, two days after his birth. The most noted son of the former president, John Kennedy Jr., who was born on November 25, 1960, was tragically killed on July 16, 1999, while flying his small private plane.

There were seven sons born to Robert Kennedy:

- Joseph P. Kennedy II, born September 24, 1952
- Robert Kennedy Jr., born January 17, 1954
- David Kennedy, born June 15, 1955
- Michael Kennedy, born February 27, 1958
- Christopher Kennedy, born July 4, 1963
- Matthew Kennedy, born January 11, 1965
- Douglas Kennedy, born March 24, 1967

David Kennedy died on August 25, 1984, in Palm Beach, Florida, from a overdose of cocaine. Michael Kennedy was killed after colliding with a tree on the ski slopes in Aspen, Colorado, on December 31, 1997.

The youngest son of Joseph Kennedy Sr., Edward (Ted) Kennedy, had four sons. Edward Kennedy Jr. was born on September 26, 1961. His right leg was amputated in 1973 because of cancer. Patrick Kennedy, born July 14, 1967, sought treatment for addictions.[4]

Strange Parallels

There are numerous strange parallels related to the tragedies, accidents, and deaths in the Kennedy clan.

- JFK died the same day as his great-grandfather Patrick— November 22 (1858 and 1963).
- JFK was buried on the same day as JFK Jr.'s birthday— November 25.
- JFK Jr. was pronounced dead on the thirtieth anniversary (July 18) of the Chappaquiddick drowning, when a young girl was drowned in Ted Kennedy's car. Ted escaped; the

girl didn't. JFK Jr., his wife, and his wife's sister all died in the plane crash that took place on July 16.

- When Robert F. Kennedy was killed in California, his wife was pregnant with their daughter Rory.

- Rory was the same girl who held her dying brother Michael on the ski slopes.

- Rory was getting married when JFK Jr. was headed to the wedding and crashed his plane.

The Reasons for the Trouble

In his book *The Sins of the Father*, Ronald Kessler traces back the many disturbing facts related to the patriarch of the family, Joseph Kennedy.[5] Old Joe was involved in many illegal activities and insider trading that made him rich—at times at the expense of others.

Insider trading

My grandfather, John Bava, was a young man during the Great Depression of the 1930s. I recall a comment he made concerning Joseph Kennedy. He said, "In the 1930s, I remember reading in the Pittsburg newspaper of how Joe Kennedy was involved in insider trading in the stock market. He would manipulate it and make huge money at the expense of others. The paper said he could have invested in the market in 1929 and prevented the crash, but he refused to do so. He let others suffer loss, then he went in and bought stock at cheap prices."

From 1930 to 1933 Joe Kennedy and Ben Smith manipulated companies to satisfy their own greed. Groups headed by Kennedy would trade among themselves to raise the prices, causing others to invest in the valuable stock, and when others would step in to purchase, they would sell their stock while it was high. The public suffered heavy losses, and many lives were ruined—but Kennedy continued to prosper. When President Roosevelt appointed Joe to head the Securities and Exchange Commission, he was asked why he had tapped such a crook. The president answered, "It takes one to catch one."[6]

The Kennedy liquor

Some of the first liquor that came to America had the Kennedy finger-prints all over it. According to *The Sins of the Father*:

> When the Volstead Acts came in 1919—no manufacturing or trans-porting of intoxicating liquors for beverages purposes, Joe ordered liquor from overseas distillers and supplied it to organized crime syndicates on the shore. Frank Costello would later say that Joe approached him for help in smuggling liquor.[7]

Joe imported Haig & Haig liquor and Dewar's liquor as medicine and formed stockpiles to secretly sell. Joe traveled with Jimmy Roosevelt to London in order to secure a liquor distributorship in London. Joe became the exclusive agent in the United States for scotch and gin from Britain.

> Besides importing scotch, Joe bought rum from Jacob M. Kaplan. Kaplan, who was from Massachusetts, made molasses and rum in Cuba and the West Indies during the prohibition.[8]

Joe eventually began buying distilleries in the United States. Eventu-ally he was selling 100,000 to 200,000 cases of Haig & Haig and 150,000 cases of gin a year. Joe's commission alone on the liquor was $500,000 a year! Finally in the 1940s, Joe sold 50 percent of the stock in the company. Franklin Roosevelt Jr. once stated, "I think Jack's father was one of the most evil, disgusting men I have ever known. Oh, I know he was a finan-cial genius, but he was a rotten human being."[9]

Possible anti-Semitism

After World War II broke out, about 24 percent of the American people thought the Jews were a menace to America. This anti-Semitism was apparent in the early days of the Kennedy clan, as seen in a letter Joe Jr. wrote from Germany on April 23, 1934:

> Hitler had taken advantage of a widespread dislike of the Jews, a dislike that was well founded. After all, Joe Jr. said, the Jews' methods are unscrupulous. Joe Jr. told his father Hitler was building a spirit in men that could be envied in any country. The brutality, the bloodshed, and marching were necessary, he said, and

the sterilization law was a good thing. I don't know how the church feels about it, but it will do away with many of the disgusting specimen of men who inhabit the earth.[10]

As Joe would later make clear, he thought the Jews had brought on themselves whatever Hitler did to them.[11]

On June 13, 1938, Joe Sr. met with the German ambassador in London. It was observed:

"In Joe's view, it was not so much the Germans wanted to get rid of the Jews that was so harmful to us, but rather the loud clamor with which we accompanied the purpose," Dirksen said. "Joe understood our Jewish policy completely; he was from Boston and there, in one golf club, and in other clubs, no Jews had been admitted for the past fifty years."[12]

Joe's anti-Semitism also has some strange parallels. Joe was born on September 6, 1888, which fell on the Jewish New Year of Rosh Hashanah. His favorite daughter, Kathleen, was killed in a plane accident in France on May 13, 1948, one day prior to Israel being rebirthed as a nation. Joe's son Robert was killed on June 5, 1968, on the one-year anniversary of the Israeli Six-Day War.

The Possible Reasons for an Alleged Curse

If we turn to the Scriptures to identify why there is a possible curse on several generations of the Kennedys, we must begin with a warning God gave to the fathers in ancient Israel:

Keeping mercy for thousands, forgiving iniquity and transgression and sin, by no means clearing the guilty, visiting the iniquity of the fathers upon the children and the children's children to the third and the fourth generation.

—EXODUS 34:7

When the patriarch of the family breaks the commandments and precepts of Scripture, unless he or the future generations repent of their sins and iniquities and turn to Christ, they will continue to experience great distress and even trouble for up to four generations. From Scripture, I suggest three reasons for the curse.

1. *Personal greed*

There is a difference between making a living and making a killing. There is a difference between honest business success and manipulation for personal greed. Joe Kennedy's history reveals his personal manipulation for personal gain at the expense of others. James warned about this greed when he wrote:

> Come now, you rich, weep and howl for your miseries that are coming upon you! Your riches are corrupted, and your garments are moth-eaten. Your gold and silver are corroded, and their corrosion will be a witness against you and will eat your flesh like fire. You have heaped up treasure in the last days. Indeed the wages of the laborers who mowed your fields, which you kept back by fraud, cry out; and the cries of the reapers have reached the ears of the Lord of Sabaoth.
>
> —JAMES 5:1–4

The Scriptures speak harshly against those who would defraud others:

> You shall not cheat your neighbor, nor rob him. The wages of him who is hired shall not remain with you all night until morning.
>
> —LEVITICUS 19:13

> Woe to him who builds his house by unrighteousness
> And his chambers by injustice,
> Who uses his neighbor's service without wages
> And gives him nothing for his work.
>
> —JEREMIAH 22:13

2. *Distributing liquor in America*

It has been pointed out for many years that Joe Kennedy not only secretly sold liquor during a time of prohibition when liquor in America was illegal, but he also ensured that he would be the first person in the Northeast to get the license once the prohibition was lifted. Only God knows the numbers of tragedies that have happened in homes and the number of men who became alcoholics as a result of the Kennedy liquor legacy. The bondage of alcohol has followed many of the Kennedy descendants.

There are numerous warnings given in Scripture concerning strong drink.

Indeed, because he transgresses by wine,
He is a proud man,
And he does not stay at home.
Because he enlarges his desire as hell,
And he is like death, and cannot be satisfied.
—HABAKKUK 2:5

Woe to him who gives drink to his neighbor,
Pressing him to your bottle,
Even to make him drunk,
That you may look on his nakedness!
You are filled with shame instead of glory.
You also—drink!
And be exposed as uncircumcised!
The cup of the LORD's right hand will be turned against you,
And utter shame will be on your glory.
For the violence done to Lebanon will cover you.
—HABAKKUK 2:15–17

It has been noted that this prophetic passage from the Bible gives a warning to anyone who would offer his or her neighbor strong drink. It says that violence will cover that person. David discovered this when he had an affair with the wife of one of his generals, Uriah. David called Bathsheba's husband from the front lines and offered this soldier time with his wife. He even got him drunk, hoping he would lay with his wife, who was pregnant with David's child (2 Sam. 11:13). Later, David set Uriah up to be killed so he could marry Uriah's wife, Bathsheba. As a result, David was told, "The sword shall never depart from your house" (2 Sam. 12:10).

God's Word came true in David's life.

- David saw his infant son die (2 Sam. 12:18).

- One of his sons, Amnon, raped his half-sister Tamar (2 Sam. 13).
- Later, Amnon was killed by his brother (2 Sam. 13).
- Another son, Absalom, became estranged from his father, and was later killed (2 Sam. 18:15).
- A fourth son, Adonijah, attempted to overthrow his own father, David, and challenged him as the king (1 Kings 1).

All these problems stemmed from David's immoral act of getting Bathsheba's husband drunk and having him killed. It is possible that the fact Joe Kennedy made much of his wealth from the first liquor to enter America brought the judgment of God upon his household, and violence followed them.

3. *Anti-Semitism*

When God birthed the nation of Israel through Abraham, He told the patriarch, "I will bless those who bless you, and I will curse him who curses you" (Gen. 12:3). History reveals that just as prophesied, all the major empires that came against the Jews, or against Jerusalem and Israel, no longer exist. The actual nations—Greece, Italy, Egypt, Iran— may continue as a modern nation, but their powerful empires fell once they touched Israel, the apple of God's eye (Zech. 2:8).

The early letters and comments of Joe Kennedy reveal his very anti-Semitic feelings toward the Jewish people in a time when Hitler was initiating the destruction of the Jewish people. This combination of greed, provision of strong drink, and anti-Semitism is a three-cord rope that ties the patriarch of the Kennedy clan into the warning of God that He will visit the iniquity of the fathers upon the third and forth generations. Hopefully, a new generation of relatives and descendants will prune the tree by repenting of the sins of the fathers and pursuing a righteous covenant with Christ.

The Curse on the Four Herods

In the New Testament many names are the same but actually refer to different people. There are two Josephs: Joseph the husband of Mary (Matt. 1:16) and Joseph who cared for the body of Jesus (Matt. 27:57–60). There were several women named Mary: Mary the mother of Christ (Matt. 1:18), Mary Magdalene, and Mary the mother of James (Matt. 27:56). The same is true with the name Herod. There are actually four different Herods named in the Scripture; all were related to one another. They are a premier example from Scripture that four generations of people could have removed a curse, but instead each generation chose to follow its own dictates, and eventually each generation suffered for its decision.

The following information is gleaned from the Jewish historian Josephus and from the Scriptures.

Herod the Great

This Herod is mentioned early in the Gospels as the Herod who met with the wise men. At age twenty-five, he took his father's place as the king of Judah in the year 37 B.C. He married a woman named Mariammne, who was very beautiful. Herod was quite jealous of her, and when he caught her in a lie, he had her killed. After her death, at times he would run through the palace screaming out her name. Two of her favorite sons were Alexander and Aristobulus; both were educated in Rome. After hearing unfavorable rumors about them, Herod had Mariammne's sons killed. Herod married a total of nine women during his reign.

In the eighteenth year of his reign, he began a massive building campaign in Jerusalem, which included adding a large addition onto the Temple Mount platform. The entire project took forty-six years to complete. It was this Herod who received a group of magi from the East, who informed him that a king of the Jews had been born. This word greatly troubled Herod, and eventually he sent an order to have all children under two years of age to be slain in and around Bethlehem

(Matt. 2). Some time later, he was smitten with a disease and died a terrible death. Josephus reports that at age seventy, Herod developed an itch and ulcerated bowels. Gangrene set into his male organs, and he developed worms. Prior to his death, he gave orders to kill a group of men so that the Jewish nation would mourn, and, at his funeral, people would think the Jews were actually mourning for him. He had himself buried on a large mountain near Bethlehem. He died in 4 B.C., shortly after he murdered the Hebrew babies.

Herod Antipas (Luke 23 and Mark 6:14–29)

The story of this second-generation Herod is mentioned in Luke 23 and Mark 6:14–29. This Herod, known as Herod Antipas, lived in the Galilee area and helped build the Roman city of Tiberius in honor of the Roman emperor. This was the Herod who had direct dealings with John the Baptist. John boldly preached against Herod's illegal marriage, and eventually Herod had John arrested and placed in prison.

At Herod's birthday celebration, a young girl was dancing before Herod, and his passions were stirred to the point he offered the girl whatever she wished, up to half of the kingdom. After consulting with her mother, she went to Herod asking for the head of John the Baptist on a silver plate (Mark 6:22–29).

It would be years later that Herod heard about the ministry of Christ and the rumor that John the Baptist had been raised from the dead (Luke 9:7). He was filled with a desire to personally meet Jesus (v. 9). Just prior to His crucifixion, Jesus stood before this Herod, but instead of repenting of his violence against John, he asked Jesus to show him a miracle, which Christ refused to do.

According to Josephus, this same Herod led his army into battle, where he and his army were destroyed. Josephus comments that Herod's death "came from God, and that very justly, as a punishment of what he did against John."[13]

Herod Agrippa I

The legacy of the Herod family tree continues. The third Herod in succession was Herod Agrippa I. According to Jewish history, he spent a lot of money attempting to buy friends in Rome and eventually left Rome and came to Judea in poverty. He was contemplating suicide when his sister gave him a job at a market. He eventually borrowed money and returned to Rome, making friends with the nephew of Gauis. Word was out that Tiberius was arrested and placed in chains in prison. Josephus wrote:

> While he waited in chains in front of the palace, a horned owl alighted on the tree on which he was leaning. Another prisoner, a German, predicted that Agrippa would soon be released and attain the highest point of honor and power. "But remember," he continued, "when you seen this bird again, your death will follow within five days."[14]

After six months in prison, Tiberius died, and Gaius took his position. Gaius crowned Herod Agrippa. This was the Herod we read of in Scripture who beheaded James (Acts 12:2). When he saw that the death of James pleased the Jews, he had Peter arrested and placed a sentence of execution on Peter, to take place after the Passover was concluded (vv. 4–7). After Peter's supernatural escape, Herod had the jailers killed (v. 19).

Shortly thereafter, he came to Caesarea for a major celebration dressed in an outfit made of silver. As the silver radiated in the bright sun, the people began to scream that he was a god. According to Josephus, that is when Herod saw the same type of horned owl sitting on a rope nearby. Suddenly a pain struck Herod, and he said, "I, whom you called a god, am now under sentence of death!"[15] This third Herod of Scripture developed severe intestinal pains and died five days later at age fifty-four after ruling for seven years.

Herod Agrippa II

The fourth Herod in succession was Herod Agrippa II, or, as Paul addressed him in Acts 26:2, "Agrippa." When he was seventeen years of age, his father died, but Agrippa was too young to take the rule. Later he was given several areas of domain. He was given the authority to appoint the high priest in Jerusalem. He was the king mentioned in Acts 25 who desired to hear the apostle Paul give his personal testimony of his conversion. After a wonderful, detailed presentation of the gospel, Paul challenged Agrippa to be a Christian. Paul also made a revealing statement to Agrippa. When speaking about Christ, he said, "For the king, before whom I also speak freely, knows these things; for I am convinced that none of these things escapes his attention, since this thing was not done in a corner" (Acts 26:26). In essence, Paul was saying to the king, "You have several generations before you who knew Christ and had direct dealings with Him. You are not ignorant of what I am saying!"

Paul asked Agrippa, "Do you believe the prophets? I know that you do believe" (v. 27).

Agrippa replied, "You almost persuade me to become a Christian" (v. 28). This Herod was the fourth generation that had been given an opportunity to believe, but instead he also rejected Christ.

1. The first Herod could have worshiped the baby in Bethlehem but instead slaughtered the innocents.

2. The second Herod could have listened to John and discovered Christ as the Messiah, but his lust ruled his convictions, and instead he slew the prophet John.

3. The third Herod paid no attention to the apostles Peter or James, but instead he killed a righteous man and was smitten by an angel of the Lord and died.

4. The fourth Herod knew the history of the previous Herods and heard a clear message of the gospel, but he chose not to become a believer.

After Acts 28, the line of the Herods disappeared from history. The four Herods reveal what can happen when men reject the opportunity to enter a new redemptive covenant with Christ. The Kennedy legacy reveals how the decision of the father(s) will have an impact upon their children.

What Would You Change on Your Family Tree?

Let me boast (in the Lord, of course) for a moment. On my mother's side of the family, my great-grandfather came from Italy. His background was Catholic, but in the 1930s he became sick unto death, and two ministers prayed for him to be healed. He was instantly healed. His two sons and two daughters all became strong, dedicated Christians. My grandfather, John Bava, was a minister, and his two daughters, now in their seventies, have served Christ from their childhood. All of their children, my three siblings and my aunt's two children, all serve the Lord. We are now raising our children in the same faith of the ancestors. This side of the family tree has produced dynamic fruit for the kingdom of God and continues to do so.

From my father's side, in the early 1950s he was the only child out of eleven living children actively serving Christ. As Dad witnessed and lived a godly life before his mom, dad, and siblings, eventually, one by one they came to the knowledge of the Lord and received Him as Lord and Savior. Several of his sisters have since gone to be with the Lord. Dad's ministry has impacted thousands of people, and he has given his children the legacy of a good name and wonderful memories of God's miracles and blessing.

This is the greatest legacy. Solomon said, "A good name is to be chosen rather than great riches, loving favor rather than silver and gold" (Prov. 22:1). At this present time, there is nothing on our family tree that I am ashamed of or embarrassed to discuss. I always pray this will continue in my life and in the lives of my precious children. However, there are things on many family trees that people would change if they could or remove. This is why we must prune our family trees.

The Process of Growing a Right Tree

The natural is a reflection of the spiritual. When a person desires to have a fruit tree that will produce fruit, there is a fourfold process necessary to bring forth eventual fruit:

1. Pollination
2. Water
3. Light
4. Pruning

The essential elements for growing a right tree involve the same process we face as we grow in our spiritual lives.

The need for pollination

Pollination is a natural process that flowers and fruit trees must experience to be productive. About 80 percent of the world's plants depend upon pollination. Small bees and other insects have pollinated one out of every three bites of food that we eat, including the spices we eat and the beverages we drink. Plants are pollinated by insects and by the wind.[16] There is self-pollination and cross-pollination. Self-pollination occurs when the flower has both the stamen and carpel (pistil), and through contacting each other in the flower, pollination is accomplished. The cross-pollination process is when pollen is transferred from one flower to another. There are some plants that require cross-pollination.

Not only does your spiritual growth require the occasional pruning or separating from some people and circumstances that are baggage from your past, but also we all require both self- and cross-pollination. We must learn to stand alone at times and self-pollinate. This is when we can take what we have learned and operate in faith, even though no other person agrees with us.

We all need cross-pollination, which occurs as we glean from one another and join our faith together to bring forth the fruit in our lives. Often believers do not fellowship with others who differ in their denominational beliefs or ideas. How can we grow in knowledge if we refuse to learn from those whose ideas may differ from ours? Being from a full-gospel background, I was raised to believe in the full work of the Holy Spirit. There are some who refuse to accept the belief in the working of the Holy Spirit today. However, when they cross-pollinate with those in the full-gospel ministry, they begin to understand the working of the Spirit.

The need for water

Water is the nourishment for all ecosystems. The human body is two-thirds water. It is recommended that each person drink seven to ten average-sized glasses of water a day. A person can actually go without food for forty days, as Christ and Moses did during their extended fasting. However, a person cannot go even one day without water without experiencing dehydration.

Rain is used as an analogy when speaking of the Holy Spirit's being poured out from heaven to earth (Joel 2:28–29). Water is used to identify the manner in which the Holy Spirit flows through a person, bringing nourishment, refreshing, and the life force that causes a believer to grow spiritually (John 7:38–39). While water drops are visible on leaves after a rain, the most important nourishment comes from the roots. Often we judge a person's spirituality by the outward manifestations we see, but the real strength is in the inner, hidden part of a person, which Peter identified as "the hidden person of the heart" (1 Pet. 3:4).

The need for light

There is no life without light. In the Creation narrative, before the Almighty created any life form—plants, animals, or man—He first created light. "Then God said, 'Let there be light'; and there was light" (Gen. 1:3). We all have physical ears to hear, but there are inner ears in our spirits where we hear the Word of the Lord and receive it. A person can hear a clear message of the gospel, and suddenly that person will understand the message and respond! This is an example of the light of the Word opening the eyes of our understanding (Eph. 1:18). If a person refuses to listen and turns away from the truth, then that person's ears become dull, and that person's understanding is unfruitful.

> But also for this very reason, giving all diligence, add to your faith virtue, to virtue knowledge, to knowledge self-control, to self-control perseverance, to perseverance godliness, to godliness brotherly kindness, and to brotherly kindness love. For if these things are yours and abound, you will be neither barren nor unfruitful in the knowledge of our Lord Jesus Christ. For he who lacks these things

is shortsighted, even to blindness, and has forgotten that he was cleansed from his old sins.

—2 PETER 1:5-9

We have also all been created with physical eyes to see; however, there are spiritual, inner eyes where we receive spiritual understanding. In Scripture we have the story of Samson, a man who allowed his spiritual eyes to become blinded so that he could no longer see the spiritual light of God. As a result he also lost his physical sight and suffered great persecution from the enemy. In his story we see many parallels to our own need to guard our spiritual eyes from the attempts of Satan to also blind us.

In Numbers 6:2-21, we find the specific and rather unusual guidelines given to Moses in the Law of God regarding a man who takes a Nazirite vow:

1. He was to drink no wine or strong drink and was limited in the types of foods he could eat.

2. He was never to touch a dead carcass, whether of a human or an animal.

3. He was never to shave his hair but was to wear his hair long as an outward sign of his vow to God

Samson was a Nazirite. Before Samson's birth his parents were informed that he would be a Nazirite (Judg. 13:5-7). As a Nazirite set apart for God, Samson was to hold to these three main restrictions and commands. As long he followed these three vows, he would be greatly anointed of the Lord. However, Samson slowly became careless with his vows, and one by one he began breaking them.

In the Scriptures, Samson stops the attack of a lion with his bare hands, killing the lion. Some time later, when he passes by the carcass of the lion, he touches the dead carcass in order to get some honey from a beehive in the carcass, and by doing so he broke the vow of not touching an unclean carcass (Judg. 14:5-9). Yet the Spirit of the Lord remained upon him. When nothing happened, Samson must have felt confident that God would bless him despite his breaking a vow. He could disobey and still maintain the anointing.

Eventually, the third vow was broken when Samson revealed to the Philistine woman Delilah that the secret of his strength was his hair. Samson's hair was braided into seven different locks on his head, and Delilah gave the fellow a haircut (Judg. 16:13–19). As the enemy came into the house, Samson, unaware that the Spirit of the Lord had departed from him, tried to shake himself free through his brute strength but could not do so. His power was not in his hair but in his covenant and threefold vow as a Nazirite. Although he broke the first part of the vow, he maintained his anointing. Even when he broke the second part, he still had great power. But once he had broken all three parts of his vow, the Lord departed from him! He had stepped out of the spiritual light of God.

The Philistines removed Samson's eyes and used him like an animal, yoking him to grind out the grain. Samson was blind, bound, and going 'round and 'round.

From a practical application, blindness in the Bible can be an analogy for spiritual blindness or a lack of spiritual understanding. People can have eyes but not see and ears but not hear. Once Samson lost his eyes, he was bound by his enemy. Once our spiritual discernment is lost, it is easy for the enemy to bring us under certain bondages of the flesh. For any person truly bound, that person's life will go in circles. He may have a desire to be free and may go a few days without sinning or following an addiction, but he will end up in the same condition again and again.

Samson had become weak. The adversary is a master at making his move when a person is vulnerable or weak. Eventually Samson's hair grew back, and he remembered his original vow to God. In his final moments, he called out to the Lord, regained his strength, and destroyed three thousand Philistines—while losing his own life.

4. Pruning the branches

Let's look at a simple process for pruning the tree. It is necessary to remove dead or fruitless branches from trees or vineyards. In a grape vineyard, the pruning process begins after the harvest and during the coldest months. It is done after the plants lose their foliage, which enables the vinedresser to see the branches needing removal from the vine. Trimming will stimulate growth prior to the spring.[17]

The grape vine is important in the Holy Land. Grapes are listed as one of the seven foods God promised to Israel (Deut. 8:8). The New Testament uses the analogy of the olive tree and the grafting process, comparing it to how a natural olive tree (Israel) received nourishment from the wild branches (Gentiles) that are grafted into the side of the natural tree. Christ called Himself the vine and said that we are the branches and must produce fruit. Any branch that is fruitless will be pruned from the vine so that the other branches will be fruitful (John 15:1–5).

If you have witnessed God's blessing but presently see no answers to prayer, no results in your work, and feel rather cold in your spirit, you may be encountering a pruning process in which the Lord is dealing with your need to separate from certain habits, bad attitudes, and people. Once you are pruned, then strength will return to your vine. You will sense both mental and spiritual relief after you make the decision to separate from the things that are pulling you down!

My wife once wrote an article for our magazine in which she shared a story related to her by her sister Shelia. Here is the original article:

> Recently, my sister Shelia was a participant in a conference in California. During the conference there was an opportunity to tour a large, beautiful vineyard. It was what the tour director said that caught her undivided attention. It was a natural law that is parallel to a spiritual law in the Scriptures. She noticed that on some beautiful vines there were red tags marking certain branches.
>
> As the tour guide was explaining the details of a vineyard, he said, "I am sure many of you are wondering why some of the branches are marked with red tags." He then explained that these were branches that were healthy, because they could produce leaves, but during the harvest time these branches did not produce fruit. They were marked while they had leaves on them, because once the

leaves fell off, it would be impossible to tell which branches were good branches and which were fruitless branches.

He stated that the branches with red tags would be severed from the vine. If these branches were not cut off, they would be detrimental to the entire vineyard. The branches that did not produce fruit would take the strength from the good vines, eventually killing the entire vine. The man said: "This branch is deceiving, because it looks like it is producing because of the leaves, but there is no fruit on it. The fruitless branch must be pruned, or it will sap the strength away from the other branches."

Jesus taught us that He is the vine and we are the branches. If a branch does not produce fruit, it is cut off, or pruned, so that it will produce fruit.

> I am the vine, you are the branches. He who abides in Me, and I in him, bears much fruit; for without Me you can do nothing. If anyone does not abide in Me, he is cast out as a branch and is withered; and they gather them and throw them into the fire, and they are burned.
>
> —JOHN 15:5–6

Often it is a person's hidden sins or inner weights that will cut off the spiritual life that proceeds from God. Unforgiveness, strife, fear, and doubt can actually shut off the blessings of the Lord from our lives. *We must nip these carnal weaknesses in the bud.* People tend to judge their own spirituality by the number of leaves they can count on their vine. However, it is fruit (of the Spirit) that the Lord is looking for in our lives, not just the show.

The Bible says that we must "cleanse ourselves from all filthiness of the flesh and spirit, perfecting holiness in the fear of God" (2 Cor. 7:1). Cleansing ourselves means we are to "lay aside every weight, and the sin which so easily ensnares us" (Heb. 12:1). Instead of asking someone to pray for your personal problems or bad attitude, get out your clippers and start nipping away! We are told to lay aside the weight and to cleanse ourselves. Sometimes God is saying, "Throw the junk in your house in the trash, put filters on the Internet, and tell the cable man to take the X-rated channels off your tube." You choose how much fruit you want in your life. You choose what type of testimony will follow you. Prune off the dead branches so the living branches will grow and mature. The fruit that those whom you love will enjoy blossoming in your life will well be worth the effort!

There are certain spiritual blessings that only the Lord Himself can give, such as salvation, the baptism of the Holy Spirit, or emotional and physical healing. When we are told to "cleanse ourselves from all filthiness of the flesh and spirit" (2 Cor. 7:1), it may seem odd, since we depend upon God alone for His cleansing power to cleanse us. However, we are responsible for what we see, hear, and say. You can prevent yourself from viewing something, from hearing something, or from speaking something displeasing to God. In this manner you have used your authority to cleanse yourself and have allowed the Holy Spirit to do those things that you are unable to do. There is nothing like seeing a beautiful fruit-bearing tree in the summer that is providing food for the hungry and shade for those in need. You can bear fruit. Begin by pruning your family tree!

Chapter 7

WHEN SATAN RETURNS TO YOUR HOUSE

When an unclean spirit goes out of a man, he goes through dry places, seeking rest, and finds none. Then he says, "I will return to my house from which I came." And when he comes, he finds it empty, swept, and put in order. Then he goes and takes with him seven other spirits more wicked than himself, and they enter and dwell there; and the last state of that man is worse than the first. So shall it also be with this wicked generation.

| MATTHEW 12:43–45 |

THIS SCRIPTURE MAKES it clear that the adversary goes house hunting. This particular verse has puzzled biblical scholars and students alike. The house referred to is not necessarily the home where you live, but it can allude to the physical body. In this passage the unclean spirit has been expelled from the house but returns to the same house, finding it swept clean but uninhabited. Eventually seven other spirits more wicked than the initial spirit join with it. Thus the condition of the person is now worse than before. This is a clear reference to Satan returning after he has been expelled—a satanic counterattack when Satan returns to your house.

Believers tend to be more guarded when they sense that a battle is looming over the horizon. We all know how to brace ourselves behind the shield of faith, strap on our helmet of salvation, grip the sword of the Spirit, and prepare to stand in the evil day. (See Ephesians 6:13–17.) But when the war is over and the battle is won, we remove the heavy armor, get some iced tea, and enjoy the latest reruns of our favorite television program. It is then that we are the most susceptible to a sudden and unexpected counterattack of the enemy. Sometimes the enemy will give up the initial loss, knowing he can nail us in the counterattack!

Counterattack Against David

When David became king over Israel, the Philistines decided to put him to an early test. They united forces and came to Jerusalem, where David and his warriors defeated his long-time foes (2 Sam. 5:12–20). The Bible says that David proclaimed: "The LORD has broken through my enemies before me, like a breakthrough of water" (v. 20). He called the place *Baal Perazim*, which means "Lord of the breakthrough." David had finally received a long-awaited breakthrough! Now he could sit back and tell his war stories, taking a long-needed vacation—right? Wrong! You would think that the Philistines became weary from being whipped by David year after year. But remember that the enemy does not become weary of assaulting you on a consistent basis because he is attempting to wear you down.

Within a few days of David's victory we read, "Then the Philistines went up once again and deployed themselves in the Valley of Rephaim (v. 22). This was the counterattack—their plan for gaining back the territory that had been lost. This time David was given different instructions from the Lord:

> Therefore David inquired of the LORD, and He said, "You shall not go up; circle around behind them, and come upon them in front of the mulberry trees. And it shall be, when you hear the sound of marching in the tops of the mulberry trees, then you shall advance quickly. For then the LORD will go out before you to strike the camp of the Philistines." And David did so, as the LORD commanded him; and he drove back the Philistines from Geba as far as Gezer.
>
> —2 SAMUEL 5:23–25

The war was the same, but the strategy had changed. The King James Bible says, "When thou hearest the sound of a going in the tops of the mulberry trees…" (v. 24). The Dake's Bible notes that in the Arabic version, the word *goings* is translated "the sound was the noise of horse's hoofs." God was revealing to David that there was an invisible army going before him to defeat the counterattack of the Philistines!

I believe the marching sounds were the sounds of angels bringing the throne of God into the battle. Ezekiel noted that at times four cherubim move the throne of God by lifting it on their shoulders. They move with such speed that the angels appear as wheels within wheels. (See Ezekiel 1:15–28.) Mystical Jews call this chapter in Ezekiel "the mystery of the Merkabah," which is the Hebrew word for "chariot." In Judaism, the throne of God is at times transformed into a chariot, borne by four living creatures.

This may be what David alluded to when he wrote, "He rode upon a cherub, and flew; and He was seen upon the wings of the wind" (2 Sam. 22:11). No doubt it was this counterattack of the Philistines that David was alluding to when he penned these amazing words. After this victory, David began preparing to bring the ark of the covenant to Jerusalem (2 Sam. 6:1–5). The golden ark was an earthly picture of God's heavenly throne.

Return of the Giants

At age seventeen, David defeated Israel's greatest adversary: a giant named Goliath. At age fifty, however, another giant almost snuffed David out. Again, it was the return of the Philistines that initiated the conflict:

> When the Philistines were at war again with Israel, David and his servants with him went down and fought against the Philistines; and David grew faint. Then Ishbi-Benob, who was one of the sons of the giant, the weight of whose bronze spear was three hundred shekels, who was bearing a new sword, thought he could kill David. But Abishai the son of Zeruiah came to his aid, and struck the Philistine and killed him. Then the men of David swore to him, saying, "You shall go out no more with us to battle, lest you quench the lamp of Israel."
>
> —2 SAMUEL 21:15–17

In his teen years, the Bible tells us that David ran *to* Goliath, but when he was older he ran *from* a giant.

As a teenager, he ran to the army to meet his brothers (1 Sam. 17:22). Later he ran toward the Philistine army to meet Goliath (v. 48), and finally, after he put one small stone in his slingshot and decked Goliath like a lumberjack felling a giant oak, he ran head-on to seize Goliath's sword and sever his head from his body (v. 51).

But by the time of the narrative in 2 Samuel 21:15–17, David was in his fifties. He is older, slower, yet still full of zeal. However, he is dealing with a new giant who has a new sword and a new strategy. I believe David was reminiscing about his earlier days, and in his mind he thought he had enough strength to endure the battle. Within moments David needed help, and he received it from Abishai, a younger soldier.

Although he had singlehandedly defeated Israel's most wanted giant thirty-three years earlier, he was now in a new season of his life. But the enemy was still bringing giants against the man of God! We must understand that the counterattacks will only stop when the coffin lid is closed at our funeral. As long as we have breath, we will encounter some form of conflict as the enemy attempts to return to regain lost territory.

Even Christ experienced this. When Christ was age thirty (Luke 3:23), Satan tempted Christ in the wilderness by questioning His relationship with God, saying, "If You are the Son of God…" (Matt. 4:3). Then at the conclusion of His ministry, while hanging on the cross, His persecutors taunted Him by saying, "If You are the Son of God, come down from the cross" (Matt. 27:40). The initial attack was in the wilderness, but the counterattack occurred when Christ was dying.

Preventing the Return of the Destroyer

In Mark 5, a naked man possessed with thousands of spirits was living in a graveyard, cutting himself, and crying out in torment. One day a tall, suntanned Nazarene stepped off a boat and met the fellow head-on. Christ commanded the evil spirits to leave the man, and the demons, knowing their time was up, requested to enter a herd of swine. The pigs eventually lost their sense of direction and headed down a cliff into the sea.

Afterward the fellow was clothed and in his right mind sitting at Jesus's feet. The man then requested permission to do something that most people who were healed in Christ's ministry had done—he wanted to follow Jesus from city to city.

For example, the two blind men from Jericho who were healed by Christ began to follow Him wherever He went (Matt. 20:34). The blind man near Jericho who was healed followed Christ (Luke 18:43). Yet, when this man healed of demonic possession wanted to follow Christ, the Lord instructed him to do something different. Christ told this man, "Go home to your friends, and tell them what great things the Lord has done for you, and how He has had compassion on you" (Mark 5:19). The Bible tells us that the man obeyed Christ and "began to proclaim in Decapolis all that Jesus had done for him; and all marveled" (v. 20).

I personally believe it is possible that this man had more than one reason for wanting to follow Christ. He desired to follow Christ not just out of appreciation, but because he had been living among family and friends when the evil spirits came upon him. Therefore he was somewhat afraid to return home, thinking that these spirits would eventually return. In other words, he was afraid of the counterattack. When Christ told him to go home and tell what the Lord had done, He revealed the key to preventing the enemy from returning—the power of the testimony. This former maniac traveled throughout the Decapolis, ten Roman-controlled cities, and began to testify what the Lord had done for him.

The Power of the Testimony

The word *testimony* in Greek is *marturia*, which means "to give evidence, including judicial evidence." It is presenting evidence of what has occurred, such as a witness in a courtroom. We use the term *testimony* to describe the witness a person gives in court. The same word is used when we say we have a testimony to tell someone about what Christ has done for us. The man of Gadera had proof of his deliverance—he carried marks on his arms and body where he had cut himself.

There is unique power in your testimony. When God has answered a prayer, met your personal need, or performed a healing or a miracle, then we should boldly testify of what the Lord has done. However, for some reason believers are often fearful of telling what God has done. I have known of individuals who received a marvelous healing but were reluctant to testify for fear that somehow the sickness would return, thus embarrassing them. One person told me, "I don't want to say too much because the enemy might get angry and attack me for it." It is common to fear that after we tell what God has done, the problem may return. In reality, we are afraid of a counterattack!

These fears are unfounded and are contrary to the Word of God. We are told in Revelation 12:11, "And they overcame him by the blood of the Lamb and by the word of their testimony, and they did not love their lives to the death."

A testimony is a form of confession. It is one of the tools we have to use in spiritual warfare. Follow the advice in 1 Peter 3:15:

> Always be ready to give a defense to everyone who asks you a reason
> for the hope that is in you.

Has the Lord healed you? Has He broken your sin bondage? Has He set you free? Then shout it from the housetops! Don't be afraid of a counterattack from Satan. Instead: "Proclaim the praises of Him who called you out of darkness into His marvelous light" (1 Pet. 2:9).

During my earlier ministry, I would often hear one believer relate to another believer how the Lord had brought a miraculous healing or a special answer to prayer. Upon hearing this, the fellow believer would encourage the person to testify publicly and give glory to the Lord on behalf of the blessing. I cannot count the number of times when a person would reply, "Well, I would like to, but I am afraid that if I testify, the enemy will hear it, and he will reverse the blessing or I will have another battle!"

Again, this is a common fear among individuals. It is based on another person's experience and not based upon Scripture. Perhaps that person had heard a believer testify of being touched by the Lord, and months or years later the same type of affliction came back upon that person. In the eyes of a faithless believer, to testify is to open the door to the enemy to know where to launch an attack.

However, as I stated above, the Bible makes it clear: "And they overcame him [Satan] by the blood of the Lamb and by the word of their testimony, and they did not love their lives to the death" (Rev. 12:11). A testimony is a verbal confession stating a fact. When Christ healed the demon-possessed man of Gadera, the cured fellow desired to follow Jesus, but instead Christ instructed him to "go home to your friends, and tell them what great things the Lord has done for you, and how He has had compassion on you" (Mark 5:19). If there was a threat that the evil spirits could come back upon the man, Christ would have never sent him back to his family. The healed man's testimony about the miracle not only prevented the enemy from returning, but it also brought great faith and hope to others in need! As Peter said, "Always be ready to give a defense to everyone who asks you a reason for the hope that is in you" (1 Pet. 3:15).

A testimony is given in a court case to allow a witness to either confirm or deny evidence against a person. A testimony is a public confession. A confession is made with words—with your mouth. There is power in a person's confession. It is written, "For with the heart one believes unto righteousness, and with the mouth confession is made unto salvation" (Rom. 10:10). The Bible further reveals that if we confess our sins, the Lord is faithful and just to forgive us our sins (1 John 1:9). Hebrews tells us to "hold fast the confession of our hope without wavering" (Heb. 10:23). The Greek word for "profession" can be translated the same as the word for "confession." Notice that we are to *hold fast* or *seize upon* the confession and not let go.

By not letting go of our faith and confession, we can keep the door closed against the powers of the adversary and against individuals who would attempt to bring us back under some form of bondage and captivity.

In a counterattack, the same faith and prayer you used to defeat the enemy the first time can be used as your spiritual weapon to conquer and overcome any form of counterattack! David picked up stones from the brook to defeat the giant, and there are still "stones in the brook," or weapons of war that can slay your giants.

Chapter 8

STAND AGAINST THE ROARING LION

But the Lord stood with me and strengthened me, so that the message might be preached fully through me, and that all the Gentiles might hear. Also I was delivered out of the mouth of the lion. And the Lord will deliver me from every evil work and preserve me for His heavenly kingdom. To Him be glory forever and ever. Amen!

| 2 TIMOTHY 4:17–18 |

PAUL WAS DELIVERED from the mouth of the lion. Scholars have two possible interpretations to this statement. First, Paul was ministering during in the time of the Roman Empire when the emperor was Nero. The historian Seneca called Nero a lion, as this vile emperor was known for inventing persecutions and gleefully enjoying the death of Christians.[1] The second possible meaning was that Paul had been condemned to die by being fed to the lions but was somehow delivered out of this punishment by some miraculous intervention from the Lord.

In the Scriptures there are several creatures on Earth that are used to paint the imagery of Satan. The oldest identification of Satan was as a serpent in Eden, and this imagery is carried though six thousand years of history, through the New Testament, to where the apostle John saw Satan as a dragon, or, as the Greek word indicates, a large serpent.

The lion is also used to compare the viciousness of Satan's attacks:

> Be sober, be vigilant; because your adversary the devil walks about like a roaring lion, seeking whom he may devour.
>
> —1 PETER 5:8

Several years ago I was speaking with a close friend, Pastor Jentezen Franklin, who had recently returned from a safari in South Africa. What he and his family had experienced during their stay is a parallel to how believers should stand against the powers of the enemy, or against Satan, who is compared to a roaring lion.

The Ways of a Lion

When Jentezen and his family checked into the safari camp, they were taken to a special house where they would stay. They were immediately warned that they should not travel out of their dwelling without first contacting an armed person to escort them to places like the dining room. They learned that there was no fence around the compound; it was open, allowing all forms of wild animal to make their way into the camp at any time. The staff pointed out that sometimes native people traveling from place to place in the surrounding areas are found dead, having been killed by a wild beast. I thought, "You call this a vacation?" At this point I would have probably packed my bags and found the next Jeep with a few armed men hanging off the sides and driven like Jehu in the Bible to the closest hotel!

The family was then informed about the most dangerous animal they might encounter—the lion. At times the campfires lit at night attract the lions. In the event that someone encountered a lion, he must never, never, never turn his back on the lion, because the moment he turns or runs, he will be attacked. Anyone running from a lion will instantly be chased down, overtaken, and slain by this king of the beasts.

Jentezen related several life-saving instructions about encountering a lion. These directions are parallels to biblical principles in dealing with Satan!

Stay together as a group.

They were told to stay together as a group and not to separate away from the group. There is greater protection when there are larger numbers of people in one group than there is when a person is alone. The spiritual application is that there is an increase in spiritual authority when individuals are united together. Christ did not send His disciples out alone; He always sent them two by two (Luke 10:1). The wise man Solomon wrote:

> Two are better than one,
> Because they have a good reward for their labor.
> For if they fall, one will lift up his companion.
> But woe to him who is alone when he falls,
> For he has no one to help him up.
> —ECCLESIASTES 4:9–10

When we stay together as one unit, we are able to cover each other's back from being struck from the blind side. The adversary may have certain limitations placed upon his plans, as in the case of Job when Satan struck Job's flesh with tormenting boils and God demanded Satan not take his life (Job 2:6), but he does not play fair; he uses his own rulebook. Just like a wild lion, the enemy comes to "steal, and to kill, and to destroy" (John 10:10).

2. Don't make any sudden moves.

The second instruction they received was this: "If you encounter a lion, do not make any sudden moves." Any sudden move would only draw attention to the individual. Sudden movement can be interpreted by a lion as a sign of fear.

The spiritual application admonishes a believer to avoid making sudden major decisions, as any sudden move could be the wrong move. In the Garden of Gethsemane, Peter, in his zeal, took his sword and sliced off the ear of a servant of the high priest. It was a sudden, impulsive move. Christ healed the man and thus destroyed any evidence of Peter's misconduct. Had Christ not healed the ear, Peter could have eventually been charged with assault and arrested for his attack.

I have seen individuals marry without seeking godly counsel. Others choose to hang out with friends who are placing destructive seed in their spirits. I have watched ministers move quickly from one church only to take a pastorate in a place where they do not fit in with the personalities of the members.

3. *If confronted, stand still and face the lion.*

The third important instruction was that if confronted by a lion, the person must stand face-to-face with the lion and stand perfectly still. Tribes in Africa who live in the bush country know that the worst mistake is to turn your back and attempt to run away from the beast. The lion reads this as weakness and immediately pursues its prey. No man can outrun a lion, but men in tribes have been able to outstand and outstare them.

When I was visiting in Kenya, West Africa, I was told about a tribe in Africa that trains their boys how to take on lions. In order to become a man in this tribe, a young boy of about thirteen is given a large spear and placed on the outskirts of the village. Eventually a lion enters the area and sees the boy. The young man will stand perfectly still, staring down the lion. Eventually the lion will make a sudden move toward the lad, who is trained and prepared to thrust the spear into the heart of the leaping lion. The key is to stand and face the lion, never turn, and keep your eyes open at all times.

Peter said we must be sober and vigilant. In other words, we must stay alert. In the wild in Africa, a person never knows when he or she will encounter a dangerous, life-threatening beast of the field like a lion.

The spiritual application is important. I have known individuals who are always running away from their commitments, their values, their responsibilities, and attempting to escape their problems. It is important to remember this: if you ever begin to run from your problems instead of facing them, you will run from difficulties for the rest of your life! The patriarch Jacob had a weakness for tricking people out of their blessings. Eventually it took a wrestling match with an angel, a change of Jacob's name, and a transformation of his character to slow him down and bring him into the fullness of his covenant blessings! When God touched Jacob's hip, He ensured that this man on the run would never be able to run again. He would need to lean on God for the remaining years of his life.

When Paul revealed that we wrestle against strong evil spirits in our earthly battle, he said we should put on the armor of God: "Therefore take up the whole armor of God, that you may be able to withstand in the evil day, and having done all, to stand" (Eph. 6:13). At the safari camp, the people staying as guests were told that if by chance they saw a lion, they should stand in one spot and face the beast. Do not, under any circumstances, take your eyes off the lion. And whatever you do, don't flinch and run.

When Peter compared Satan to a roaring lion, he said we must "resist him, steadfast in the faith" (1 Pet. 5:9). The word *resist* in Greek is *anthistemi*, meaning "to stand against and oppose."

4. *Wave your arms and speak in a loud voice (make noise).*

The fourth instruction for dealing with a lion was that if you are standing face-to-face with one, then at some point raise your hands as high as you can and begin yelling and making loud noises. The reason is that the noise can be confusing to the lion, and when you raise your hands, you appear larger than you really are.

There are numerous examples in Scripture revealing the importance of raising one's hands. Israel once won a major battle against Amalek when Moses kept his arms raised (Exod. 17:11–12). When Moses raised his hands with the rod of God, the sea was opened (Exod. 14:16). The high priest raised his hands when speaking the priestly blessing (Num. 6:24–26). Jesus bought salvation when He stretched His hands across the wood of the cross!

We are told, "I desire therefore that the men pray everywhere, lifting up holy hands, without wrath and doubting" (1 Tim. 2:8). When we pray, lifting up our hands, we are surrendering to God and allowing Him to take control of our situation!

5. *The enemy is defeated by words!*

A loud noise can confuse the lion. Believers are taught the power of our words when we use them in earnest, passionate intercession.

> Assuredly, I say to you, whatever you bind on earth will be bound in heaven, and whatever you loose on earth will be loosed in heaven.

Again I say to you that if two of you agree on earth concerning anything that they ask, it will be done for them by My Father in heaven. For where two or three are gathered together in My name, I am there in the midst of them.

—MATTHEW 18:18–20

Stopping the Intimidation

Some time ago our ministry purchased seventy-eight acres of farm property to construct a special youth ministry and a gathering place for youth and future conferences. Part of the initial process was when a group of talented builders constructed a beautiful new facility from an old barn, which is used for special prayer meetings. Near the barn is a creek, lots of trees, and tall grass.

There are three things about an old farm that I do not like: rats, ticks, and snakes—especially snakes, and I mean any kind of snake! One evening I was in the barn and turned to see a snake about five feet long. I suddenly froze but then reached for a metal pole. I began to hit the snake as it crawled about six feet away. Then it opened its mouth like it was going to strike me. I moved the pole near its mouth so it would bite down on the pole. Eventually I pushed the serpent into an area where it fell into a hole underground.

I immediately called my dad and told him about this huge snake. He asked me one question (he was raised on a farm): "What was the color of the snake?" I told him it was a black snake. He replied, "Brother, leave those black snakes alone. They won't hurt you and will actually eat rodents. We were told growing up that they can also keep some of those mean snakes away from you!" I realized at that moment that I knew nothing about snakes and that I was intimidated by *every* snake—both the *good* and the *bad*.

Both the image of a snake and the roar of a lion can bring intimidation. Intimidation plays upon the imagination, the same way the giants caused the Hebrew spies to view themselves as grasshoppers. It will not always be the lion itself but the roar of the lion that intimidates, just as it is the fiery darts of Satan that hit your mind. That is where the real battle is. This is why each believer must put on the "helmet of salvation" (Eph. 6:17) to protect his or her mind and must continually renew his or her mind to build barriers against the strongholds of intimidation.

The true Lion is Christ, the "Lion of the tribe of Judah." The imagery shows us that Christ has conquered all of the powers of the enemy and is our spiritual leader in all of our struggles.

Chapter 9

REVERSE THE ATTACKS

And the LORD restored Job's losses when he prayed for his friends. Indeed the LORD gave Job twice as much as he had before.

| JOB 42:10 |

H E WAS CONSIDERED the greatest man in the East. He had ten children, all who owned houses, along with a massive business portfolio that included:

- Seven thousand sheep
- Three thousand camels
- Five hundred yoke of oxen
- Five hundred female donkeys

Thus Job's personal story reveals in vivid detail how Satan moved against a righteous person and set an ambush. But as we can see in the Book of Job, God can and will reverse the attack when the righteous make the proper decision in the midst of their adversity.

Invisible Bodyguards

The Book of Job is believed to be the oldest book in the Bible. It is the first book to introduce Satan as a heavenly being that sets out to kill, steal, and destroy (Job 1:6; John 10:10). The story begins with a heavenly counsel meeting between God and the sons of God—a term used four times in the Bible to identify angelic beings.

During this session in the heavenly court God is boasting on Job, saying that there was none like him on the earth who feared God and shunned evil (Job 1:1). Satan answered, insisting that Job feared God out of an ulterior motive. God had blessed him so abundantly that if Job's wealth and family prosperity were destroyed, Job would curse God (vv. 9–11). Satan also revealed that he had been near Job's property but could not penetrate the hedge that surrounded the man, his family, and his possessions.

This hedge is interesting. It was something that Job could not see with his natural eyes, but both God and Satan saw it and knew it existed. Thus the hedge was invisible to the natural eyes and visible in the spirit world. I believe it was an encampment of angels assigned to protect Job and his possessions. The Bible says, "The angel of the LORD encamps all around those who fear Him, and delivers them" (Ps. 34:7). Angels are invisible to the human eye but completely visible to the spirit world. They can appear in the form of horses of fire and chariots of fire (2 Kings 6:17). Angels can circle people to protect them from danger (2 Kings 6). Satan was unable to penetrate the invisible bodyguards surrounding the property of the righteous man Job!

What Formed the Hedge?

Was there something Job did that helped form this hedge? I believe the answer is found in the first chapter of Job. There were times when Job's ten children were feasting, and Job would offer special sacrifices on the altar on behalf of his children, lest they sin against God:

> Now his sons would go and feast in their houses, each on his appointed day, and would send and invite their three sisters to eat and drink with them. So it was, when the days of feasting had run their course, that Job would send and sanctify them, and he would rise early in the morning and offer burnt offerings according to the number of them all. For Job said, "It may be that my sons have sinned and cursed God in their hearts." Thus Job did regularly.
>
> —JOB 1:4–5

I believe these blood sacrifices were the key to Job's protective hedge. This pattern can be seen in several biblical accounts. First, in the Exodus story when the blood of slain lambs was sprinkled on the doors of the Israelites to prevent the destroyer from entering their homes (Exod. 12:22–23).

In the time of David, a destroying plague was stopped when David placed sacrifices on the altar. When God saw the blood offering, He stopped the destruction of Jerusalem (1 Chron. 21:26–27). Under the old covenant, blood sacrifices had power to release a person from guilt and transgressions. Thus the sacrifices of Job were an important part of God maintaining the hedge of protection around Job.

Notice that Job's motive for the sacrificial offering was his fear that his children may have cursed God in their hearts (Job 1:5); thus he offered sacrifices continually. This may be why Satan told God, "Stretch out Your hand and touch all that he has, and he will surely curse You to Your face!" (v. 11).

The Blood Is Removed

God removed the hedge to prove to Satan that Job would stay faithful to him despite his financial and family losses. The nomadic tribe called the Sabeans invaded Job's land and seized his donkeys and oxen (Job 1:13–15). Immediately after Job heard this report from a servant, lightning began striking and consumed Job's seven thousand sheep (v. 16). No sooner had Job received this news than a third servant arrived, announcing that three bands of Chaldeans had invaded the land, stealing three thousand camels (v. 17). The worst news suddenly followed: a whirlwind has struck the home of the oldest son, collapsing the building on all ten children, and all were killed (vv. 18–19).

It is important to note that when the animals were removed, Job had no sacrifice to place upon the altar. Without blood, there was no possibility of creating the protective hedge. It was after the removing of the blood sacrifices that Satan was able to get to Job's children! Throughout the Old Testament, the adversary was always after the blood sacrifices. Cain offered fruit from the ground, and Abel brought forth the blood sacrifices. In anger Cain killed his brother because of his offering

(Gen. 4:5–8). When Moses and the Hebrews were departing from Egypt, Pharaoh demanded they leave their animals in Egypt (Exod. 10:24). When the temples were destroyed, the sacrifices were also stopped. Without the shedding of blood, there was no remission of sin, and without sacrificial blood, the Israelites would be weakened spiritually and unable to please God and receive atonement for their sins (Heb. 9:18–22).

Both redemptive and protective power was released through the blood. When Noah built an altar and offered blood, God confirmed that the earth would be preserved from a future global flood (Gen. 8:20–22). Abraham built an altar, and God covenanted for a new nation through Abraham (Gen. 12:7). Lamb's blood restrained the destroyer in Egypt (Exod. 12). When the blood was gone, the hedge was lifted.

The Second Wave

During the first wave of attacks Job maintained his integrity and his faith in God. After hearing of the losses, he said: "The LORD gave, and the LORD has taken away; blessed be the name of the LORD" (Job 1:21). Scripture says that Job did not sin (v. 22). He did not curse God or blame God; however, the second wave of attacks was just over the horizon.

A second counsel meeting took place in the heavenly court. God was boasting about Job's integrity when Satan recommended a second attack, this time on Job's own physical body. Satan suggested that once Job's body was sick and his health failing, he would curse God to his face (Job 2:5). Suddenly Satan was permitted to smite the body of Job with boils from head to foot (v. 7).

It was following this strange sickness that Job's wife said, "Curse God and die!" (v. 9). Through Job's wife Satan was making another attempt to get Job to speak evil toward the Lord. In much the same way, Satan persuaded Peter to speak out in error to Christ, after which Jesus rebuked him, saying, "Get behind Me, Satan!" (Matt. 16:23). Following Job's sickness, Job's three closest friends came to comfort him, but when they saw him they went into shock because his sickness had severely altered his physical appearance.

For seven days Job said nothing. And then we read where he opened his mouth and began to curse.

> After this Job opened his mouth and cursed the day of his birth. And Job spoke, and said: "May the day perish on which I was born, And the night in which it was said, 'A male child is conceived.'"
>
> —Job 3:1–3

> Let them curse it that curse the day, who are ready to raise up their mourning.
>
> —Job 3:8, KJV

Job never cursed God, but he cursed himself. This was uncharacteristic of him. He did not sin against God but was speaking evil of himself. Suddenly, after cursing himself, he cried out:

> For the thing I greatly feared has come upon me, And what I dreaded has happened to me.
>
> —Job 3:25

In my earlier ministry I taught that Job was afraid that he would lose everything he had and at some point had confessed his fear publicly. However, the only thing Job feared was that his children would curse God. He realized that he was falling into the snare of cursing his own life, which God had given him.

Hope in the Middle of the Storm

When we enter an unexpected struggle, we need to keep our spiritual ears open. God will send us a special word of encouragement through a sermon, a song, or an individual. In the midst of Job's tragedy and sickness, the Lord sent this word to Job:

> If you return to the Almighty, you will be built up;
> You will remove iniquity far from your tents.
> Then you will lay your gold in the dust,
> And the gold of Ophir among the stones of the brooks.
> Yes, the Almighty will be your gold
> And your precious silver;
> For then you will have your delight in the Almighty,

And lift up your face to God.
You will make your prayer to Him,
He will hear you,
And you will pay your vows.
You will also declare a thing,
And it will be established for you;
So light will shine on your ways.

—JOB 22:23–28

The Almighty was promising a restoration of financial blessing in the form of gold and silver to Job, if he would make his prayers to God, keep the promises he had made in the past (pay your vows), and make a decree (a confession) that God would establish His blessing on his life. Today we would say, "Begin praying for a divine reversal, and begin decreeing that God is going to bring you out of the negative situation you are in."

Later, Job received this word:

Surely there is a mine for silver,
And a place where gold is refined.
Iron is taken from the earth,
And copper is smelted from ore.
Man puts an end to darkness,
And searches every recess
For ore in the darkness and the shadow of death....
As for the earth, from it comes bread,
But underneath it is turned up as by fire;
Its stones are the source of sapphires,
And it contains gold dust.
That path no bird knows,
Nor has the falcon's eye seen it.
The proud lions have not trodden it,
Nor has the fierce lion passed over it.

—JOB 28:1–3, 5–8

In the Bible silver represents redemption. In this passage the speaker is revealing that you don't find precious stones or gold lying on the ground, but they are discovered by digging deep into the ground in the dark pits under the earth. The writer seems to be saying that he doesn't understand why he (Job) is experiencing what he is, but if he will keep digging in the darkness, he will discover a vein of silver, or a vein of redemption. He is told that He (God) will set an end to the darkness!

Another powerful part of this passage is when the speaker says that there is a path that no bird knows and that no falcon's eye has seen. In the New Testament parable of the sower planting the Word of God, the birds attempt to devour some of the seed (Mark 4:4). The interpretation is that Satan steals the word that is sown (v. 15). There is, however, a spiritual path that is far away from the eyes of the seedeaters. There is also a path on which the fierce lion cannot walk. Peter describes Satan as a roaring lion (1 Pet. 5:8). Job 28:8 reveals there is a path that the roaring (fierce) lion will be unable to tread upon. This was an encouraging word to Job to continue to believe for a divine reversal; God would place him on a new road with a new direction.

Suddenly God Shows Up

For several months Job's three friends attempted to explain to Job the reasons he had lost his wealth, family, and health. Some believed it was God getting the pride out of his life. Others insinuated it was a hidden sin of some sort, and the troubles were a form of God's chastisement. Finally God Himself spoke to Job out of a whirlwind, giving him a profound revelation.

A spiritual principle was established in the Law of Moses concerning the restoration of goods and stuff, which would happen if the thief could be discovered and exposed.

> If a man delivers to his neighbor money or articles to keep, and it is stolen out of the man's house, if the thief is found, he shall pay double.
>
> —Exodus 22:7

Earlier in the story of Job, Job had said that the Lord gave and the Lord took away. During his trials he was unaware that Satan was the instigator of all his difficulties. Thus someone had to reveal the real thief to Job. Since no one knew of the secret meeting between God and Satan in the heavenly court, the Lord Himself came down to reveal to Job who his real enemy was!

This leads us to two of the most unusual chapters in the entire Bible. Job 40 deals with a strange creature called Behemoth, and Job 41 shows God revealing the power of something called Leviathan. God describes Behemoth as a creature whose bones are like pieces of brass and iron (Job 40:18). The most interesting creature, however, is Leviathan.

Leviathan is mentioned in other biblical references, such as Isaiah 27:1, where he is described as "Leviathan the fleeing serpent, Leviathan that twisted serpent." He is alluded to in Psalms as a multiheaded dragon that will be broken (Ps. 74:13–14). In the New Testament Satan is symbolized as a seven-headed dragon (Rev. 12:3). In the original Greek the word *dragon* is *drakon* and actually refers to a serpent. The link between the seven-headed Leviathan and the seven heads of the dragon in Revelation is unmistakable. God told Job that Leviathan made the deep to boil, and no earthly weapon could defeat him. God identified Leviathan as the king over all the children of pride. (See Job 41.) God was revealing to Job that it was Leviathan, the old serpent the devil, who had initiated the attack against him!

It is important to understand that God revealed or exposed the thief because if the thief could be found, then he must restore double of what he had stolen!

Restoring the Blood on the Altar

After God revealed the source of the trouble, he then rebuked Job's three friends, informing them that they were all wrong in their theological opinions of why the trouble came (Job 42:7). After this, a restoration process was initiated.

> And so it was, after the LORD had spoken these words to Job, that the LORD said to Eliphaz the Temanite, "My wrath is aroused against you and your two friends, for you have not spoken of Me what is right, as My servant Job has. Now therefore, take for yourselves seven bulls and seven rams, go to My servant Job, and offer

up for yourselves a burnt offering; and My servant Job shall pray for you. For I will accept him, lest I deal with you according to your folly; because you have not spoken of Me what is right, as My servant Job has."

—JOB 42:7–8

First, Job prayed for his friends who had spoken evil of him (v. 8). Second, Job's friends brought sacrifices to offer on an altar (v. 8). Third, Job's friends brought a special offering to him of gold (v. 11).

This process reveals important spiritual principles. First is the principle of forgiving those who have offended us. Christ made it clear that we would not experience God's blessing if we allowed unforgiveness to rule in our spirits. Not only would our prayers be hindered, but also our financial giving would not be blessed (Matt. 5:23–24; 6:14–15). Job prayed for his friends, and this released God's blessing to begin to flow toward Job.

Job had no animals, but his friends did. The Almighty instructed the three friends to bring seven bulls and rams and offer them on an altar. When the blood flowed again, and the sweet fragrance of the burnt offering arose toward heaven, it was enough to place the hedge back around Job! In the beginning of Job's troubles, Satan had seized all the animals that could be used as sacrifices, such as the sheep. Now, however, the altar was restored, and God could legally replace the hedge around Job's life.

We then read the following:

> And the LORD restored Job's losses when he prayed for his friends. Indeed the LORD gave Job twice as much as he had before.

—JOB 42:10

Double for Your Trouble

Notice that Job received twice as much. Why double the blessing? First, we saw the principle from the Law of Moses that if the thief was exposed, he must restore double of what he had stolen. God exposed the thief as Leviathan (Satan), and thus the blessing to Job would be double. Also we saw that Satan had twice told God that Job would curse

Him if the blessings and health of Job were removed. Job suffered two major waves of attacks, and twice he did not curse God. Therefore God restored double for his faithfulness! God used those close to him to help recover Job's wealth by giving him an offering of gold.

We read where everything was doubled in the latter half of Job's life:

In the Beginning (Job 1:3)	The Double Portion Blessing (Job 42:12)
7,000 sheep	14,000 sheep
3,000 camels	6,000 camels
500 yoke of oxen	1,000 yoke of oxen
500 female donkeys	1,000 female donkeys

This list reveals that every animal was doubled. When we read the list of children Job fathered after the trial, we discover he had seven sons and three daughters (Job 42:13). This was the same number of children mentioned who were killed during the initial attack (Job 1:2). I always felt the number should have been doubled, similar to the way the livestock numbers literally were twice as much. As I meditated on this contradiction, I suddenly realized he did have double the children. He had seven sons who went to be with the Lord during the trial, and seven other sons born to him after the trial. He also had three daughters in heaven, and three new daughters who were born to him after his double blessing was initiated! This was a great revelation for me, since it reveals that when our family members go to be with the Lord, they continue to be identified as our family! Paul said we would know even as we are known (1 Cor. 13:12).

Job lived 140 additional years after this period of testing (Job 42:16). Some suggest that he was 70 when the trial came, and if this is correct, he lived double the number of years after his restoration than he lived before the trials began.

How does this apply to you? The terrible disaster Job experienced and his amazing comeback hold several keys for us to discover in our own challenges and battles.

First, when the loss came, Job did not sin by blaming God for something He did not do. Solomon wrote, "Do not be rash with your mouth, and let not your heart utter anything hastily before God" (Eccles. 5:2). He also instructs, "Do not let your mouth cause your flesh to sin...[lest] God be angry at your excuse" (v. 6). Often when trouble strikes, our first question is, "Why me, Lord?" This is a common reaction and is not necessarily a sin. However, becoming angry with God will bring you into a spiritual condition of unforgiveness toward God Himself!

Second, Job was misinformed and even verbally insulted by his closest friends. It would be easy for Job to tell them to get out of his life and never visit him again. But instead he listened to their complaints and gave his own personal opinions. He was instructed to pray for his friends, who had not spoken what was right! This sounds familiar to Christ's command: "Pray for those who spitefully use you and persecute you" (Matt. 5:44). Forgiveness not only releases the people we hold captive in our mental prisons of unforgiveness, but it also opens a door for God to bless us for our obedience.

Third, while the Book of Job has always been considered a *faith book*, there is a hidden thread revealed in the story about the power of a blood sacrifice. We no longer bring lambs, goats, and bulls to the house of God. Can you imagine the noise and the smell that would cause while the pastor was preaching? However, we do have authority through the blood of Christ to defeat the powers of the enemy. Job needed blood on the altar, and through Christ, we can confess the power of His forgiving, cleansing, and healing blood (Rev. 12:11).

Although we do not bring grain, oil, wine, and animals to present to God on the altar, we do present our financial gifts, our praise, and our prayers at the place where we meet to worship God.

This powerful story reveals that God is able to reverse the attacks of the enemy and cause your "latter end to be greater than your beginning"!

Chapter 10

EVICT THE ENEMY FROM YOUR HOUSE

All Scripture is given by inspiration of God, and is profitable for doctrine, for reproof, for correction, for instruction in righteousness, that the man of God may be complete, thoroughly equipped for every good work.

| 2 TIMOTHY 3:16–17 |

IF I WERE to ask you, "What is the most powerful spiritual weapon to remove the authority and influence of the adversary from your home and your life?", what would you say?

May I suggest that there would be four main answers given by most believers? They would be:

1. Quoting Scripture

2. Experiencing the anointing

3. Rebuking the devil

4. Having strong faith

Let's examine these four in more detail.

Quoting the Scriptures

Christ was tempted by the devil for forty consecutive days. After Christ hungered, Satan came and tempted Him to turn stones to bread, to throw Himself down from the wall at the temple, and to bow down and pay homage to Satan himself (Matt. 4:1–10). During each of the three temptations, Christ quoted three different scriptures written in Deuteronomy 6. Suddenly, in the midst of the temptation, Satan reveals that he also can memorize and quote Scripture.

When Satan tempted Jesus to throw Himself down from the pinnacle of the temple, the adversary began quoting a passage found in Psalm 91 to undergird his opinion that Jesus could jump without harming Himself:

> Then the devil taketh him up into the holy city, and setteth him on a pinnacle of the temple, and saith unto him, If thou be the Son of God, cast thyself down: for it is written, He shall give his angels charge concerning thee: and in their hands they shall bear thee up, lest at any time thou dash thy foot against a stone.
>
> —MATTHEW 4:5–6, KJV

This passage is found in the Old Testament in Psalm 91:11–12. Since Psalm 91 is a psalm detailing God's ability to protect His people, the enemy wanted Christ to jump (actually to attempt suicide), and if he was God's Son, then God would send angels to cushion His fall and He would be unharmed. In reality the enemy actually misquoted the actual verse in Psalm 91 by adding a phrase that is not in the original text. Psalm 91:12 reads, "Lest you dash your foot against a stone."

According to Matthew's account, the words *at any time* are added to the text by Satan; the original quotation in Psalm 91 simply says, "Lest you dash your foot." The additional phrase "at any time" implies that under any and all circumstances the angels would be with you. Thus Satan was telling Jesus to jump off a three-hundred-foot wall in Jerusalem (the pinnacle of the temple), because any time you jump, the Lord will protect you! This is called *presumption*, or a false assumption.

The enemy knows the Bible quite well and has assigned his own false prophets to use the Scriptures for their own deceptive, false teaching. The Bible even says that at times Satan transforms himself into an angel of light (2 Cor. 11:14). We know the Bible is the sword of the Spirit (Eph. 6:17) and is a spiritual weapon to defeat the enemy, yet the enemy himself quotes the Word.

So, is the anointing of God upon a believer's life a major weapon against Satan?

Does the Anointing Alone Defeat Satan?

There are those in the Pentecostal and charismatic faiths who believe that a powerful anointing is the main weapon that will defeat the enemy. I once heard a noted television minister make a statement that sent shivers down my spine. He screamed over a microphone, "I am so anointed that the devil cannot touch me!" Yet, just a few weeks later, he began encountering a series of attacks against his ministry that were almost unbearable.

The anointing is unique. It is the *unction* from the Lord (1 John 2:20, KJV). It is the energy and the very life of God that is released through the laying on of hands and prayer, and it can bring deliverance and healing to those oppressed by the devil (Acts 10:38). When a minister is preaching with the anointing, he is bold, defiant against the adversary, and fearless. Yet Elijah, the mighty man of God who took on 850 false prophets, after the anointing lifted from him ran from Jezebel and sat depressed under a juniper tree, asking God to kill him (1 Kings 19:4).

The anointing is a great gift that accompanies a Spirit-filled life. However, King David made an interesting observation when he said, "I am weak today, though anointed king" (2 Sam. 3:39). When Christ was baptized in water, the Holy Spirit came upon Him and led Him into the wilderness where He was tested by the devil (Matt. 4:1). The anointing does not exempt you from attack but, in fact, can actually attract attack. After all, Satan was originally the anointed cherub. He certainly understands the power of the anointing. It takes the anointing to break the yokes of sin (Isa. 10:27); however, the anointing is not a barrier to prevent attacks.

So, what about rebuking the enemy?

Will Rebuking the Devil Defeat Him?

Jesus had rebuking power. He rebuked the storm (Matt. 8:26), rebuked demons (Matt. 17:18), and rebuked the fever afflicting Peter's mother-in-law (Luke 4:39). Even the disciples understood the authority released by rebuking Satan, seen when they attempted to rebuke the spirits in an epileptic child (Mark 9:17–19). The disciples learned later that some spirits respond only to intensive fasting and prayer (Matt. 17:21). The hindrance with the epileptic child had been the disciples' own unbelief. Fasting and prayer would have increased their faith and authority level over the powers of the enemy. I must confess that there have been times when I have rebuked the enemy, and at that particular moment I didn't see any direct response. Perhaps it was weak faith or a weak confession (Heb. 10:23).

So, is faith the greatest weapon against the enemy?

Does Using the Right Kind of Faith Alone Stop Him?

In the 1980s there was a strong Word of Faith movement in which ministers taught and emphasized the message of faith and personal confession. The emphasis on the faith message was either received or criticized as extreme by Christians in North America. Those who became engulfed in the message often taught that any sickness, financial difficulty, or problem was a result of a lack of faith. When a person gave his or her offering and didn't see a return on that giving, the problem was said to be a crack in that believer's faith armor.

While researching this subject, I read James 2:19, which states, "You believe that there is one God. You do well. Even the demons believe—and tremble!" Suddenly I realized that the demons have more faith than some alleged Christians have. Demons believe that Jesus is the Son of God, and some religious folks do not (Luke 4:41). Demons know Christ can heal, and yet numerous preachers preach that miracles have ceased. The kingdom of darkness believes in the abyss, and the demons know they are going there, but even many Christians deny the existence of hell (Luke 8:31). It is a sad commentary when fallen spirits, which are doomed for perdition, have more faith in God, Christ, and the power of God than do some theologically lame unbelieving believers.

Without faith it is impossible to please God (Heb. 11:6). Paul wrote, "Above all, taking the shield of faith with which you will be able to quench all the fiery darts of the wicked one" (Eph. 6:16). You must believe with your heart and confess with your mouth in order to be saved (Rom. 10:10). Every man has a measure of faith (Rom. 12:3). There is also a special gift of faith that manifests at times (1 Cor. 12:7–10). Faith is also a fruit of the Spirit (Gal. 5:22). Is faith the greatest weapon in defeating the enemy? If so, what happens when you have little faith (Matt. 8:26) and you pray, but your faith is weak and faltering?

The Most Important Weapon

Early in the life of Christ, when the Roman soldiers slew all the infants they found in Bethlehem, Satan made an attempt to kill Jesus. Men in His hometown of Nazareth attempted to throw Christ off a cliff (Luke 4:29–30). Later a storm struck the sea of Galilee when Christ was in a boat that became full of water yet never sunk—another attempt by Satan to kill Christ (Mark 4:37–38). On another occasion men planned to stone Christ when He claimed to be the Son of God, but again He escaped (John 10:31–39). During the forty-two months of Christ's ministry, we can see the invisible hand of the enemy guiding the subtle attacks against Christ. On one occasion—the Garden of Gethsemane, Satan himself was present, but not even he had any influence or control over the situation. Read the account in these three translations:

> I will not speak with you much longer, for the prince of this world is coming. He has no hold on me.
> —JOHN 14:30, NIV

> Hereafter I will not talk much with you: for the prince of this world cometh, and hath nothing in me.
> —JOHN 14:30, KJV

> I will not talk with you much more, for the prince (evil genius, ruler) of the world is coming. And he has no claim on Me. [He has nothing in common with Me; there is nothing in Me that belongs to him, and he has no power over Me.]
> —JOHN 14:30, AMP

Christ was identifying Satan as the prince of this world (2 Cor. 4:4). The Bible says that in the garden, Christ entered into agony, and "His sweat became like great drops of blood falling down to the ground" (Luke 22:44). The stress and pressure on Christ were almost unbearable. The sins of the world were being placed upon Him in the garden (2 Cor. 5:21), and the sinless Lamb of God was feeling the burden of the entire world upon Him. Prior to these three hours in the garden, Christ wanted His disciples to know that the enemy was coming, but what they were about to see was not Satan attacking Him. It was the plan of God—not Satan. The adversary was coming, but he had no hold on Christ, nothing in Him, and no power over Him. This was one moment that Satan had no power over Christ, because the sin placed on Christ was not His own but the sins of others being placed upon Him.

Our greatest weapon is the power of righteousness, or being in right standing with God. Satan could not hold on to Christ and had no power over Him as Christ was walking free from sin (John 14:30). When we are free from walking in sin, we are also free from guilt and condemnation, which is one of Satan's most powerful tools to stop our confidence in our relationship with God (1 John 3:20–21). If we abide in sin, the enemy holds on to us.

When Christ healed a man, He later saw the fellow and made an unusual statement:

> Afterward, when Jesus found him in the temple, He said to him, See, you are well! Stop sinning or something worse may happen to you.
>
> —JOHN 5:14, AMP

James teaches us that when the elders in a church pray for the sick, anointing them with oil in the name of the Lord, the prayer of faith will bring healing, and God will raise them up. He also adds, "And if he has committed sins, he will be forgiven" (James 5:14–16). In Christ's ministry He continually connected forgiveness of sins with being healed (Matt. 9:2–6). The fall of Adam in the garden produced sin and sickness, and Christ came to defeat sin and bring healing for mankind. This is why we read, "By whose stripes you were healed" (1 Pet. 2:24).

An Extreme Example

Years ago in the church my father was pastoring at that time, he was conducting an afternoon business meeting when suddenly he heard a voice interrupting him, screaming, "Come out of him, you devil!" He was stunned to see a woman in the church publicly rebuking him.

Dad answered, "Sister, I don't know what you are doing, but this man quit lying at age seventeen when Christ saved him!"

The woman continued to rave and eventually left after calling Dad a liar. The following morning when she got up, she could not speak. Thinking it was laryngitis, she did nothing and went on with her day. Imagine her shock thirty days later when she was still unable to speak!

The strange phenomenon continued into the second month. Dad recalled the scripture about how Zacharias doubted the angel's message that his wife was pregnant and was struck dumb, unable to speak, for nine months because of unbelief (Luke 1:20). This woman in Dad's church had offended the Holy Spirit and was under divine retribution. Even the doctors were unable to explain or treat her condition. One specialist wanted to charge $16,000 to examine her to discover the cause. She continued to come to church in that pitiful condition.

I was preaching a revival at Dad's church when the Holy Spirit spoke to Dad and said, "Her children need her, and if you will pray for her tonight, I will heal and restore her voice. She will never repent to you, but I will heal her because of her children, who are crying to me to help their mother." Dad called her out during the choir music and asked Mom to come to the front with her. He told her what the Lord said, and he asked Mom to forgive her, which Mom did. The following morning she was healed completely. Yet instead of humbling herself, she took on an arrogant spirit. As a result, she and her family began suffering, and she was later killed in a terrible auto accident.

This is a prime example of what is meant by the words in John 5:14: "Stop sinning or something worse may happen to you" (NIV). Walking in obedience is the most powerful weapon we have in our daily spiritual arsenal. No blessing of any type is released into our lives without faith.

We may say we have faith, but faith without works (obedience) is dead (James 2:20).

The Threefold Process

Since every living person is a spirit, soul, and body, the attacks of the enemy will manifest against our spirit, soul, and body. God has provided a spiritual action that will impact each individual area of our tripartite temple.

1. *Repent and come to Christ.*

Just as Satan had nothing to hold Christ with in the garden, so repentance will shut the door on the access the enemy has in our spirits. To repent not only means to be regretful or sorry for your actions, but it also means to turn and to change your mind about your destination. Often in church, seekers will come to the altar, repent of their sins, pray a prayer, and then exit the church only to continue in their old manner of living. We need to teach seekers not just to ask for forgiveness but to plan on a new lifestyle, new friends, and an exciting journey free from the sins and bondages of their past.

2. *Renew your mind from the world's corruption.*

Scripture teaches that we must be "renewed in the spirit of your mind" (Eph. 4:23). *To renew* means "to reform or to renovate." W. E. Vines comments on Ephesians 4:23:

> The renewal here mentioned is not that of the mind itself in its natural powers of memory, judgment and perception, but "the spirit of the mind," which under the controlling power of the indwelling Holy Spirit directs its bent and energies Godward in the enjoyment of fellowship with the Father and with His Son, Jesus Christ, and of the fulfillment of the Will of God.[1]

3. *Resist the enemy, and he will flee.*

James also wrote, "Therefore submit to God. Resist the devil and he will flee from you" (James 4:7). The word *resist* is used nine times in the New Testament in the King James Version. The word means "to stand against and oppose." In the natural, the human immune system is designed to fight off germs and viruses that could weaken the body. When the immune system is weakened, the body is more susceptible to sickness. The immune system works in and through the blood.

There are men who raise dangerous and deadly reptiles, including snakes. Some have been bitten so many times that their blood has built up immunities to the poison. When the sins of the world were laid upon Christ, He experienced a bite from the serpent. However, the precious blood of Christ became immunized against the power of sin, and when we receive His blood through faith and redemption, sin no longer has dominion in our body and spirit.

In the following scriptures, John tells us that a believer will not practice a lifestyle of sinning if the seed (Word) of God is dwelling in his heart. Each believer is to "keep himself," which means "to guard, to keep on eye on to prevent a loss." The phrase paints an imagery of guarding an expensive treasure to prevent a thief from entering and stealing it. It is our responsibility to keep things in check to prevent the wicked one from gaining access.

> We know that whoever is born of God does not sin; but he who has been born of God keeps himself, and the wicked one does not touch him.
>
> —1 JOHN 5:18

> We know [absolutely] that anyone born of God does not [deliberately and knowingly] practice committing sin, but the One Who was begotten of God carefully watches over and protects him [Christ's divine presence within him preserves him against the evil], and the wicked one does not lay hold (get a grip) on him or touch [him].
>
> —1 JOHN 5:18, AMP

In this first part of this chapter we have discovered the power of God's Word to help us to evict the enemy from entering our spirits and homes. There is another powerful tool that can be used—the power of worship and praise.

Using Music to Change the Atmosphere in Your Home

As young children, if we were verbally insulted by someone, we would say, "Sticks and stones may break my bones, but words will never hurt me." Now that I am older, I have come to understand that whoever came up with that little ditty was either unable to hear or had no friends and no contact with the public! In reality, one of the most powerful weapons in the world is the weapon of words. Solomon stated, "Death and life are in the power of the tongue" (Prov. 18:21). Wars are started with words, and peace treaties are initiated with words. Marriages are covenanted though verbal vows, and divorces occur because of negative words and strife. Words create the atmosphere around you.

Years ago I was ministering in a church where I knew nothing about the congregation or any internal difficulties they were experiencing. However, when I walked onto the platform, I could sense in my spirit a very tense atmosphere. As I ministered, I began dealing with the issue of strife and unforgiveness. I noticed that several of the people could not look me in the eyes when I made eye contact with them. The longer I preached, the tighter the atmosphere became. After the service the pastor informed me that everything I said hit the target, and he shared with me that several people had began a rebellion against his ministry, and the church was on verge of a split. I knew by the atmosphere that something was wrong—words had formed a spiritually dark cloud over the congregation!

The same is true with your home. Tension is formed when angry, negative words are released. The psalmist taught that bitter words are like arrows from a bow. There is no greater blessing than a home where the peace of God prevails and those who lie down can have sweet sleep (Prov. 3:24). One of the continual compliments my wife receives from friends who sleep in our guest room is, "We slept so well; there is such peace in this house." Christ taught that when believers stayed in the home of other believers, they were to ask the peace of God to rest on the home (Luke 10:5–6).

Sleepless Nights on the Road

I have traveled continually since I was eighteen years of age. In my earlier ministry the churches I visited were mostly small, rural congregations. I would stay in the pastor's home during my entire stay. As the ministry grew and invitations were received to minister in larger churches, the pastor would usually provide a hotel room to ensure our privacy. My wife and I have been blessed to stay in some very nice facilities, many moderate ones, and, on occasion, a few that would keep you awake wondering if the tires on your car would be there in the morning!

In our earlier days we were invited to preach for a friend who was starting a new church in Tampa, Florida. The income at the time was low, and they provided us a hotel room on the main road. Each night our infant son would awaken at 12:30 p.m. sharp, screaming as though someone was harming him. I would awaken about every hour, and there was a very uneasy atmosphere in the entire area. We saw a great spiritual breakthrough among the people, but I was relieved to depart from that particular area because of the very depressive atmosphere we were encountering. While this was a rare experience, a couple of cities had some type of negative atmosphere that made it difficult for my wife and me to sleep. Occasionally I would literally have the most bizarre dreams throughout the night. When waking up, I would ask my wife, "Where is all this coming from? I don't have anything like this on my mind, and yet I am having weird nightmares and dreams."

I wanted to know what I could do to help change the atmosphere where we were staying. I heard about a well-known gospel singer and musician who followed the same routine when staying in hotels around the world. He carried a cassette player and numerous worship cassettes, and, upon arrival, as he unpacked, he plugged in the player, popped in a praise and worship tape, turned up the volume, and then headed out to lunch or dinner. The praise and worship music filled the room while he was away. He called this *purging the atmosphere*. After hearing this, I decided to imitate his idea. I carried praise and worship cassettes and anointed messages from various ministers and played them from the time I awoke until the time of the service each evening. The music and messages literally changed the atmosphere where we stayed.

Remember that Scripture teaches us that David's music (playing a harp) brought refreshing and peace to a tormented king (1 Sam. 16:23). If music had this effect in David's life and ministry, why would it not have the same effect today?

A Revelation of Music

During this time I began a biblical study to determine the power of music. The first song led me to the moment when God created the world. Job was asked a series of questions:

> Where were you when I laid the foundations of the earth?
> Tell Me, if you have understanding.
> Who determined its measurements?
> Surely you know!
> Or who stretched the line upon it?
> To what were its foundations fastened?
> Or who laid its cornerstone,
> When the morning stars sang together,
> And all the sons of God shouted for joy?
>
> —Job 38:4–7

In Hebrew, the word *morning* in the phrase *morning stars* is *boker* and alludes to the *dawn* and, generally, to the morning. This could connect with the name Lucifer, found in Isaiah 14:12, an early name referring to Satan. Lucifer is called the "Son of the morning" (Isa. 14:12). The Hebrew word *Lucifer* is *heylel*, which means, "to shine, boast, or praise." Many scholars believe that by comparing Isaiah 14:12–14 with Ezekiel 28:13–16, we discover Satan may have been a worship leader in heaven prior to his being expelled. Ezekiel describes this anointed cherub as being created with *tabrets*, *pipes*, and *timbrels*—all forms of musical instruments or sounds.

The power of music can be observed when we hear an old song. Oftentimes when I have been watching a program or listening to the radio, suddenly I hear an old song and can instantly remember where I was when the song was being played more than thirty years ago! Certain songs bring back precious memories. My wife and I have a special song that is our song, and when we hear it, we immediately think of each other!

Music's effect on the emotions

Numerous tests have been conducted that demonstrate the physical, mental, and even spiritual effects of music. According to the Institute of HeartMath, 144 individuals completed a psychological profile before and after fifteen minutes of music. The four types of music tested were grunge rock, classical, New Age, and designer.

Each group experienced unique and specific emotional responses to the music they heard. Those listening to grunge rock showed a significant increase in hostility, sadness, tension, and fatigue. Those listening to designer music seemed relaxed and experienced mental clarity and vigor. The group listening to New Age music had mixed emotions, including some increase in relaxation along with reductions in mental clarity and vigor. Those listening to classical music experienced a reduction in tension and vigor. The study presented a rationale for the use of music to reduce stress, fatigue, and negative affect, and to enhance emotional well-being and mental clarity.[2]

Music's effects on the memory

Sara Kirkweg, with the Department of Psychology at Missouri Western, has conducted a study that indicates that music stimulates certain parts of the brain. Music was shown to enhance memory in patients with Alzheimer's and dementia. There are three basic types of memory—sensory memory, short-term memory, and long-term memory. Kirkweg and others have concluded that short-term memory can retain about seven bits of memory. (Bits are units of information such as numbers, phrases, or words.)[3] Oddly, there are seven main keys on a keyboard, from the note C to the note B.

People have long known that music can trigger powerful recollections, but a recent brain-scan study has discovered what part of the brain causes these recollections. "What seems to happen is that a piece of familiar music serves as a soundtrack for a mental movie that starts playing in our head," said Petr Janata, a cognitive neuroscientist at University of California–Davis. "It calls back memories of a particular person or place, and you might all of a sudden see that person's face in your mind's eye." According to Janata, "This latest research could explain why even Alzheimer's patients who endure increasing memory loss can still recall songs from their distant past." It is Janata's hope that his and other studies could encourage practices such as giving iPods to Alzheimer's patients, possibly providing real-life testament to the power of music. "It's not going to reverse the disease," Janata said. "But if you can make quality of life better, why not?"[4]

Music's effect on plant life

Studies have even been conducted to determine the effect of music on plants. Dr. T. C. N. Singh, of the Department of Botany at Annamalai University in India, discovered that music can affect the growth and development of plants. As early as the 1950s, Singh discovered that plant protoplasm moved faster in the cell as a result of the sound produced by an electric tuning fork. He concluded that sound must have some effect on the metabolic activities of the plant cell.

"Dr. Singh began a series of experiments on a large number of species, such as common asters, petunias, cosmos, and white spider lilies, along with food plants such as sesame, radishes, and sweet potatoes." For several weeks, just before sunrise, he played music lasting half an hour, scaled at a high pitch, with frequencies between one hundred and six hundred cycles per second. As a result of his research, "he was able to state that he had proven, beyond any shadow of doubt, that...sound waves affect the growth, flowering, fruiting, and seed-yields of plants."[5]

The effect of music on the physical body

The entire body is linked to electric impulses. The ears pick up sound waves in the air and change them into electrical impulses. Impulses move

147

up the nervous system into the neurons through electricity. The brain produces electromagnetic waves (brain waves), which can be measured by certain electronic medical equipment. Even the human heart responds to electric impulses, as proven by the use of pacemakers.

Rhythm in music can also affect the brain and the body. Marie-Louise Oosthuysen de Gutierrez, an educational brain researcher in Mexico City, Mexico, has documented some amazing research done by Russian biophysicist and molecular biologist Pjotr Garjajev and his colleagues, who have explored the vibrational behavior of DNA. Their research suggests that "DNA are resonate structures that possess the linguistic patterns of language and the vibrational frequencies which respond to light and radio waves. Language and music are in our genes!" These researchers were able to determine that "music activates multiple brain regions, which is why it has such a global impact on us—memory, immune response, stress response, and our emotions." From her research on Garjajev and his colleagues, as well as her own additional research, Gutierrez concludes, "Music has such a widespread influence on us (and other animals and even plants), calming us down and reducing stress hormones, to stimulating us through all levels of arousal to euphoria!" She believes that the power of music should be part of every school's curriculum to assist with "math, language, and reading skills. Music should be used more extensively in sports training as it improves the brain's ability to conceptualize space and also teaches rhythm and fluid execution of movement (from gymnastics through ball control in football)."[6]

If you don't believe that music can create a mood, then try playing, "I'm Dreaming of a White Christmas" in the middle of summer. Or try playing "Jungle Bells" at a funeral. What about "Jesus Loves Me" instead of the National Anthem at the Super Bowl? What about "The Star-Spangled Banner" at Saddam Hussein's funeral as his family members stand with their hands over their hearts? Perhaps "The Wedding March" would be nice while the undertaker closes the casket. Songs fit certain occasions because they were written for the occasion and because they create a mood and a memory.

Saying or Singing the Word

When a person takes voice training or a speaking class, the instructors continually remind the students to sing and speak from the diaphragm, which takes the pressure off the vocal chords. Don Channel, a song-writer, singer, and musician, once showed me the difference between *singing* and *saying* the Word of God. Placing your four fingers lightly over the diaphragm, simply say aloud three or four times: "Hallelujah." You can barely feel the diaphragm move. Now sing the word "Halle-lujah" in a loud voice and hold the sound for about five seconds. It is possible to actually feel the diaphragm moving when you sing—much more than when you simply speak.

Why is this interesting? When Jesus was unlocking the revelation about worshiping God in spirit and in truth, He was sitting at a well with a woman from Samaria (John 4:6–24). The wells in Christ's time were underground cisterns that either contained a natural spring or, in many cases, held rainwater. Each well had a large stone covering that had to be removed each time someone dipped his or her bucket into the well to bring forth water. The cover ensured that the water remained pure from outside impurities.

Later at the temple, during the Feast of Tabernacles, the priests performed a water-drawing ceremony. At dawn the high priest descended from Jerusalem's Water Gate to the pool of Siloam and dipped a golden vessel into the flowing (living) water. A team of priests followed him, playing flutes, cymbals, harps, lyres, and bells. The elders and members of the Sanhedrin danced and juggled torches. After the priest reached the large gathering of people at the Temple Mount, he would pour water on the brass altar and proclaim, "With joy we draw waters from the wells of salvation" (Isa. 12:3).[7]

It was in this setting of the water-drawing ceremony, on the last day of the feast, that Jesus made a profound prophecy:

> On the last day, that great day of the feast, Jesus stood and cried out, saying, "If anyone thirsts, let him come to Me and drink. He who believes in Me, as the Scripture has said, out of his heart will

flow rivers of living water." But this He spoke concerning the Spirit, whom those believing in Him would receive; for the Holy Spirit was not yet given, because Jesus was not yet glorified.

—JOHN 7:37–39

Jesus said that out of your belly, or out of your innermost being, would flow this living water of the Holy Spirit. It is interesting that Christ said the river begins in your "belly" (v. 38, KJV). Man is a tripartite being of body, soul, and spirit (1 Thess. 5:23). All spiritual blessings begin within the human spirit. Solomon wrote, "The spirit of man is the candle of the LORD, searching all the inward parts of the belly" (Prov. 20:27, KJV). The physical heart is the center of the human body, and the belly is the center of the human spirit. We sense many emotions deep in our belly area. When we are afraid, grieving, and angry, we can actually feel a stirring in the pit of our stomachs. This is because the center of emotions for the human spirit is located in this area.

Don Channel stated that the diaphragm is similar to the stone covering over the well of water. When we sing praise to God, it opens the covering (the diaphragm), allowing a flow of the Holy Spirit to move though us, thus releasing a faith-filled atmosphere around us!

Singing has a dimension of its own. Anyone can open his or her mouth and appear to be praising God, but that person's heart may not be connecting with what they are saying with the mouth. This was a problem with the hypocritical Pharisees in Christ's time. Christ said, "These people draw near to Me with their mouth, and honor Me with their lips, but their heart is far from Me" (Matt. 15:8). Their praise was coming from the head and not from the spirit.

A person can sit in a dry atmosphere in a dry worship service and say, "Praise the Lord," and feel absolutely nothing. However, if that same person stands and sings out a praise song, something begins to occur; the lid on the well is removed, and the living water begins to flow. This is not to say that when we pray or worship without singing, that we are not experiencing the same level of God's presence. Prayer is another dimension. However, it is interesting to note that in the Jewish synagogues when the Scriptures are read, they are actually chanted by a cantor in a rhythmic manner. Prayers are often prayed in a low moaning, rhythmic type of flow. In Judaism, the inner song is important in prayer and worship.

Paul revealed the importance of music and singing and how it assists in stimulating the Holy Spirit within us:

> And do not get drunk with wine, for that is debauchery; but ever be filled and stimulated with the [Holy] Spirit. Speak out to one another in psalms and hymns and spiritual songs, offering praise with voices [and instruments] and making melody with all your heart to the Lord.
>
> —EPHESIANS 5:18–19, AMP

When we sing to ourselves and to the Lord, the well of our spirit is opened, allowing the presence of the Lord to move in us, upon us, and around us.

The Power of the Trumpet

The adversary is keenly aware of the power of musical instruments in worship. Satan was originally created as an anointed cherub, a special angel assigned to guard the presence of the Lord. Cherubim protected the gates of the Garden of Eden (Gen. 3:24), and two golden cherubim sat on the lid of the ark of the covenant (Exod. 25:18–20). Ezekiel saw cherubim carrying the throne of God in Ezekiel chapter 1.

Ezekiel revealed insight into the pre-Fall history of Satan and what his assignment was in heaven:

> You were the seal of perfection,
> Full of wisdom and perfect in beauty.
> You were in Eden, the garden of God;
> Every precious stone was your covering:
> The sardius, topaz, and diamond,
> Beryl, onyx, and jasper,
> Sapphire, turquoise, and emerald with gold.
> The workmanship of your timbrels and pipes
> Was prepared for you on the day you were created.

You were the anointed cherub who covers;
I established you;
You were on the holy mountain of God;
You walked back and forth in the midst of fiery stones.
You were perfect in your ways from the day you were created,
Till iniquity was found in you.
By the abundance of your trading
You became filled with violence within,
And you sinned;
Therefore I cast you as a profane thing
Out of the mountain of God;
And I destroyed you, O covering cherub,
From the midst of the fiery stones.

—EZEKIEL 28:12–16

The description given to this anointed cherub begins by describing nine gemstones that formed his covering. These nine stones are also found on the breastplate of the Old Testament high priest, whose golden breastplate held twelve stones identifying the twelve tribes of Israel.

The prophet then described how the cherub had been created with timbrels and pipes, and Isaiah added that Lucifer had viols as a part of his musical gifting (Isa. 14:11, KJV). I suggest to you that this angel was created to lead the praise and worship of the angelic hosts before the throne of God prior to the creation of man.

Musicians know that all musical instruments are divided into four different categories:

1. Wind instruments

2. String instruments

3. Percussion instruments

4. Brass instruments

The wind instruments are blown with the mouth, the string instruments are plucked with the fingers, and the percussion instruments are played by beating with the hands.

This anointed cherub had three of the four main musical groups created within him. The pipes are associated with the wind instrument, the viols with the stings, and the timbrels with the percussion instruments. Years ago my friend Phil Driscoll pointed out that there was one instrument group that was never given to Lucifer, and that was the brass or the horns.

In the Old Testament there were silver trumpets prepared for the calling of the camp and the journey of the assembly (Num. 10:1–2). The most common trumpets, however, were the natural trumpets made from the horns of animals, called *shofars* in the Hebrew. These consisted of the ram's horns, which are the small circular horns of a ram and the larger horns of the antelope. As Driscoll pointed out, God never gave Lucifer the horn as one of his instruments since God reserved the voice of the horn for Himself!

For example, in the Old Testament when God's voice was heard, it was often compared to the sound of a trumpet by those who heard it (Exod. 19:16). At the return of Christ, He will return "with a shout, with the voice of an archangel, and with the trumpet of God" (1 Thess. 4:16). The apostle John was on the island of Patmos when he received his apocalyptic vision. He writes:

> After these things I looked, and behold, a door standing open in heaven. And the first voice which I heard was like a trumpet speaking with me, saying, "Come up here, and I will show you things which must take place after this."
> —REVELATION 4:1

To John the voice was like a trumpet, and yet it was the voice of a heavenly being speaking to him. When God created Lucifer, He limited him in several areas. This angel, according to Ezekiel 28, had nine stones as his covering. However, twelve precious stones covered the breastplate of the high priest, meaning that Lucifer was three stones short of a full load! He was created with three main instruments, but God reserved the trumpet for Himself. This was so that when the trumpet sounds, we will know the heavenly sound, which cannot be duplicated or imitated by the enemy!

Praise Can Rattle Your Cage

It is difficult, if not impossible, to get a decent night's sleep after being beaten and placed in wooden stocks in an inner prison. When Paul and Silas were arrested and beaten for preaching the gospel, they were unable to sleep, and they began singing. What started as a duet quickly became a *trio*—God made it a trio by sending an earthquake that shook the prisoners loose from their chains and broke down the bars holding them in! The incident was so supernatural that the head jailor was converted to Christ, and later, his entire family received the gospel (Acts 16:23–34). Anointed music can break the stronghold that surrounds a person!

This was true in the life of King Saul, the first king of Israel. Saul became violently jealous of David because of his military success against Goliath and his new recognition among the people. An evil spirit began troubling Saul, and the tormented king attempted to assassinate David on several occasions. David, however, understood the power of anointed music. He would take his harp and play music in the presence of the king. The Bible says:

> And so it was, whenever the spirit from God was upon Saul, that David would take a harp and play it with his hand. Then Saul would become refreshed and well, and the distressing spirit would depart from him.
>
> —1 SAMUEL 16:23

Three specific things occurred when David ministered before Saul:

1. Saul was refreshed.
2. Saul was made well.
3. The evil spirit departed.

Music such as praise and worship songs, Southern gospel, instrumental, and songs on CD by anointed singers and musicians not only can minister to you, but they can also create an atmosphere in which you can dwell—even when traveling or isolated from home and friends.

Chapter 11

BIND DEVILS AND LOOSE SAINTS

And I will give you the keys of the kingdom of heaven, and whatever you bind on earth will be bound in heaven, and whatever you loose on earth will be loosed in heaven.

| MATTHEW 16:19 |

WHAT IF THE scales covering your spiritual eyes could be removed, and like a large screen at a theater, you could see into the invisible realm of angels and demons? Throughout Scripture angelic messengers were sent from the heavenly temple to the earthly realm to unveil divine revelations and reveal warnings and instructions to the early patriarchs, the prophets, and the priests. The same scriptures indicate that opposing spirit rebels—identified in categories such as demons, evil spirits, unclean spirits, prince spirits, and rulers of the darkness of this world—are present on the earth to hinder, disrupt, and even destroy the purposes of God and eventually the souls of men. As Christ warned, "The thief cometh not, but for to steal, and to kill, and to destroy" (John 10:10, KJV). These strategies for many major spiritual conflicts originate in the cosmic realm between angels of God and angels of Satan.

Cosmic Conflicts—Angelic Wars

Throughout the Old Testament God assigned His personal messengers, angels, to exercise spiritual authority over the forces of the adversary, including Satan himself. The Book of Jude indicates that after the death of Moses, Satan desired the body of the man of God, and Michael the archangel was assigned to descend to Mount Nebo and resist the plot of

Satan. After the conflict God personally buried the body of Moses, in my opinion to prevent the children of Israel from discovering his corpse and building a memorial to this saintly leader. (See Deuteronomy 34 and Jude 9.)

The tenth chapter of Daniel is a classic example of angelic wars in the cosmic realm, or the second level of heaven. This chapter mentions two of God's angels, Michael and an unnamed angel (many believe it was Gabriel), that were being hindered for three weeks from delivering the understanding of a vision to Daniel (Dan. 9:21; 10:1–13). Two opposing evil prince spirits, identified as the *prince of Persia* (Dan. 10:13) and the *prince of Greece* (v. 20), were engaging God's messengers in a struggle to prevent spiritual understanding from reaching Daniel. These two evil spirits, just like angels, were invisible to the human eyes; however, they were visible and tangible to all other spirits in the spirit world. In this biblical account these satanic agents were hindering an answer to prayer by restraining the angel of the Lord in the second heaven, thus preventing him from reaching Daniel (Dan. 10:1). Only when Michael the archangel was commissioned, after twenty-one days, to restrain the wicked prince spirit controlling Persia was the meaning to a vision from God clearly revealed to Daniel. Notice that Daniel exercised no spiritual authority over the situation, but the archangel Michael was given special authority to resist and restrain the demonic angel of Persia.

A third example of angelic—satanic—conflict was when the Jews returned from Babylonian captivity to rebuild the temple. As Joshua the high priest stood on the ruins of the temple platform to minister, an angel of the Lord was assigned to stand with him. Suddenly, Satan (the adversary) appeared on Joshua's right side to resist his priestly ministry. The reason: the priestly garments of the high priest were unclean, since there had not been an active priesthood in Jerusalem during Israel's seventy years of Babylonian captivity. Satan was making accusations against Joshua the high priest and initiating a resistance to prevent the sacred services of God's house from proceeding. The prophet Zechariah saw an angel from the Lord appearing near Joshua and rebuking Satan (Zech. 3:1–5).

Since Satan is also an angel (a fallen angel), and Michael, Gabriel, and other ministering spirits in heaven are also angels, then the angels of the Lord cannot rebuke Satan by using their own authority. In the spirit realm, it would be compared to two five-star generals in a conflict, with one attempting to exercise complete authority over the other. If one general receives orders from the president of the United States—the commander in chief over all branches of the US military—the order from the commander given to one general will supersede the previous instruction given to the other military general. Both generals have the same level of authority. Satan was "the anointed cherub" that "was on the holy mountain of God" and walked back and forth in the midst of "fiery stones" (Ezek. 28:14). He was created with a breastplate of nine precious stones and had "timbrels and pipes," indicating some form of internal musical ability that many scholars believe were linked to his role as director of the worship of the angels in heaven upon the holy mountain (v. 13). Satan was a unique, high-level creation; thus an archangel, such as Michael, needed to exercise authority given directly from God Himself when dealing with Satan.

This is why when a high-ranking angel of the Lord rebuked Satan, the angel at the temple said, "The LORD rebuke you..." (Zech. 3:2), and why Michael the archangel said to Satan in the plains of Moab, "The Lord rebuke you!" (Jude 9). On one occasion Satan stood up to provoke David to number the men living in Israel (1 Chron. 21:1). However, in the process of initiating the census, David disobeyed God, ignoring the Law of Moses, which instructed the leader to collect a half of silver shekel from each man over twenty years of age, which was the "price for redemption" (Exod. 30:11–16). Because of David's national sin, a death plague struck Israel. And more than seventy thousand men were slain within a short time (1 Chron. 21:14). To stop the death angel, David ascended to Mount Moriah, where Abraham had offered Isaac hundreds of years earlier, and built an altar upon which he placed a blood offering as atonement. In this instance, it was blood upon the altar that prevented the destruction of Jerusalem. David had no "spiritual authority" over the plague, other than dependency upon the blood sacrifice. For four thousand years the sons of Adam leaned upon angels and blood sacrifices to restrain and stop the power of sin, death, and satanic agents assigned to their destruction. This process remained until the revelation of Christ's ministry in Israel when the Messiah came and demonstrated His power over all the powers of the enemy (Luke 10:19).

Jesus—the Original Exorcist

The New Testament clearly identifies various types of spirits active among the people in Christ's time. We read of foul spirits (Mark 9:25, KJV), unclean spirits (Mark 1:23), evil spirits (Luke 7:21), spirits of infirmities (Luke 13:11), and seducing spirits (1 Tim. 4:1, KJV). These evil entities could cause deafness, weakness in the body, sickness, disease, epilepsy, and various tormenting mental conditions (Mark 5:1–13; 9:25).

In Judaism there was no one person who was an exorcist—an individual given the ability to cast out evil spirits with spiritual authority. However, there was a belief in evil spirits and that they could be tricked into being expelled. One method used was to establish communication with the demon(s) to discover the name of the particular spirit in order to *trick it* to come out. The rabbis in Christ's time were familiar with this method, and this may be one reason why in Mark 5:9, when confronting a man with more than two thousand evil spirits, Christ demanded to know the name of the chief demon controlling the other spirits inside the tormented man. Christ asked the spirit, "What is your name?" The reply was, "My name is Legion; for we are many" (v. 9). Once Christ took authority over the dominant chief spirit controlling the other spirits and commanded it to be expelled from the fellow's body, the other less powerful spirits that were a part of this organized gang of body invaders immediately were expelled from the tormented man.

Years ago in Israel, a tour guide explained that it was taught among the ancient rabbis that one of the signs of the Messiah would be His ability to exercise control over spirits that caused a person to be deaf and dumb, since a command for the spirit to reveal its name would not work because the person was deaf and could not hear. Therefore only the Messiah could command a deaf and dumb spirit to depart from a person. In Matthew 12, Christ demands a deaf and dumb spirit to leave the body of a person (Matt. 12:22). Immediately the afflicted person could both hear and speak!

This miracle impressed the eyewitnesses, and they began to ask, "Could this be the Son of David?" (v. 23). The term *Son of David* is a phrase used to identify the Jewish Messiah as the descendant of King David. Those present at the healing service were so impressed with the miracle because they knew that only the Messiah would have power to expel a spirit from a person who could not even hear the words that were being spoken—however, the evil spirit heard and obeyed. The religious Pharisees immediately said that Christ was casting out devils by the power of devils and that He was Himself a devil (v. 24). The religious zealots were fearful that the multitudes would follow Christ and declare Him as Messiah. Thus they attempted to place fear in the followers of Christ by saying He was aligned with Beelzebub, a chief demon.

This miracle is significant, since it is the first instance in the Scriptures of a man (Christ) having complete authority over the world of evil spirits! Christ did not perform exorcism using ancient roots and spices, and He had no holy water or special diets to help remove the demonic presence from one possessed. He simply used His WORDS! This is why an officer of the chief priest who had been sent to arrest Christ returned empty handed and declared, "No man ever spoke like this Man!" (John 7:44–46). Christ exorcised evil spirits by His word and healed the sick by a simple faith command or a brief prayer.

Discern *Real* Evil

As we begin to deal with the use of spiritual power and authority in the life of a believer, we must first learn to discern what is actual *spiritual warfare* and what is the result of simply living on an earth that has multitudes of unconverted and unregenerate human beings. I have heard some sincere believers say, "The devil gave me a flat tire!" I reminded those individuals that the nail they ran over in the road actually gave them the flat.

Someone once stated, "The devil gave me a speeding ticket while I was coming to the revival." The first thing to remember is that when you break the law and travel above the speed limit, you have opened the door—not to a devil—but to a police officer in a blue uniform with blue lights pulling you over and presenting you a *bill* for being in such a hurry.

I once laughed when a fellow who was eating tacos drenched in hot sauce, accompanied by a pile of sliced jalapeño peppers, suddenly cried out, "Wow, pray for me, because the devil is giving me severe indigestion." It was no time to rebuke the devil; it was time to quit setting his *temple* on fire with the hottest liquids and foods in the restaurant.

Years ago, when old-timers had a difficult day and then came to church to *testify*, they would announce, "The devil has been on my back all day, bless His name." I used to picture a small evil spirit with both arms clamped around the person's neck, jumping up and down on the back of that old saint. Then I thought, "Why did you let the devil ride around all day and not just tell him to get off your back?" After all, Jesus said, "Get behind Me, Satan!" (Luke 4:8), which Stone's Unauthorized Version translates the verse to say, "Hey, Devil, get out of my way and leave me alone; I'm not playing games!"

The *real* battle is not the daily *flesh and blood* struggles we have, like burnt toast, running out of coffee, a dead battery in the car, or a migraine headache. These circumstantial situations come and go on a daily basis. The real struggle is against the satanic power of temptation to affect the mind, creating formations of imagination that create spiritual strongholds. There is also the aspect of emotional and physical struggles that hinder the believer, and, at times, can be generated by spiritual powers. The secret battles or the internal conflicts that create roots of bitterness, unforgiveness, strife, fear, and other works of the flesh are where the real struggle begins or ends. However, the adversary can, at times, create a situation or a circumstance near or around you to get you off track. This is the purpose of a "deceiving spirit," which Paul warned Timothy would be active in the latter times (1 Tim. 4:1). The Greek word for "seducing" (KJV) is *planos*, and it can allude to an imposter that deceives. To *seduce*, in a spiritual sense, means "to pull a person away from the truth." The reason deception works is because people either ignore or reject the truth.

The First Principle in Warfare: Possess the Right Knowledge

The first principle of victory during warfare is to have the right information or knowledge. Be informed about your enemy. The following story illustrates the importance of being properly informed. Years ago I was ministering in Florida under a large, two-thousand-seat tent with canvas "walls" hanging around the edges. During the service, someone attempted to start a fire on the outside by burning a rope and part of the canvas tent. Smoke suddenly appeared in the back, and the pastor's wife came running to the platform while I was preaching, whispering into her husband's ear, "The tent is on fire outside…Someone has tried to burn us down tonight." He simply smiled and sat there very calmly, and the service went on. Nothing notable happened to the tent, and the service concluded later with a great altar invitation and the dismissal prayer.

After the service my wife and I were sitting in the pastor's office with the pastor and his wife when I heard the pastor's wife say to her husband, "I cannot believe that you just sat there when I said the tent was on fire! What would you have done if suddenly the entire tent would have been engulfed in flames?"

He began to laugh, which only accelerated the tension. She said, "It's not funny!"

He replied, "Woman, calm down. This tent is completely fireproof, and the city would have never allowed me to use it for a public meeting without a certain type of fabric that is flame retardant. The little fire was not going to burn down this tent, and I knew it. But it was funny watching you get all excited." At that moment we all had a good laugh. *She saw the fire, but he had the knowledge!*

Warfare is not so much about what we *see* as it is what we *know*. Notice these verses:

> For the weapons of our warfare are not carnal but mighty in God for pulling down strongholds, casting down arguments and every high thing that exalts itself against the knowledge of God, bringing every thought into captivity to the obedience of Christ, and being ready to punish all disobedience when your obedience is fulfilled.
>
> —2 CORINTHIANS 10:4–6

Prepare With the Right Armor

Notice that strongholds are for the purpose of exalting themselves against the *knowledge of God*. We must understand that spiritual knowledge becomes our spiritual weapon—but not just any knowledge. It indicates knowledge that deals with knowing the enemy, understanding his strategies, and knowing what weapons to use with each separate attack. This is why there are different parts to the armor of God (Eph. 6:13–18).

The helmet of salvation covers the entire head where the mind is located and protects us during certain mental attacks Satan brings, including the feelings of condemnation, guilt, and fear. If we understand that there is "no condemnation to those who are in Christ Jesus, who do not walk according to the flesh, but according to the Spirit," then Satan's mental assaults fail (Rom. 8:1).

The breastplate of righteousness covers the vital organs, including the heart, and prevents evil from penetrating the inner sanctum of our spirit. Christ said:

> Are you also still without understanding? Do you not yet understand that whatever enters the mouth goes into the stomach and is eliminated? But those things which proceed out of the mouth come from the heart, and they defile a man. For out of the heart proceed evil thoughts, murders, adulteries, fornications, thefts, false witness, blasphemies. These are the things which defile a man, but to eat with unwashed hands does not defile a man.
>
> —MATTHEW 15:16–20

When our hearts are left unguarded, the floodgates of iniquity are opened for all forms of temptation to enter.

Our spiritual armor also includes *gospel shoes*; this is called "having shod your feet with the preparation of the gospel of peace" (Eph. 6:15). In this verse Paul uses the shoes of a Roman soldier for an analogy. In Roman times, the shoes of the soldiers had spikes underneath, giving soldiers the ability to stand firm in their battle stance and not be knocked down by the blows of the enemy. This is how a believer can "withstand in the evil day, and having done all, to stand" (v. 13).

Paul wrote, "Above all, taking the shield of faith with which you will be able to quench all the fiery darts of the wicked one" (v. 16). The Roman soldiers had two types of shields. One was small and round and was attached to the soldier's loin belt. It was more for beauty and could be used in one-on-one combat. The word *shield* here in Greek is *thureos* and is a word used for a door—or for a door-shaped shield. This was a large shield that covered much of the body of the soldier. This shield could be lined up alongside the shields of other soldiers, forming a wall of protection. Large groups of soldiers used these shields, often to cover the heads of the troops when they were near a city wall and rocks were being thrown down by the enemy. These shields, combined with the helmets that covered the heads, resembled the shell of a turtle. Thus, the shield of faith is a type of faith that can be used individually or linked with the faith of other believers to endure the arrows of the enemy.

Paul spoke about the "fiery darts of the wicked one" (v. 16). These darts were arrows with metal tips that were dipped in a flammable substance and lit seconds before they were released from the bow of the enemy. In order to quench the darts once they hit the shield, a Roman soldier would dip his leather-covered shield in water before the battle and take olive oil and rub it into the shield, thus taking the dryness out of the leather and making it more difficult for a fiery arrow to burn the shield!

Levels of Testings

In a believer's life, there are many different types of arrows or *darts* sent from the enemy. These arrows can be classified in three levels: the common testing, the seasonal testing, and the hour of testing. The Bible teaches, "No temptation has overtaken you except such as is common to man" (1 Cor. 10:13). For example, all men experience temptation in some form. To occasionally be *stressed out* is a *common testing*. To occasionally battle fear is also common among man. The common testings come and go and are easier to defeat if we use our shield of faith.

The next level is a *seasonal test*. After Satan tempted Jesus during the forty days in the desert, we read, "He [Satan] departed from him for a season" (Luke 4:13, KJV). Satan challenged Christ on His deity, questioning if He was the "Son of God" (v. 3). More than three years later at the crucifixion, we see the same attack coming from the people and from one of the dying thieves, "If You are the Son of God..." (Matt. 27:40).

I have discovered that tests and temptations move in seasons. For example, a believer can be delivered from a habit, such as smoking, and go for months without any desire to smoke. Then one day that person gets up and senses a strong *force* or desire to go back to the habit. If the individual understands that this is a seasonal attack, he can endure the season, and within a short time the pressure will be removed. Remember that seasons come and go—they change. What you battle today can be removed tomorrow.

The third and most difficult level of testing is the *hour of testing* mentioned in Revelation 3:10 (KJV), which will come upon the whole earth. The hour of testing is when a family member or a circumstance causes a situation—or a personal attack arises from within your mind— that tests your faith and your confidence in the Word of God. Such an example is when Job, the wealthiest man in the East, suddenly lost his entire livestock, ten children, and his health (Job chapters 1 and 2). He went from a millionaire to a pauper in a short time. Your *hour of testing* could be the sudden death of a child, a deadly disease that is snuffing the life from a companion, or a major car accident that causes a loved one to become physically disabled. At some point in our lives, each of us will have an *hour of testing.*

Each level of testing is initiated with darts and arrows sent to attack the mind and turn the heart from the Lord. When trouble comes, we will either turn to God or turn away from Him. The shield of faith must cover us at all times. Only an active faith can quench the fiery darts. Just as water and oil were elements used to soften the tough dry leather covering the shield of the soldier, the "washing of water by the word" (Eph. 5:26) renews the spirit of our mind by cleansing our thought process, and the oil of the anointing of the Holy Spirit not only breaks yokes of bondage (Isa. 10:27) but can also rise up within us and put out the carnal fires from the mental arrows that can cause burning with thoughts of lust, greed, anger, or other works of the flesh.

Paul wrote that we are not ignorant of the enemy's devices (2 Cor. 2:11). Ignorance breeds darkness in the mind and prevents understanding. This is why spiritual darkness is an effective weapon. When the thought process of men becomes stained with the tar of sin, and the light of truth cannot penetrate their thoughts, men remain in their sin, bondage, and unbelief and accept their captivity as a part of their life. A person will never change what he or she permits and will never be free from the habits he or she accepts. Only when a person is confronted with the light of the truth can the rays of God's delivering power penetrate into that man or woman's thinking and create a reservoir of knowledge that leads to the prison doors being opened! Knowledge is a weapon. The enemy has difficulty deceiving a person who knows the strategy and understands how to defeat the assault.

There Is Peace in *Knowing*

Jesus could sleep peacefully in a boat that was rocking up and down, moving sideways in the wind, and being slapped with waves because He had already given a clear word: "Let us cross over to the other side of the lake" (Luke 8:22). The pronoun "us" indicated Christ's intention that everyone in the small ship would make it to the destination. This *spoken word* was sufficient to bring peace to Christ in the middle of a violent storm. The disciples, however, were afraid of drowning and questioned Christ's concern for them. The disciples' eyes were upon the storm, but Christ's eyes were upon the destination.

When Lazarus was sick unto death, Christ continued ministering until his friend Lazarus died. Christ was not only late for the final good-bye, but He also missed the funeral! Why did Christ take His time (four days) to travel to the graveyard and raise Lazarus? In the Jewish beliefs, there is a tradition that the soul of a departed person can actually roam the area for three days. However, on the fourth day, the soul and spirit take their final journey to their eternal abode. Thus, on the fourth day, according to this tradition, the soul of the departed could never be resurrected, as it enters its permanent eternal abode. I believe Christ waited until the fourth day to raise Lazarus because there would be no possible way (in the eyes of the religious Jewish leaders) that such a resurrection could occur.

The sisters of Lazarus shared their disappointment that Christ allowed Lazarus to die. In the story, "Jesus wept" (John 11:35). Why would He weep when He knew He would bring Lazarus out of the tomb? I believe He wept because of the unbelief and criticism coming from Lazarus's two sisters, Mary and Martha, who knew Christ could raise the dead but didn't believe it was possible for Lazarus. Christ, however, had knowledge that the others did not. Martha told Christ she knew Lazarus would be raised at the future resurrection (v. 24). The Lord is the resurrection and life, and He had power not only to raise Lazarus from the dead, but in the future He would also raise Himself from death's grip!

When a believer knows the promises God has for his or her life, that person can live in confidence and without fear, knowing the future outcome. In Acts 12, James was beheaded, and Peter was next on the chopping block. Peter was arrested, placed in a prison, and was awaiting his execution following Passover. Yet we read that when the angel entered Peter's prison, Peter was soundly sleeping. Could you sleep knowing you would be beheaded at sunrise? Peter's inner *peace* was based upon a prophetic revelation Christ gave him before His ascension.

The apostle John records a conversation between Christ and Peter, where Christ informed Peter that he was young and would be old, needing assistance from others:

> Jesus said to him [Peter], "Feed My sheep. Most assuredly, I say to you, when you were younger, you girded yourself and walked where you wished; but when you are old, you will stretch out your hands, and another will gird you and carry you where you do not wish."
> —JOHN 21:17–18

At the time of Peter's imprisonment, he was still rather young in age and fully capable of traveling on his own. Because Peter had received a direct prophetic word about his future from Christ, and the Lord predicted Peter would live to be an *old man needing the assistance of others*, this promise of a long life no doubt brought peace to Peter as he lay down to sleep in the prison. It was not the right *time* for Peter to depart this life! That same night the angel of the Lord walked undetected through the jailhouse, loosed Peter from his chains, and led him through the iron gates to his freedom. Peter had knowledge that his enemies did not have. The plans of his enemies would fail, because Peter had a sure word of prophecy from the Savior Himself! Even in the life of Christ, men attempted several times to take His life, but Scripture says, "His hour was not yet come" (John 2:4; 7:6; 7:30; 8:20). It is impossible to defeat a man who knows his purpose and his final destiny! In these cases the weapons of the adversary failed because the knowledge of the future was greater than the plans of the enemy (Acts 12:1–12).

As previously stated, Paul instructed that we be not "ignorant of [the devil's] devices" (2 Cor. 2:11). The Greek word for "devices" is *noema* and alludes to a person's inner intentions or inner thoughts. We can understand how the adversary thinks by reading through four thousand years of biblical history and observing the various types of attacks and strategies the enemy and his cohorts use against men and women in the Bible. From the green trees of Eden to the Judean wilderness, the serpent has crawled through time, setting snares and traps for the righteous. Hosea reminded Israel, "My people are destroyed for lack of knowledge"

(Hosea 4:6). Spiritual ignorance is the greatest tool of the kingdom of darkness. Entire nations are bound by strange beliefs and bizarre superstitions because of lack of truth.

The Powers of the Enemy

Since our warfare is against numerous spirit rebels, how do believers deal with spirits? There are two important words in the New Testament that indicate two strong weapons for dealing with all of the power of the enemy. They are the words *power* and *authority*. In the English translation of the Bible there is one word used for both power and authority, translated as the word "power." However, in certain passages in the Greek language with which the New Testament was written, there are two different words often translated as the word "power." In Acts 10:38, Luke wrote, "How God anointed Jesus of Nazareth with the Holy Spirit and with power, who went about doing good and healing all who were oppressed by the devil, for God was with Him." In Luke 10:19, Christ said, "Behold, I give you the authority to trample on serpents and scorpions, and over all the power of the enemy, and nothing shall by any means hurt you." In Acts 10:38 the word *power* is the Greek word *dunamis*, which alludes to miraculous power. In Luke's Gospel, the word *power* is the Greek word *exousia* and alludes to having judicial authority.

The Difference Between Authority and Power

The following illustrates the difference between *power* and *authority*. A trucker arrives at a truck stop, and the six-foot-four-inch truck driver exits the rig, only to be attacked by four five-foot men hiding behind some bushes. In anger, the trucker grabs his attackers and begins slamming them down in four different directions. He uses brute force and human *power* to initiate his defense against his assailants.

The same trucker gets back into his large rig and begins driving through side roads in the state of Virginia. As he is cruising on the long stretch of a country road, he spots in the distance a police car with its blue lights spinning and sees a police officer waving frantically. The trucker puts on his air brakes and comes to a halt a few feet away. He gets out of his truck as his blood pressure rises like steam from a burning volcano. He screams, "What are you doing! I could have had an accident. I ought to…" Suddenly the tiny policeman flashes his badge and the trucker shuts up. The policeman was small in statue, but he had the *authority* of the county, the state, and the federal law enforcement agencies standing behind the power of his badge. To attack this policeman was to bring on the wrath of the entire law community that would legally defend this officer from a rural community.

One man used *power,* and the other used *authority.* Both power and authority were used in the ministry of Christ. The healing power of Christ was manifested through His physical touch. He laid His hands upon the sick, and when people touched Him in faith, the Bible says that "virtue" left His body and entered into the sick, bringing healing (Mark 5:30, KJV). The English word *virtue* is *dunamis,* the same Greek word that is used for *power* in Acts 1:8: "You shall receive *power* when the Holy Spirit has come upon you" (emphasis added). This power is an inward energy of the Holy Spirit or, as some say, the *anointing of the Spirit* that is released through the hands of an anointed person when praying for a person who is sick, diseased, oppressed, or in spiritual bondage. Just as the woman with the issue of blood could feel in her body the healing power of Christ, the power of the Holy Spirit can be felt when an anointed individual begins to pray for another person through the laying on of hands. The power of God is released through the hands and through the touch.

Authority, however, is released through words. When a minister preaches with authority, then the congregation can sense the presence of God through the authority of his message. Jesus "spoke as one having authority" and not as the average religious leader of His time (Matt. 7:29). Once a Roman centurion besought Christ to heal his servant. As Christ was walking with him toward the sick man's house, the Roman soldier said:

> Lord, I am not worthy that You should come under my roof. But only speak a word, and my servant will be healed. For I also am a man under authority, having soldiers under me. And I say to this one, "Go," and he goes; and to another, "Come," and he comes; and to my servant, "Do this," and he does it.
>
> —MATTHEW 8:8–9

In Roman times a centurion commanded and directed a *centuria*, or *century*, which consisted of between eighty to one hundred men. According to the Roman historian Vegetius, a Roman centurion had to be educated, have letters of recommendation, and be at least thirty years of age. They were selected for their size, strength, and skill with weapons. The centurion understood military authority and could command any man in his regiment to follow any order, and he would do so without question. This Roman military leader understood that Christ had divine and supernatural authority with His words over sickness, disease, and death. He told Christ to speak the healing word only, and his servant would be healed. Perhaps this man knew the Scripture promise in Psalm 107:20: "He sent His word and healed them."

This is how the evil spirits were cast out by Christ. The kingdom of darkness was fully aware that Christ had complete authority over them. When Christ commanded an unclean spirit to "come out," he could not argue, debate, or go on strike and refuse to follow the rules. Christ even gave an order for thousands of spirits to possess a large herd of swine— all of whom later drowned themselves in the Sea of Galilee. Imagine, demons needing *permission* to go into a herd of wild pigs!

Our Authority to *Bind and Loose*

After witnessing numerous supernatural miracles, including Christ's dominion over the demonic realm, the Lord began to transfer this same power and authority to His followers. We read:

> Assuredly, I say to you, whatever you bind on earth will be bound in heaven, and whatever you loose on earth will be loosed in heaven. Again I say to you that if two of you agree on earth concerning

anything that they ask, it will be done for them by My Father in heaven. For where two or three are gathered together in My name, I am there in the midst of them.

—MATTHEW 18:18–20

In the setting of this passage, Christ was dealing with how to treat an erring brother. He mentioned that if two brothers in the assembly have a fault with one another, then they are to go to one another and, as we say today, "iron out" their differences. However, if one refuses to hear, then the other is to bring in two or three witnesses to hear the entire discussion. If the unforgiving brother refuses to hear, then he is to be exposed before other believers in the church so others will not follow the fellow in his rebellion and create confusion in the body. If the rebellious member continues in his rebellion, he is to be treated with the same disdain as a heathen or a "tax collector" (Matt. 18:15–17).

In this setting Christ then reveals that whatever is bound on earth is bound in heaven, and whatever is loosed on earth is loosed in heaven. Some theologians say these rules of spiritual engagement of binding or loosing have nothing to do with dealing with the forces of darkness but only allude to dealing with an erring member in the church. Actually, in rabbinical thought, to *bind* something was to *not allow* it or to forbid it. To *loose* something was to *permit it*, or to allow it to occur. Thus the new interpretation would be, "Whatever you forbid on earth is forbidden in heaven, and whatever you allow on earth is allowed in heaven."

Using this concept, the Roman Catholic Church leadership has believed that Peter was the first pope and was given the keys to expel or allow a person into the kingdom. The theology then says this authority was passed on to subsequent popes, cardinals, and bishops in the church. In brief, if a member is expelled from the church, then that person is removed from the kingdom of heaven; but if he or she is received by the church, he or she will be received in the kingdom of heaven. In reality, this idea gives human men the power to forgive sins instead of giving full authority of forgiveness to the High Priest of heaven, Jesus Christ, who alone is able to forgive sins (Acts 4:12).

There are several difficulties with this being the only interpretation to binding and loosing. First, Christ did not say, "Whosoever you bind" (meaning the person in the church), but, "Whatsoever you bind…" *Whatsoever* can allude not just to persons but to situations that arise in the spirit realm. The authority of binding and loosing is actually demonstrated in the ministry of Christ.

A woman called a "daughter of Abraham" was bound by a spirit of infirmity. The Greek word for "infirmity" is *astheneia* and can allude to being weak and feeble in mind, body, or spirit. This unnamed woman had suffered for eighteen years and was unable to lift herself up. She continually walked in pain, doubled over. Christ called her forward and said: "Woman, you are loosed from your infirmity" (Luke 13:12). When Christ laid His hands upon her, she was instantly healed. His words loosed the spirit of weakness from her, and His hands released the power of healing into her body. The word *loosed* is the Greek word *apoluo,* meaning "to let go, release, and set at liberty." In a second example, a young boy unable to speak was brought to Christ, and Christ loosed "the string of [the boy's] tongue," and he was instantly able to speak (Mark 7:35, KJV). These two examples reveal how Christ used His authority to *loose* the sick and afflicted from their infirmities.

On one occasion Christ was dealing with an evil spirit, and the demon was manifesting by using the voice of the possessed man and disrupting a synagogue service. Christ commanded the evil spirit to "hold your peace," which could correctly be translated to indicate that Jesus said, "Be quiet!" (Mark 1:25, NIV). If this incident was occurring today, a person might say to the demon, "Shut up!" Christ forbade the evil spirit to speak out in public. He was *binding its authority* by not allowing the demon to manifest verbally. In another example, Christ was casting out an evil spirit from a young child with epilepsy. We read:

> When Jesus saw that the people came running together, He rebuked the unclean spirit, saying to it, "Deaf and dumb spirit, I command you, come out of him and enter him no more!"
> —MARK 9:25

What is allowed in binding and loosing is what *God* allows, and what is not allowed is what *God does not* allow. In this passage in Mark, the evil spirit is commanded not to return and afflict the young child. Christ's authority restrained the spirit from reentering the epileptic boy who had just been released. The heavenly Father ensured that what Christ did not allow was not allowed. In other words, God watched over the words of Christ to ensure that the evil spirit never returned.

These two examples reveal the spiritual aspect of binding and loosing the powers and influences of the adversary. The spiritual authority that Christ gave to believers enables them to "bind devils and loose saints!"

I Met the Wild Man of Dallas

Many years ago I was attending a denominational conference in Dallas, Texas. As always, I was one of the last persons to leave the large convention center. I arrived at my car in the outdoor parking lot, which was parked beside my father's car. Dad was also preparing to leave with Mom and my little sister. Dad and I were standing next to the cars and talking, and I noticed a group of Hispanic believers witnessing to a rather large white man who was standing on the sidewalk gripping his T-shirt in his hand. I commented, "Isn't that great, Dad? While others are out eating, these people are helping to reach a lost soul!"

Almost immediately, I heard a man screaming profanity, and I saw the large man begin hitting and screaming at the Hispanic believers as they scattered like leaves in the wind.

Suddenly "the wild man of Dallas" (as I referred to him) began walking down the sidewalk about thirty yards from our cars. He was cursing God and Christians. I could see my father's face turn red as his blood pressure began rising. I said, "Dad, don't say anything; the man looks drunk or on drugs and is dangerous."

As the man continued in his rage, the profanity got worse, and he made contact with Dad, who by now had told Mom and my sister to lock themselves in the car, and me. Suddenly Dad had all he could take, and he screamed out, "Mister, you need God in your life!"

I said, "Dad, what are you doing?" The wild man turned and made his way into the parking lot. For some reason he stopped within two feet of me and screamed, "I don't like you. I'm gonna let you have it!" A fear seized me because this man was high as a kite, dangerous, and ready for a fight.

Suddenly an unction of God's Spirit overwhelmed me, and I looked at this demon-possessed man and yelled, "I bind you in the name of Jesus! You cannot lay a hand on me, you foul, unclean spirit. I command you to shut up in the name of Christ!" The boldness was not me but was rising up like a river behind a dam that was about to break.

The angry man began cursing me and screaming. He said he would bust the teeth out of my mouth and other violent actions that I will not repeat. As he spewed his sewage from his mouth, a righteous indignation rose up like a fire within me, and I resisted his words with, "No, you won't, because the power of God on me can overpower the evil in you!" I drew an imaginary line on the pavement with my right foot. I demanded, "Come on and cross this line if you can! The anointing on me will defeat you if I have to!"

He ranted, raved, and cursed, but every time he attempted to cross the line, he was restrained by some *invisible force*. Within a few minutes the Dallas police arrived and, after seeing the fellow, placed him in a police car and removed him from the property.

After the incident, I was suddenly left slightly weak and thought, "Oh my, what did I just do? That was crazy, because this fellow could have let me have it!" The boldness a person has when the anointing and presence of the Holy Spirit is upon him is amazing, and when the same anointing begins to lift, he suddenly realizes just how weak and human he is when the anointing is not present! David understood this when he wrote, "I am weak today, though anointed king" (2 Sam. 3:39).

For me, this is a personal example of the authority of binding, or not allowing, the adversary to act out his will and desire in that negative and dangerous situation. Spiritual authority is part of the inheritance of a believer when he enters into the redemptive covenant of Christ. When you pray for a loved one to be saved, you are moving in your spiritual authority. If you intercede for the protection of a child and ask angels to surround that child on his or her journey, you are exercising your legal rights and spiritual authority. When you pray and begin to rebuke a foul sickness off another believer who is too weak to pray for himself or herself, you are following the instructions of the apostle James to anoint the sick, pray over them the prayer of faith, and God will raise them up (James 5:14–15). To some extent, all prayer is a form of using the authority given you to approach God's throne and take dominion over the powers of the enemy. Jesus said it this way:

> And Jesus came and spoke to them, saying, "All authority has been given to Me in heaven and on earth."
> —MATTHEW 28:18

> Behold, I give you the authority to trample on serpents and scorpions, and over all the power of the enemy, and nothing shall by any means hurt you.
> —LUKE 10:19

> But as many as received him, to them gave he power [authority] to become the sons of God, even to them that believe on his name.
> —JOHN 1:12, KJV

> To open their eyes, and to turn them from darkness to light, and from the power of Satan unto God, that they may receive forgiveness of sins, and inheritance among them which are sanctified by faith that is in me.
> —ACTS 26:18, KJV

When the adversary attempts to bring his baggage into your house, put a *return to sender* notice out and refuse his offer! The adversary certainly wants to keep a believer in spiritual ignorance as it relates to spiritual authority. The promise of binding and loosing definitely has more practical application for a believer than what many theologians have interpreted. The power of God comes through the Holy Spirit and is released by prayer and laying on of hands. The authority of a believer is released by speaking the Word of God. It is a central blessing as a believer to be able to exercise your authority by *binding devils and loosing saints*!

Chapter 12

REVERSE PROPHECY FROM AN EVIL SPIRIT

The thief does not come except to steal, and to kill, and to destroy. I have come that they may have life, and that they may have it more abundantly.

| JOHN 10:10 |

IN THE MID 1980s, my wife and I were ministering in Gastonia, North Carolina. I would spend all day in study and prayer. One day I was in the church sanctuary praying for the night service. The pastor came to me and asked me if a woman who was a member of his church could briefly speak with me, as she seemed quite distressed. I agreed, and the woman came in and sat on the front pew. She said, "For many years I have battled depression, and I mean very severe depression. I sew at a local factory and have fought this battle of mental anxiety for years."

She continued, "Several weeks ago I heard the voice of the Lord speaking to me saying, 'Today I am setting you free!' All of a sudden the pressure broke, and I began to weep and rejoice. I was literally free in my mind for the first time I can remember! This new freedom continued for several weeks." Her countenance changed as she commented, "But this morning I felt it like a weight again, and I heard the devil say to me, 'I'm back!'"

At that moment my own spirit was suddenly charged with two words for her. First I said, "The devil is a liar, and the truth is not in him, so why are you listening to him when he is a liar?" Then I said something that was quickened to her spirit and brought her to her feet rejoicing. I said, "The word that the Lord gave you three weeks ago is the same word

He is giving you today. His Word is eternal and cannot be changed. If He freed you, then you are free indeed according to John 8:36."

This type of mental attack happens to thousands of believers every day! God has given us His Word, but the enemy has a word of his own that he is attempting to place, or replace, in your mind. The problem is that too many Christians don't recognize the voice they are hearing and don't know how to deal with what they are hearing.

The Devil Believes and Can Prophesy

I may surprise you when I say that the devil has more faith than some so-called Christians! For example, some alleged Christians say that hell does not exist, but evil spirits not only know hell exists but also know they are doomed to spend forever in the confines of the underworld (Isa. 14:12–15; Luke 8:26–31). Some *secular* Christians believe that Jesus was a good man but not the Son of God. Even evil spirits recognized Jesus as the Son of God on many occasions (Luke 4:41; 8:28). While some Christians identify the events of biblical prophecies as mere myths, allegories, or metaphors, Satan will one day be cast down to earth in great anger, knowing he "has but a short time" (Rev. 12:12). While some churches are filled with zombie-like members who reject any form of emotion in their worship, even devils will bow down and worship when they are in the presence of Christ (Mark 5:6–9). Perhaps the enemy's greatest *gift* is *his ability to release his own personal prophecy* in the life of a believer!

If this statement sounds odd and difficult to comprehend, then consider this rather unusual example. The Old Testament prophets, such as Isaiah, warned that Jerusalem would be destroyed by her enemies— through an invading army (Jer. 25:11). Many years later, one king from Assyria named Sennacherib knew this prophetic warning and attempted to make it a *self-fulfilling prophecy.* In other words, the invading king planned to intimidate the Jews to give up their city by saying he was the very king the Lord had warned them would defeat the city. (See 2 Kings 18:17–37.) The king sent an *ambassador* making false prophetic claims to Jerusalem to demand the Jews to capitulate and hand Jerusalem over to

Sennacherib. This false prophet named Rabshakeh even told the Jewish leaders, "The LORD said to me, 'Go up against this land, and destroy it'" (v. 25). Rabshakeh went to the upper hill where all of the Jews would view him from the wall of the city and even spoke in the Hebrew language (v. 28) so that all of the Jews within Jerusalem's walls could understand his words and spread the prophecy of coming doom and destruction. His goal was to frighten the entire populace, thus making them give up— since *God* had already predicted Jerusalem's defeat.

Here are the facts. Isaiah's and Jeremiah's prophecies of Jerusalem's destruction and the Israelites' seventy years in captivity was referring to the future king of *Babylon* and not the king of *Assyria*. Twisting this prophecy for personal benefit is about as ridiculous as an alleged incident when Saddam Hussein sought out a group of psychics and astrologers prior to the Gulf War, who informed Saddam that he would defeat the invading allied armies in the coming war. Saddam believed a false prediction, was humiliated and defeated, and would, in the second war, be captured hiding in a hole and later executed by hanging.

The false prophetic interpretation *backfired* on the false prophet and this Assyrian king when an angel of the Lord marched secretly through the camp of the Assyrians. By morning there were more than one hundred eighty-five thousand Syrians lying dead across the hills surrounding Jerusalem (2 Kings 19:35–37). While the real prophecy came from God, the twisted and false prophecy was used to intimidate the Jewish people.

Have You Received a Prophecy From the Devil?

A *prophecy from the devil* is when the adversary throws mental or verbal darts through the words of others or darts of thoughts into your mind, attempting to get you to agree and submit to the *predictions* you are hearing. Perhaps you will recognize one or several of the negative predictions below that may have crossed your own mind at some time:

- You know that disease runs in your family and is hereditary. That pain that you are feeling is no doubt cancer—can't you see it is in the same area of your body where your father suffered?

- Divorce runs in your family, and the arguments and disagreements you are having with your companion are going to lead to a divorce—just like the rest of your family—so get prepared for divorce court!

- Nervous breakdowns run in your family. That nervous feeling that you are having is the early stage of a complete breakdown, which you are going to experience in the future.

- You will never be blessed with any form of prosperity. Just look at your relatives; none of them are blessed financially. Poverty is a part of your family, so just get used to it.

- You may as well just quit praying for your children. You see the condition of your sister's kids and your brother's kids. It's just this generation. They are all on alcohol and drugs, so just get used to it. Maybe in the end they will make it.

- Addictions are a part of your family, and you know the baby you are having may end up an addict. Why don't you just abort it so it won't have to put up with some of the negative things you had to put up with?

- Your son will end up in jail just like the other men in your family who have failed in the past.

Often people will hear such statements in their minds but not recognize they are the fiery darts of the enemy. Eventually these thoughts are accepted as truth, and we position ourselves to receive the negative outcomes with comments like: "Well, the times are different now, and these problems are all a part of life and growing up," or, "This is part of my DNA, and there is nothing I can do about it." The enemy desires for you to *agree with his predictions* for you instead of resisting and rebuking the thoughts.

During the forty days of temptation, Satan challenged Christ's position as the *Son of God*, demanding some miraculous proof to *prove* who He was. He commanded Christ to turn rocks into edible pieces of bread. Afterward Satan ordered Him to jump from the pinnacle (southeastern corner) of the temple and see if angels cushioned His fall. Satan finally offered Christ the kingdoms of the world if He would bow and pay homage and worship to him (Matt. 4:1–10).

First, Christ refused to prove to Satan that He was the Son of God, because He *knew* who He was! Christ refused to turn stones into bread, but later on during an outdoor crusade, Jesus took a boy's lunch and multiplied bread to feed more than five thousand men (Mark 6:35–44). Christ refused the challenge to jump from a tall wall and *tempt God* to send angels for supernatural protection. However, the Lord later stepped on the water and began walking on the sea toward His disciples, thus defying the very law of gravity that should have sunk Him like a rock to the bottom of the deep lake (Matt. 14:24–26). As far as owning the kingdoms of the world, I am certain Christ already knew the prophecy of Daniel that reads:

> I was watching in the night visions,
> And behold, One like the Son of Man,
> Coming with the clouds of heaven!
> He came to the Ancient of Days,
> And they brought Him near before Him.
> Then to Him was given dominion and glory and a kingdom,
> That all peoples, nations, and languages should serve Him.
> His dominion is an everlasting dominion,
> Which shall not pass away,
> And His kingdom the one
> Which shall not be destroyed.
> —DANIEL 7:13–14

Satan's third recorded temptation was to give Christ the "kingdoms of this world." Since the Roman Empire was ruling the known world, and the highest position in Rome was the emperor, the temptation of Satan was actually, "If You will worship and follow me, then I will make You popular and help You achieve the control of the world's kingdoms—or of the Roman Empire." This was not the reason Christ came. He came as the Lamb of God to suffer. On one occasion when the people rose up and wanted to make Him king, He refused and instead escaped to a private hideaway away from the overzealous multitudes. It was not *time* for Him to become a king (John 6:15). Becoming king at that moment would have preempted the redemptive covenant from being initiated for all of mankind.

Because Christ knew who He was, then the temptations of the enemy had no influence upon Christ. For many believers, the only biblical insight for living they receive is the two hours on Sunday when they may attend a local church. Because so many North Americans who attend church often do not privately read their own Bibles at home, they are not informed about who they are in Christ and the spiritual authority they have in the Word.

The Day Satan Gave Me a Prophecy

I have rarely related this story publicly but was impressed that it would be an eye-opener to someone reading this book. In the early 1990s, I was returning from a Holy Land tour and felt impressed to go on an extended fast. After returning home, I received a strange and unexpected phone call from a former well-known minister who had fallen into an addictive bondage that eventually caused him to lose his church, his ministry, his family, and his personal integrity. I recalled that when I was a teenager, he was one of the most dynamic ministers and pastored a very large, growing congregation.

The voice on the other end of the line said, "Perry, this is [he gave his name]. I am calling to ask you to go pray; then call me back after the Lord gives you a word for me. Here is my phone number…" My phone number was unlisted, and I have never found out how he knew my phone number.

I went to a bedroom and began praying. Within fifteen minutes I heard the Spirit of the Lord impress me, "This man is at the lowest point he has ever been and is contemplating suicide. He is making one final effort for someone to reach him." I ran to the phone, called the number, and repeated what I had heard.

He replied, "That's right. God did speak to you. Now what are you going to do about it?"

I asked him where he was calling from in the town and told him I would come and pray for him. He gave me the address and apartment number. Before leaving, I told my wife, Pam, "Pray until I return. I feel this is a major spiritual battle."

I didn't know what to expect, and as I knocked on the door, he answered. He was in his forties but looked much older because the drugs and sin had worked their damage upon his body. I was invited in, and I started the conversation by asking about him and what he had been through. Shortly into the discussion, I saw for the first time in my life how evil spirits can possess someone who has drifted far from God. His countenance began to change, and his voice inflection as well. Another entity took over his voice and began to mock me and laugh at me. I prayed under my breath, and the evil spirit knew what I was doing. Suddenly, this man returned to himself and carried on a conversation, almost in tears.

At first I thought he was high on some type of drugs. However, he confessed that he had not taken anything prior to our meeting. It was as though he had a split personality. However, I had witnessed demonic possession before and knew how a person's voice could be altered by the unclean spirit. As this evil entity spoke and then the minister returned to a normal conversation, I was reminded of the story of King Saul.

When the evil spirit troubled Saul, he would be relieved when David played the harp. However, he would suddenly turn against David, making death threats and throwing javelins at him (1 Sam. 16:14–23; 18:10–11; 19:9–10). Suddenly I felt like little David in the presence of a tormented King Saul, and I was becoming somewhat concerned that he could become violent with me.

The cursing and the threats had become so intense that I was about to walk out the door when suddenly the evil spirit said this: *"I know how old you are, and I will do the same thing to you that I did to him in two years!"* A cold chill ran up my spine, and I know my mouth dropped open. I felt such spiritual indignation, I jumped up from the chair and began to rebuke the demonic power in him and commanded the spirits to leave him alone. I then told the man that he needed help from God, and he should leave the town and go to a Christian rehab center to receive spiritual counseling and spend time with God believing for a new beginning. I then walked out the door.

As I drove home, the *prophetic words* of the evil spirit began to play over and over in my mind. Why did it say? "I know your age." At the time I was thirty-one years of age, and in two years I would be thirty-three. Suddenly that is when I remembered that the addiction problems began to come upon this minister at about the same age that this spirit had predicted my own demise—age thirty-three.

At that moment I had one of two choices. I could live the next two years in a state of dread, not knowing what terrible attack lay around the corner. I could spend sleepless nights wondering what snare the enemy had laid and how it appeared that I too would fall into the trap and bring destruction to my life. Or I could resist this prediction, call the devil a *liar*, and expect God to give me strength and wisdom to overcome any situation that would arise.

As I approached my home, a third strategy of victory came to me. I began to laugh out loud, and I spoke out into the atmosphere, "Devil, you really are very foolish! You should have kept your plans secret and never have told me. That way I could have been surprised and overwhelmed. Now you have given me the time frame, and I will have all of my ministry partners praying and will watch and pray to defeat your plan!" My mistake was that I never followed up with this strategy. After a few months I forgot about it, as I was very busy preaching three- to five-week revivals back to back across the nation.

Entering a dark hole of depression
About two years later, in the month of May, I will never forget waking one morning with the darkest cloud of depression on my mind I had

ever experienced. After several days of no relief, I began to have a strange desire to quit the ministry. Later in the month of June I traveled with a group of friends to the former communist nation of Bulgaria for an evangelistic outreach. While in the nation, I was suddenly seized by what I call a suicidal spirit that seemed to linger like a dark shadow for several days. This cloud of oppression was like inviting a spirit of hopelessness into your life. At the time I had forgotten about the prophecy from the evil spirit and was trying to claw my way out of this dark pit of depression with my own strength. After two months, I suddenly recalled the two-year-old prediction of the enemy and thought, "Oh my, it's been two years, and I failed to discern this as a spiritual attack, thinking it was only some mental stress I was under!"

At the time that the eyes of my understanding were opened, I was ministering nightly under a big tent in Anniston, Alabama. That night I stopped preaching and began to explain to the seven hundred people present what I had been encountering. I told the congregation of the staggering depression and the feelings of utter hopelessness. When I ended my confession, the altars immediately filled up with men and women who were fighting a similar battle. After praying for these seekers, I was dripping with perspiration and making my way from the tent to the church on the hill, preparing to change from my wet clothes, when a group of close friends stopped me and said, "Where do you think you are going?" They continued, "You are not leaving this tent until we anoint you with oil and rebuke and bind this spirit that is attacking you." One person grabbed a bottle of olive oil and began pouring it on the top of my head. A second person began rubbing it in, and suddenly I felt the hands of my friends on my head and shoulders, and they were rebuking the powers of Satan and commanding my mind to be free. About ten minutes later, when I arrived at the church, I looked into a full-length mirror. My hair was sticking up, oil was all over my suit, my tie was sideways, and sawdust from the tent floor was sticking all over my pants. I thought, "Stone, you are a sight. God must be laughing right now!"

The following morning I felt some relief, and I knew the strong pressure-like vice was slowly slipping. However, it would be a few weeks later, at home, when I awoke one morning and the dark grip around my mind was gone just as suddenly and quickly as it had arrived. I jumped from the bed and inside felt like a man who had been confined to a wheelchair and was instantly able to walk! I took a shower, dressed, and drove to my two-thousand-square-foot office on Broad Street in downtown Cleveland. I walked over to my desk, gripped my black leather Bible in my right hand, shook it in the air, and yelled, "Tell the enemy that Stone is back!" I was free. The plan of the enemy failed.

I would later learn that the fallen minister I had prayed for two years earlier had experienced depression. His own father had committed suicide. This depression had led the fallen minister into chemical dependency and addiction, which led to alcohol and other sins of the flesh. The root cause of his attack was a spirit of depression that affected certain family members. In our own family, on both my father's and my wife's sides, there have been relatives who experienced mental and emotional breakdowns. I believe that at age thirty-three there was an assignment against me to bring me down mentally, emotionally, physically, and finally spiritually. But it was canceled because I exposed the attack and refused to submit to this prophecy from the devil, and I opened my heart to prayer warriors who cared enough to stand in the gap for me until the victory was manifest.

That night after exposing the details of what I was experiencing to those in the tent, one of our close friends came to me and said, "You did something that is a great spiritual lesson for others to learn."

I asked, "What was it I did?"

She replied, "You exposed a secret attack to the light, and now the enemy has nowhere to hide!"

I pondered her words and realized how powerful this statement was. If you are in a struggle, and you *hide* the problem or don't admit you have a struggle, then the enemy can always sneak in the door undetected and unrestrained, because no one is resisting him in prayer. One of the first principles of freedom from addiction is to first admit that you are an addict. When you admit to your problem and begin to expose it to the light, the enemy's cover is blown, and the spotlight is shined on his path.

It is virtually impossible for an attacking army to win a battle when the opposing forces know the entire battle plan of their enemy!

The Prophecy Simon Peter Had to Reverse

A powerful example of the reversal of a plan of Satan involved the life of Simon Peter. Christ asked His disciples, "Who do men say that I...am?" (Matt. 16:13). Each disciple gave a response, naming various prophets from the Bible, including Isaiah and Jeremiah. Peter suddenly announced, "You are the Christ, the Son of the living God" (v. 16). Jesus told Peter that the Father in heaven had revealed this revelation to him. Christ further predicted, "Upon this rock I will build my church; and the gates of hell shall not prevail against it" (v. 18, KJV). The following statement by Christ is very significant to this story:

> And I will give you the keys of the kingdom of heaven, and whatever you bind on earth will be bound in heaven, and whatever you loose on earth will be loosed in heaven.
> —MATTHEW 16:19

On the surface it seems Christ was saying that He would build the church on the *foundation* of Peter. However, He was actually saying He would build the church on the revelation that He (Christ) was the "Son of the living God." This truth would initiate the redemptive covenant of forgiveness of sins and eternal life to all who believed. However, just several verses later, Peter gave a prediction, telling Christ that He would not die and suffer! Christ rebuked Peter, saying, "Get behind Me, Satan!" (v. 23). One moment Peter received a revelation from God, and shortly thereafter, Satan threw a fiery dart in his mind that was certainly not from God!

Months prior to the crucifixion Jesus warned Peter, "Satan has asked for you, that he may sift you as wheat" (Luke 22:31). Wheat can be sifted numerous times, as it was done when the priests at the temple sifted the flour made from wheat ten times before baking the bread for Pentecost. The purpose of sifting Peter was to shake his faith, which is clear from Christ's next statement: "But I have prayed for you, that your faith should not fail" (v. 32). The attack against Peter was to *sift and shake his faith*. In reality, every spiritual attack that you encounter is designed to hinder, sift, or destroy your faith.

When you support the work of God financially and later lose your job, the event is designed to make a person question, "Why did the Lord let me lose my job when I tithe and give offerings?" I knew of a respected minister who began a six-week series on God's promises for your health and healing, and before he completed the teaching, he was lying in a hospital bed suffering with cancer (that was in 1985, and he is still living as of the time I write this book). Why was Peter targeted above the other disciples? I believe Satan heard the prediction about Peter being given the "keys to the kingdom," and the adversary perceived that Peter had a significant future in the kingdom. The enemy put a target on Peter to wreck his faith, causing him to lose confidence. If Peter had not repented and gained back his spiritual integrity, he may have felt condemned and unworthy to stand before the Jews on the Feast of Pentecost and preach three thousand souls under conviction (Acts 2).

Satan had a plan—to sift him as wheat. Jesus, however, said, "I have prayed for you, that your faith will not fail!" Christ did not wait until Peter was cutting off the ear of Malchus in the Garden of Gethsemane to begin His intercession on Peter's behalf (John 18). Christ stood in the gap through prayer before the strategy was set, and it was His prayer that prevented Peter from falling into a pit from which he may have never returned. Whenever you sense a burden to pray, you may not always know who or what you are praying for, but the Holy Spirit knows and makes intercession for you "according to the will of God" (Rom. 8:26–28).

How to Reverse Satan's Prophecies

Satan's plan is simple; he comes to kill, steal, and destroy (John 10:10). He kills through disease and sin, he steals through robbing us of our blessings, and he destroys individuals through unforgiveness, strife, and bitterness. The adversary is called a "thief" (John 10:10) because he sneaks into the circumstances of a believer in the same manner that a thief presses into a guarded or protected house—by overpowering the spiritual strong man in the house. We see his manner in the following:

> When a strong man, fully armed, guards his own palace, his goods are in peace. But when a stronger than he comes upon him and overcomes him, he takes from him all his armor in which he trusted, and divides his spoils.
>
> —LUKE 11:21–22

As believers, we guard our most valued possessions, which includes our companion, children, grandchildren, and the tangible blessings such as our homes and valuables and family heirlooms. When the palace (house) is protected, everything is in peace. A person is a *strong man* because of his prayer life, active faith, and a dedication to God's Word. Notice what happens however. A being *stronger* than the strong man enters the house and takes the *armor* from the head of the house in order to divide the spoils—or bring division in the home! Only when a strong spirit can strip a believer of his or her armor can that spirit enter the house and bring division. In Matthew's Gospel, he alludes to the same scripture and says the strategy of the strong man entering the man's house is to "spoil his goods" (Matt. 12:29). The Greek word for "goods" in this passage is unique, as it is not the normal biblical word for "property" or "possessions" but is the word *skeuos*, which is translated eleven times in the New Testament English translation as the word *vessel*. Oddly, the same Greek word is used in the verse when it speaks of the "wife, as to the *weaker vessel*" (1 Pet. 3:7, emphasis added). Today, one of the greatest divisions is caused by the increasing rifts between a husband and wife that end on a road of separation—the spoiling of the goods! Any time the adversary can enter the home through the door of strife, contention, jealousy, and mistrust, he will impact the goods and divide the house.

To prevent what I call these demonic *home invasions*, it is necessary for the believer to be "strong in the Lord and in the power of His might" (Eph. 6:10). We must be spiritually stronger than the strong men outside of our house who are forming their strategies to get inside and divide the spoil. What weapon must we wield to hinder and stop the plans of the archenemy? The answer is to *speak out* the Word in faith.

For example, when a believer has suddenly been assaulted by a physical sickness, he must turn to the Scriptures, which give hope and promise for healing. These passages include, but are certainly not limited to, the following. Notice these numerous scriptures can be combined to form a *paragraph prayer.*

> *Lord, according to* Exodus 15:26, *you are the Lord who heals Your covenant people. You revealed to the prophet David that You forgive all my iniquities and You heal all of my diseases* (Ps. 103:3). *Father, I can receive my healing because Christ was wounded for my transgressions and bruised for my iniquities, and with His precious stripes I am healed* (Isa. 53:5). *Lord, I thank You that Christ Himself took my infirmities and carried my sicknesses through His atoning work* (Matt. 8:17).

When you quote healing scriptures in this manner, there is always going to be someone who reminds you that they had a friend or knew someone who tried this *method* of using Scripture, but that person died anyway. In response, there are numerous reasons, including the sovereignty of God, as to why certain things happen the way they do. However, this should not prevent a believer from quoting the Holy Scriptures. After all, Christ is our example, as seen in each of the three temptations Satan offered. Christ countered the enemy with scriptures from Deuteronomy that applied to the situation He was experiencing (Deut. 6:5, 16; 8:3).

Today many good people are living under additional stress, leading to oppression, depression, and negative mental thoughts. Instead of accepting this and saying, "I'm just like my mother and father…They really struggled with mental oppression and depression," use the written promises of God to counter the prophecies of the enemy.

> *Father, in* Isaiah 26:3 *You have given me the promise that You would keep me in perfect peace if my mind would remain upon You. Today I am thinking about Your goodness toward me.*

Christ promised in John 14:27 *that He would leave His peace with me, and His peace He would give me, and by faith I receive the peace He promised for my thoughts and my mind. I am also thankful, Father, that in* 2 Timothy 1:7 *You tell me that You have not given me a spirit of fear, but one of power, love, and a sound mind.*

The Lesson From the Mayor

Many years ago as a teenaged minister, I was preaching in a city in Alabama. At that time the mayor and his wife attended the local church where I was ministering. I remember him being a fine, upstanding person in the community, and his wife was a very godly, praying Christian woman. I recall her telling me of a very public attack that was designed by a group of individuals to remove him from his position. Accusations were even made in the local news, of which she said none were true, but the lies were having a mental effect on her husband, who was greatly distressed by the negative publicity.

She said that she wrote out specific scriptures and key promises of God, including the passage that no weapon formed would prosper and every false word would be void (Isa. 54:17). She placed the scriptures on paper and taped them to the bathroom mirror, as this would be the first thing he would see each morning. Other passages were placed inside his shoes, in his important books, and in other places where he walked or worked each day. They literally fought this battle by using the Word of God, holding the Lord to each of His promises. As time passed, those who rose up against him were removed, and he was reelected for another term! One word from God that becomes quickened or made alive within your spirit can change the outcome of your situation!

Dead Men Can't Preach

As a young preacher living in Virginia, I was mentored by a powerful man of God named Marion H. Kennedy. Bishop Kennedy related to me that when he was a young boy, he was stricken by a terrible sickness that doctors said would lead to his early death. On this occasion, Kennedy was severely ill, and the doctor was called to the home to examine the lad. The prognosis was made to get Marion to a hospital immediately, as he could pass very soon. Suddenly, Marion heard the voice of the Lord say, "Marion, I am calling you to preach My Word!"

He called his mother to his bed and said, "Momma, I just heard from the Lord."

"What did He say?" she asked.

Marion replied with a smile, "He told me I was called to preach!"

His mother turned to the doctor and said, "Doc, you can leave now, as you are no longer needed!" The doctor argued, saying they should not delay getting the boy to a hospital as the worsening of his condition could lead to death.

Sister Kennedy replied, "Doctor, dead men can't preach, and God called my boy to preach, so he is not going to die!" Marion didn't die; in fact, he lived a strong, healthy life to his mideighties!

What do you *know* that is a faith promise? When young Timothy was being criticized for being placed as a young pastor in a church of older, more experienced saints, he became intimidated with a spirit of fear. Paul told him that God did not give him a spirit of fear, but of power, love, and a sound mind (2 Tim. 1:7). He also instructed him:

> This charge I commit to you, son Timothy, according to the prophecies previously made concerning you, that by them you may wage the good warfare.
>
> —1 TIMOTHY 1:18

Paul had given Timothy a personal prophecy concerning God's will for him to be pastor of this great congregation. He reminded the young minister not to neglect the gift given him and the prophetic word spoken over him (1 Tim. 4:14). Fear was paralyzing the gift because Timothy was feeling intimidated by the elders, a much more knowledgeable and experienced group of believers in his congregation. Paul revealed that a spoken word, or a prophetic word, can be used as a weapon to defeat fear and intimidation.

This Plane Won't Crash

At age eighteen I was excited to be invited to preach a youth camp in Nebraska. Prior to flying out, I was ministering in a local church in Virginia when several people had a bad "feeling" about my trip. A few reminded me that a similar plane had crashed in Chicago a few days earlier. In fear, I called to cancel my speaking at the camp based on *someone else's fears*, which were spreading over my heart like dust in a storm into my own mind. The camp director begged me to come, so I headed on to the Roanoke airport *knowing* something bad would happen to me. After getting on the Eastern Airlines plane, I later arrived at Chicago—the very airport where the plane crash had occurred. Standing at the gate window, I heard these conversations: "I hope they check the bolts on these engines." "I'm really afraid to fly now." "Hey, does that look like smoke coming from the engine?" Hearing these comments only added to my apprehension. Fear was being fed without my permission!

At that moment I began to hear a conversation within me, which I believe was the Holy Spirit speaking to me. The voice said, "Who opened the door for you to go to Nebraska?"

I thought to myself, "The Lord did."

The inner voice replied, "If the Lord opened the door to go, then why would He allow something to happen to stop what He has already planned for you to do?"

Instantly faith shot into my spirit like an adrenaline rush. I stepped on the plane and said, "You all are the luckiest people in Chicago, because a King's kid just got on board this flight. Nothing will happen from Chicago to Nebraska because I'm on board, and I am on assignment from God!"

Some would suggest this sounds a little arrogant or proud, but it is neither—it is simply confidence. It is not confidence in myself but trust in the Word of the Lord and His promises. You can never reverse a satanic prophecy unless you have a prophecy or a promise that can counter what the enemy is predicting. Go to God's Word. There is a promise for any and every need you will ever have in your life.

Shut Out the Lies

If you knew a person close to you was known for continually lying and telling stories that were actually not true, I am certain you would place no confidence in that person's words. Why is it, then, that believers will continually say, "The enemy is telling me this, and he is telling me that"? The Bible identifies the adversary as a "liar and the father of it [lies]" (John 8:44). Why, then, do we dwell on the suggestions pouring into our minds that are the product of the world's greatest liar? If we know that the darts burning into our thoughts and emotions are coming from the enemy, and the enemy is a liar, then shut out the liar and close the door on the lies. Use the phrase Jesus said to Peter when the enemy attempted to throw a lie—that Jesus would not die—at Christ. The Lord demanded, "Get behind Me, Satan!" Truth should lead you, and all lies should remain behind you!

Chapter 13

ATMOSPHERIC WARFARE—FULL MOONS AND NEW MOONS

So let no one judge you in food or in drink, or regarding a festival or a new moon or sabbaths, which are a shadow of things to come, but the substance is of Christ.

| COLOSSIANS 2:16–17 |

THERE IS A theory that the full moon often brings out the worst in people, including violence, crime, arguments, accidents, and so forth. It has been called the *lunar effect,* or the *Transylvania effect.* Having many personal friends in the medical field, I have asked them if there is any increase or decrease in activities in the emergency room and mental hospitals or in the birthing process during a full or new moon. While they all indicate there are few actual studies that can confirm or deny the activities centered around the moon cycles, there is definitely more activity in mental hospitals and in the birthing process during a full and a new moon.

A report by the *Journal of the American Veterinary Medical Association* stated that injuries and illness among pets seem to be 23 percent higher for cats and 28 percent higher for dogs during or near a new moon. British researchers found a lunar link to how many humans were bitten by animals during a full moon, while studies in other nations saw no link.[1] Some maternity units in hospitals add additional staff during full moon cycles. There are more false labor pains during full moons, sending many women to the maternity unit, only to discover it was not the time for the arrival of the infant. Nurses have told me that the full moon is a likely link to when a pregnant woman's water will break.

The theory is that the gravitational pull of the full moon has an effect on the amniotic fluid in the same manner as it affects the tides in the sea.[2] Because the human body consists of as much as 80 percent water, many believe that we tend to hold more water in our bodies during a full moon, which may contribute to accounts related to mood changes during the full moon.[3]

From a natural perspective, there may be an answer as to why there is more mental pressure during the full and new moon. During both cycles, the earth, moon, and sun are lined up, resulting in higher tides than usual. The difference is that during the full moon the earth is between the moon and the sun, and at the new moon the moon is between the sun and the earth. During the full moon the light of the sun is reflecting on the moon, giving a slight glow from the night sky. On the new moon there is total darkness in the night, except for the stars visible on a clear night.[4]

The War in the Heavens

Scripture indicates there are three levels of heaven: the clouds, the stars, and the temple of God, which is positioned beyond the stars (Isa. 14:13–14). Adam was given dominion over the birds of the air in the first level of heaven (Gen. 1:26). Numerous stronger spirits, called *principalities*, which have been given dominion over certain governments on the earth, exist in the second level of heaven (Eph. 1:21; 6:12; Col. 2:10). The third heaven is the home of the righteous dead and is the location of the heavenly paradise in 2 Corinthians 12:4–7.

The second heaven is where there are invisible battles occurring between an archangel named Michael and the angels of Satan. We read:

> And war broke out in heaven: Michael and his angels fought with the dragon; and the dragon and his angels fought, but they did not prevail, nor was a place found for them in heaven any longer. So the great dragon was cast out, that serpent of old, called the Devil and Satan, who deceives the whole world; he was cast to the earth, and his angels were cast out with him.
>
> —REVELATION 12:7–9

This type of spirit war between good and evil—Michael and his angels, and Satan and his angels—is called *a combat myth* by some liberal scholars and is said to be taken from some pagan mythology. I find it difficult to understand why men who are allegedly intelligent have such a desire to pick and choose what they do or don't believe, basing their lack of faith upon their personal prejudices and interpretations. The above passage from Revelation 12 is the account of a real conflict that will unfold during the middle of the seven-year Great Tribulation. These types of heavenly battles, recorded in Revelation 12 and Daniel 10, are a part of the atmospheric conflict in the heaven.

The Earthly Conflicts and the Moon

There is, however, another strange phenomenon that cannot be explained with natural or scientific explanations. It is the bizarre activity that is witnessed in nations like India when there is a new moon.

The main religion in India is Hinduism, an ancient religious belief that accepts practically anything in nature, animals included, as a god. There are rat temples in India where a white rat is the center of the worship, and literally thousands of rats multiply and live in the temple, being fed by the Hindu worshipers. Those of the Hindu persuasion accept thousands of idol gods. This idolatry opens a door to evil spirits. Missionaries who minister in India often tell stories about the demonic powers that manifest all the time in the massive crowds that gather when Christians are witnessing through singing and preaching.

Each month during the new moon, missionaries have noted that literally thousands of people in India experience demonic manifestations, including violent shaking, levitating, foaming at the mouth, eyes rolling in the head, and other physical, visible marks that identify demonic oppression or possession. During the new moon cycle, one of the leading Christian pastors in India places large bright lights in an open field for the purpose of allowing thousands of people to sit under the bright lights. For some reason, the light helps to prevent the demonic powers from manifesting as strongly. Many have come to Christ as the result of these bright lights he uses as an opportunity to preach a clear gospel message.

From a more personal view, I am always able to determine when the moon is on full cycle; throughout my lifetime I have endured severe headaches on the right side of my head during the full moon cycle. I don't ever need to look up into the night sky—I can always tell because of the three days of pressure I feel on right side of my head. I realize that these changes are certainly not a sign of some type of monthly spiritual warfare that is unleashed. There is a good explanation for this phenomenon: there is simply more pressure on the earth during the full moon, and the physical body—and, for some, the mind also—can feel the effects of the atmospheric changes that occur a few days each month.

What is the strange connection to the new moon and such activity in the spirit world? I am convinced that something unseen but very real must take place during the time of the new moon. Whatever it is that takes place, God Himself was aware of it, and He placed special new moon sacrifices.

The Moon—Israel's Heavenly Sign

Most nations in the ancient world based their calendars on the cycles of the sun. However, God required Israel to organize their calendar and feast days on the cycle of the moon. The rabbinical reason for God choosing the moon was that all other nations tended to worship the creation, and there were many sun worshipers on the earth. Thus the moon was chosen for Israel. Another symbolic reason is that the moon is the lesser light, and God was going to take a lesser nation, Israel, and raise it up as a light in a dark world.

The moon enters four major phases in a twenty-nine-and-a-half-day period of time:

- From dark to half, called a quarter moon—new moon
- From half to full, called the full moon—first quarter
- From full back to half—full moon
- From half to darkness, called the new moon—last quarter

Jewish sages believe the moon is a reflection of the nation of Israel. It takes almost fifteen days for the moon to be renewed from dark to full, and another fifteen days to decline from a full moon back to a new moon. The imagery of Israel is hidden in this cycle. Israel began with Abraham in a time when the world was filled with spiritual darkness. Fifteen generations later, the kingdom of Solomon became the fullness (full moon) of the kingdom of Israel. In Israel's history, there was no other king like Solomon, who built the most expensive and impressive temple, perhaps, in world history! After Solomon's death, his son Rehoboam was placed on his father's throne, and his arrogance and lack of wisdom split Israel into the northern and southern kingdom. Fifteen generations later, representing the fifteen-day period when the light of the moon is headed to decline and darkness, Israel was carried into Babylonian captivity. Thus the light of Israel was darkened like the moon during the new moon.

The seven feasts of Israel were all centered upon the cycles of the moon. In fact, the Hebrew word for "month" is *chodesh*, the same word used for "moon." The new month is called *Rosh Chodesh*, or "the head of the month." In ancient times the months were determined when the tiny silver sliver of the moon was spotted by two witnesses and confirmed in Jerusalem when the two witnesses reported their sighting to the Sanhedrin, who immediately informed the high priest. The high priest then sanctified the beginning of the month. The first feast of Israel was Passover, which was celebrated on the fourteenth day of the first month. The days were numbered from the moment the sliver of the moon was seen to reappear in the dark night. Thus, the Passover occurred on a full moon. About fifty days later was the Feast of Pentecost.

The final feast of Israel, the Feast of Tabernacles, began on the fifteenth day of the seventh month. The fifteenth day was when the moon was again full. There is one feast whose feast day could only be determined at the time of the new moon. That was the Feast of Trumpets, called *Rosh Hashanah*, which means "the head of the year." Today, Rosh Hashanah is the first day of the secular Jewish New Year. In ancient times this feast day began the first day of the seventh month. However, the first day was the beginning of the month and could not be determined until the end of the new moon and the reappearing of the moon in the sky.

> Blow the trumpet at the time of the New Moon,
> At the full moon, on our solemn feast day.
> For this is a statute for Israel,
> A law of the God of Jacob.
> —PSALM 81:3–4

It is interesting that God established a new moon offering. The phrase "new moon" is mentioned nine times in the Old Testament and is also alluded to by Paul:

> So let no one judge you in food or in drink, or regarding a festival or a new moon or sabbaths, which are a shadow of things to come, but the substance is of Christ.
> —COLOSSIANS 2:16–17

In Ezra 3:5, the Hebrew priests presented continual burnt offerings, both for the new moons and for all the set feasts of the Lord that were consecrated. The new moon offering included a bull, a ram, and a lamb, along with a drink offering of wine as a monthly burnt offering at each new moon during the year (Num. 28:14). Based on two scriptures, Amos 8:4–5 and 1 Samuel 20:5–25, individuals were not permitted to sell on the new moon or on the Sabbath, and there were certain meals to be eaten during the new moon. The period of the new moon lasted about two days, during which the night had no reflection from the moon.

Many of Israel's main feasts would fall on the full moon, or near the middle of the month. This included the three spring Feasts: Passover (the fourteenth of Nissan), Unleavened Bread (the fifteenth of Nissan), and Firstfruits (the sixteenth of Nissan). The Feast of Tabernacles began on the fifteenth of Tishrei, which was the full moon. The new moon was the beginning of the month for the Hebrew nation, a time of importance in the monthly cycle.

Moonstruck

In the time of Christ, a person who was experiencing epilepsy was called *moonstruck*, as the symptoms and manifestations were the greatest during the time of the full moon. In the Gospel of Matthew we read where a father came to Christ on behalf of his son and said:

> Lord, have mercy on my son, for he is lunatick, and sore vexed: for ofttimes he falleth into the fire, and oft into the water.
>
> —MATTHEW 17:15, KJV

The name of this disease came from the Latin name of the moon, *Luna*. It has the same origin in the Greek, the language of the New Testament. The belief was that the person suffering from seizures was affected more or less by the increase or decrease of the light of the moon.[5] The father said that often the spirit within his son would throw him into the fire or the water. It was apparent that this young man's life was in danger, as deep water could cause him to drown and fire would burn him. Christ revealed that the son was under the control of a spirit. When the lad was set free from this demonic power, he was cured.

The New Moon and the Spirit World

The spiritual principle is clear—evil men love spiritual darkness, and righteous men love spiritual light. When darkness covers the earth, the world of sinners comes alive. Of course, people who are working jobs during the day are unable to sin as much during work hours. However, drug addiction, prostitution, alcohol consumption, partying, and crime all occur during the night. As it is written, "Men loved darkness rather than light, because their deeds were evil" (John 3:19).

In the ancient world the beginning of the day was at six in the morning, and the conclusion of the day was at six in the evening, or a period of twelve hours. After sunset the moon could be seen, and from six in the evening to six in the morning the light of the moon was present. The sun was the greater light, and the moon was the lesser light (Gen. 1:16). During the night, when the faint light of the moon is glowing in the darkness, there is just enough light to see something close in front of you. However, when the moon is hidden during a new moon cycle, there is complete darkness.

The new moon cycle does appear to be a time when there is some sort of spirit activity taking place, as God required a sacrifice during the new moon. The sacrifice on the altar was for setting apart the new month. However, in the Old Testament, certain offerings also served as protective hedges against spiritual attacks.

Blood in the Morning and the Evening

Most people begin their day about six in the morning (if they live in an average community). The average arrival time home from work is between five thirty or six in the evening. This means that from our rising up to our sitting down is about twelve hours, the same timeframe that Jesus called a day.

After entering our homes, we will spend about twelve hours, which includes dinner, relaxing, some prayer time, and sleeping, until we wake up at six in the morning and repeat the cycle. The two most important moments occur when we begin our day and when we conclude our day.

Our entire workday can be ruined with a bad report, an argument, or a negative event. Our sleep in the evening can also be disrupted with conflict, stress, strife, and confusion. If you had lived in the time of the tabernacle or temple, you would have known that God required the priest to offer a sacrificial lamb in the morning and another lamb in the evening.

I have used this spiritual principle of the beginning and ending of a day in the following manner. When beginning my day, I confess in prayer my need for God's protection over my family and myself. I can recall my own father praying over his children in this manner, saying:

Father, keep them from harm, danger, and disabling accidents.
I approach the heavenly throne through the blood of Christ and

ask for protection in Christ's name through the authority that is in the blood of Christ.

If the blood of a simple, pet lamb in Egypt could keep the death angel out of the homes of the Hebrew people, how much more can the blood of Christ restrain the influences and selective attacks against our own family!

Chapter 14

TAPPING INTO THE SPIRIT WORLD

No temptation has overtaken you except such as is common to man; but God is faithful, who will not allow you to be tempted beyond what you are able, but with the temptation will also make the way of escape, that you may be able to bear it.

| 1 CORINTHIANS 10:13 |

I T WAS A chilly November night in 1988 when I was welcomed into the personal office of a chief Jewish rabbi near the famed Western Wall in Jerusalem. While there, I received an unexpected answer to a question I had carried in my mind for over twelve years. My discussion with the rabbi led to a conversation where I asked him why each night about midnight he came to his office to pray until the sun rose each morning.

He explained to me about a Jewish mystical belief that God's presence visits the earth in a unique manner each morning about two hours before sunrise. Those who were up and praying at that time would receive a divine inspiration, strength, revelation, or would sense the presence of the Almighty in their midst. Needless to say, this was a new theory for me, but afterward I began to research some interesting passages from the New Testament and saw a correlation to what the older rabbi believed.

During many years of ministry I observed that it was common for me to awake at exactly three o'clock in the morning. During my evangelistic travels, on a consistent basis I would awaken and look at the digital clock on the dresser to see the time—exactly 3:00 a.m. Not 2:59 or 3:01, but exactly 3:00 a.m. I would share this information with other believers and discovered that they too were having the same experience. At times

I would minister on early-morning intercession and was amazed when I would ask a large congregation of believers, "How many of you often wake up at three o'clock in the morning?" At times, up to 90 percent of the congregation would raise their hands, affirming the same experience I had for many years.

Those who study the question of why so many people awake at three in the morning have their own theories, such as it is the caffeine in our drinks or noises we are hearing subconsciously that awaken us each night. Others suggest that our energy levels are lowest at this time, and our awakening is caused by a surge of the hormone cortisol a few hours early.

A Chinese interpretation points to the *Horary Energy Cycle*. In Chinese medicine, the body is believed to go through a twenty-four-hour energy cycle where each energy center peaks during a particular period of time. If someone consistently wakes up at 3:00 a.m., then there may be a problem with the liver (1:00–3:00 a.m.) or lung (3:00–5:00 a.m.) meridian and the corresponding organs.[1]

I began to research the Scriptures to see if there was a biblical precedent related to a 3:00 a.m. experience. I discovered that in the time of the Romans, which was the time of Christ, the Jews divided the day into two halves—twelve hours and twelve hours. The Jewish day began at six in the morning and concluded at six in the evening. This is why Jesus answered, "Are there not twelve hours in the day?" (John 11:9). This division is based upon the Creation story, where we read how God divided each of the six creative days by saying, "So the evening and the morning were the first day" (Gen. 1:5).

However, the Romans divided the time of the day into four watches:

1. From six in the evening to nine at night was the first watch.
2. From nine at night to midnight was the second watch.
3. From midnight to three in the morning was the third watch.
4. From three in the morning to six in the morning was the fourth watch.

In the Scriptures we read where Christ said that His second coming could be during any of these watches, and we should remain alert to His sudden and unexpected arrival:

> Blessed are those servants whom the master, when he comes, will find watching. Assuredly, I say to you that he will gird himself and have them sit down to eat, and will come and serve them. And if he should come in the second watch, or come in the third watch, and find them so, blessed are those servants. But know this, that if the master of the house had known what hour the thief would come, he would have watched and not allowed his house to be broken into. Therefore you also be ready, for the Son of Man is coming at an hour you do not expect.
>
> —LUKE 12:37–40

The Fourth Watch

After understanding the various watches during the Romans' time, I noticed a phrase in a passage I had read hundreds of times. Now, however, it took on a new meaning:

> And when He had sent the multitudes away, He went up on the mountain by Himself to pray. Now when evening came, He was alone there. But the boat was now in the middle of the sea, tossed by the waves, for the wind was contrary. Now in the fourth watch of the night Jesus went to them, walking on the sea. And when the disciples saw Him walking on the sea, they were troubled, saying, "It is a ghost!" And they cried out for fear.
>
> —MATTHEW 14:23–26

This event occurred at the Sea of Galilee, a beautiful lake where even today fishermen earn their living netting and selling fish to local restaurants. Large mountains surround this lake, and the view from the top of the mountains is breathtaking. The Bible teaches that Christ often arose a great while before day to pray and, on one occasion, led Peter, James, and John to a high mountain (Matt. 17:1).

> And in the morning, rising up a great while before day, he went out, and departed into a solitary place, and there prayed.
>
> —MARK 1:35, KJV

> And when he had sent the multitudes away, he went up into a mountain apart to pray: and when the evening was come, he was there alone.
>
> —MATTHEW 14:23, KJV

> And it came to pass in those days, that he went out into a mountain to pray, and continued all night in prayer to God.
>
> —LUKE 6:12, KJV

Mark tells us that He prayed "in the morning," while Matthew says, "when the evening was come," and Luke adds He "continued all night in prayer." Thus we discover that Christ understood something about late night and early morning intercession and prayer. The real nugget, however, is seen in Matthew 14:23–26, where we read that He had been praying during the "fourth watch" when He walked on water to the disciples.

The fourth watch began at three in the morning! There is a practical reason the disciples were in a boat at such an early time; several disciples, including Peter, had a lucrative fishing business when Christ called them into full-time ministry (Luke 5:3–7). Fishermen who fish the Sea of Galilee do so several hours before the sun rises, and some fish all night long. Peter revealed this when he said, "We have toiled all night and caught nothing" (v. 5). The reason for night fishing is because the fish will come closer to the surface at night and cannot see the nets spread out by the fishermen.

Thus, in Christ's time, most fishermen were already up and fishing at the beginning of the fourth watch. This was when Christ would spend hours in prayer. After discovering this, I wondered if Christ knew something about the fourth watch, or three o'clock in the morning, that we are unaware of today. Was there something special or uniquely supernatural about this time period that provided the best opportunity to pray, and if so, why?

A Revelation From a Jewish Rabbi

In November 1998 this was the question I asked a rabbi, named Zvi, while visiting late at night in the office of former Israeli rabbi Yehuda Getz. I asked the rabbi why he and Getz would come to the Western Wall area so late at night and remain awake until near sunrise, studying and praying. The rabbi explained to me a mystical belief that God visited the earth several hours before sunrise.

He told me of a strong Jewish tradition stating that several hours before the sun rises, God restrains the presence of evil and visits the earth with His divine presence. The timeframe begins about three in the morning and continues until just before sunrise. In the days of the temple, the time of the morning Tamid offering ranged from 3:45 a.m. to about 5:00 a.m., which was before sunrise and during the fourth watch of the night.[2]

Upon hearing this, I began to realize that moving throughout the world there are demonic spirits called "rulers of the darkness of this age" (Eph. 6:12). Most evil acts, including robberies, murders, prostitution, and other dark vices, occur during the night. The darkness serves as a covering to hide the particular evil being preformed. I also was aware that most parties, inner-city prostitution, drinking, and drug abuse peak just prior to three in the morning. Thus many people are asleep or off the streets prior to three in the morning. Could this be one reason why evil appears to be restrained or limited—since spirits work through people, and most of the people performing the evil acts are winding down and off the streets by then?

I also recalled what I had heard from numerous nurses. It is a known fact that three in the morning is a pivotal time for anyone who is sick or in a critical condition. One of my ministry partners from Virginia, Ellen Kanode, directs several hospitals in Virginia. She has confirmed to me that three in the morning is often the timeframe when a person will begin to experience a recovery or face death. It has remained a mystery as to why, but even fevers tend to break after three in the morning.

The third interesting concept involves Jacob wrestling with an angel, recorded in Genesis 32. We read that he wrestled a man, but it is clear this man was an angel of the Lord. We read:

> And Jacob was left alone; and there wrestled a man with him until the breaking of the day.
> —GENESIS 32:24, KJV

Notice the phrase "breaking of the day." This refers to the rising of the sun, which is the conclusion of the fourth watch! The angel finally demanded, "'Let Me go, for the day breaks.' But he said, 'I will not let You go unless You bless me!'" (Gen. 32:26). Why was the angel concerned about ending the wrestling match prior to the sunrise? Why was he willing to wrestle with Jacob during the fourth watch but wanted to depart as the sunlight was inching its way over the eastern horizon?

The story of Lot and the two angels sheltered in his home also presents a point of interest. Two angels in the form of men entered Lot's house to warn Lot of destruction coming to his city. After the men of Sodom attempted to rip the door of Lot's home off its hinges to seduce the two men, the Sodomites were smitten with blindness by the two messengers of the Lord (Gen. 19:11). The angel instructed Lot to get out early in the morning prior to the sunrise. This may have been to sneak out of the city and not be seen by the violent men who could harm him and his family. By rising early and departing out of the plains toward a high mountain, Lot escaped the fiery judgment. We read:

> The sun was risen upon the earth when Lot entered into Zoar. Then the LORD rained upon Sodom and upon Gomorrah brimstone and fire from the LORD out of heaven.
> —GENESIS 19:23–24, KJV

Lot departed before the sun rose and entered the safe haven of Zoar as the sun was rising on the earth. We can deduct that he departed the city during the fourth watch, somewhere between three and six in the morning, because by 6:00 a.m. the sun would be rising, signaling the end of the fourth watch.

Tapping Into the Spirit World

Very early in my ministry I learned the uniqueness of the fourth watch, especially three in the morning and its link to the spirit world. I was called into the ministry at the age of sixteen, after an all-night prayer meeting with three older friends at a church my father pastored in Salem, Virginia. By age eighteen, I had a rather busy itinerary, preaching one to four weeks in extended revivals in rural communities throughout Virginia, West Virginia, and Maryland. I began spending long hours in prayer and often days in fasting, which was unique for a person my age. I knew I had the attention of the Lord, but soon I discovered I also had the attention of another world.

One night in July 1978, after preaching in Weynoke, West Virginia, I went to my room at 12:30 a.m., exhausted and wanting to rest. As I lay down, the room began closing in on me. I lay there praying and eventually went to sleep. The same strange sensation was repeated the following night. This time a strange presence entered the room. I eventually brushed it off.

Several weeks later I was ministering at my grandfather's church in Gorman, Maryland. My grandparents lived in the small community of Davis, West Virginia, located in the northeastern part of the state. Late one night I slipped into the bed and thought I had lain down on a bed of bugs. It felt as though hundreds of small insects were crawling over my legs. I recall flinging back the covers and turning on the light, only to discover the sheets were white and spotless. Turning off the light, I expected normality, only to experience the same strange physical sensation. The second time was enough! I jumped from the bed, grabbed the pillow, and slept on the couch downstairs. At first I reasoned that this was some strange phenomenon that would pass. I reasoned incorrectly.

The Dark Presence

Leaving West Virginia, I returned home to Salem, Virginia. I was soon entrenched in intensive Bible study, prayer, and fasting, often studying eight to fourteen hours a day. At the time, my bedroom was also my personal study, equipped with a simple desk, a chair, light stand, and seemingly endless stacks of books, notebooks, research helps, and Bibles. Late one night in July 1978, I turned off the light and fumbled my way through the dark to the lower bunk bed. Within a few moments, a very negative dark presence entered the room. This time it was so tangible I felt I could reach out and touch it. I began to rebuke the presence, saying, "I rebuke this presence in the name of the Lord Jesus Christ." In an instant, the presence lifted.

The following night, unexpectedly, the same manifestation occurred. After retiring for the night, this dark presence again hovered in the atmosphere. It was not in my psyche, but it was tangible. I noticed that the presence did not depart upon my rebuke. It seemed to linger until slowly it slipped into the darkness. I was uncertain of what this presence actually was. I had been a Christian since I was a child, and I had never encountered such a real, invisible presence. A mild feeling of fear would overtake me when this force was near. I knew I had spent ample time studying scriptures relating to the supernatural realm of evil spirits, but I had little knowledge in personally dealing with this dark presence that seemingly came and went at will. This led me into a very detailed, complex study of the spirit world. I thought arming myself with this information would automatically shield me from this invisible entity. Instead, these unnatural visitations accelerated.

Two months later, in September 1978, this presence took on a visible form. Late one morning I was awakened by a loud buzzing noise in my ears. I became aware of the strange sensation that I was unable to speak or physically move my body. Immediately, I heard deep male voices that were cursing me, using every form of profanity imaginable. This was not my imagination; it was very real. I had never read of such encounters and was unfamiliar with how to stop these intrusions. Unable to speak, my mind began to rebuke the evil powers. The rebuke worked. My body was loosed, and silence followed, although it was some time before exhaustion led into sleep. It became troubling to me that these manifestations and audible voices speaking into my ear continued several times a week.

The Manifestation of an Evil Spirit

These paranormal attacks become more common and frequent into the late fall months. They included the weird buzzing noises, the helpless sensation of being paralyzed, and audible voices mocking me, cursing the Bible, blaspheming Jesus Christ, and threatening me with physical harm. Let me emphasize: This was not my mind playing tricks or an overworked imagination. This was real, very real. Eventually the attacks took a new level. Late one November night, after ministering at the North Danville Church of God, this spirit became visible in an upstairs room where I was sleeping, waking me up. It was then I saw for the first time what I was dealing with. The presence was covered with a dark shroud, similar to a long, thick robe often seen worn by a Satanist or by witches. The face was dark, and a dark hood hung low over the face, covering the head and most of the face. This physical manifestation engulfed me in the worst kind of fear I had ever experienced. Although the presence left after a few seconds, the fear froze not just my body, but like a cold knife it cut into my very spirit, leaving me feeling like ice on the inside. I turned on a light and was unable to sleep.

I began to think these attacks were seasonal—that they would shortly pass. Again my reasoning was incorrect. These mental and spiritual invasions from another realm only increased in magnitude and intensity. Soon I would be awakened throughout the night. Often two and three times a weeks this tormenting force would manifest. Strange sounds, voices, footsteps, and physical manifestations became my unwelcomed and unwanted visitors.

Why Was This Happening to Me?

As these troubling attacks persisted, there were several things I knew for a fact:

- I knew I was called to preach, and no intimidation would change my mind.

211

- I knew I was living right and was spending time with the Lord.
- I knew that sooner or later, like Job, I'd get some explanation as to why this was happening.

Yet these three facts did not change the questions that began to haunt my mind and were not answered as the weeks turned into months:

- Why was this happening to me when no one else I knew was having these experiences?
- What could be the purpose for the Lord permitting this to continue on and on?
- Would this be an attack I would encounter on and off for the rest of my life?

The third question troubled me the most. I became deceived into thinking that these demonic manifestations would be something I would encounter the remaining days of my life and ministry. I began to believe this was my thorn in the flesh (2 Cor. 12:7) and that the Lord was going to allow this spirit to follow me for some unknown reason the rest of my ministry. Paul had written that a messenger of Satan had been given to him to buffet him. I was not Paul, but I assumed that if a messenger (angel) of the enemy was attacking Paul, then why should I be any different? If fact, I began to expect these attacks on a consistent basis. *Needless to say, if you expect the enemy in your house, he will gladly accommodate your expectations!*

A Possible Explanation

I recall going to my father, a seasoned man of God, and explaining what I was encountering. He discerned it was a supernatural attack and an assignment from a demonic power. He felt I was fasting and praying and the Lord was opening my eyes into the spirit world. The adversary was attempting to stop something God was planning in my life. This still did not answer my questions: *What is the purpose? What am I supposed to learn from this?*

Five months after the initial attack, I was ministering in Blacksburg, Virginia, for Pastor Jim Angle. Jim was a unique man of God whose ministry focused on deliverance and healing. After detailing the events, Jim looked at me and said, "Perry, the Lord has been boasting about your dedication as a young man to Him in the same way God bragged on Job in the Book of Job, chapter 1. Satan has said to the Lord, 'Let me test Perry, and he will give up and fail you.' That is what is going on. You are being tested for a season."

Jim's observation put steel in my back and set my face as a flint to endure and eventually overcome these intrusions. I knew the Bible taught spiritual authority over all the powers of the enemy and revealed that when Jesus rebuked Satan, the enemy departed from Him (Luke 4:13). I was fully aware of the scriptures that promised spiritual power. Yet I also knew, according to the Book of Job, that there are seasons when God allows a person to be tested. Could the enemy frighten me away from fasting and praying for long seasons? Would I back away from preaching on defeating the enemy and victory in spiritual warfare? Was this a form of spiritual intimidation to make me say, "I don't want to have a global ministry if I have to deal with these tormenting spirits?"

The Roar of the Lion

I once heard Dr. E. L. Terry explain that the roar of a lion can be heard up to five miles away. He noted that the roar of a lion can actually paralyze some animals with fear. There literally are small creatures that cannot move when they hear the roar of a lion, because the sound is so intimidating. In much the same way, these manifestations and strange voices were impacting me; I was paralyzed with fear.

> Be sober, be vigilant; because your adversary the devil walks about like a roaring lion, seeking whom he may devour.
> —1 PETER 5:8

I was ignorant of this new strategy, and the enemy was gaining an advantage, literally wearing me down mentally and physically. The enemy will gain the advantage of us if we remain ignorant of his devices and strategies (2 Cor. 2:11). One day I came across one verse of Scripture that I seized upon and thrust into my spirit. It became my rope to hold on to:

> No temptation has overtaken you except such as is common to man; but God is faithful, who will not allow you to be tempted beyond what you are able, but with the temptation will also make the way of escape, that you may be able to bear it.
>
> —1 Corinthians 10:13

Deep inside I knew these tormenting manifestations could not last forever. God would make a way of escape (1 Cor. 10:13). For six consecutive months, from July to December 31 of 1978, I lived a life of mental torment, while at the same time I was seeing great revivals in local churches throughout the East Coast.

The Night the Lord Came Into the Room

After several months I found myself dreading the night. I often slept with a nightlight on or played gospel music on a stereo until I could fall asleep. Finally the holiday season was in full swing, and Mom's relatives were staying with us in Salem, Virginia. My brother and I were sleeping downstairs in my room. Our beds were opposite each other. On December 31, 1978, I recall praying and asking the Lord to not allow even one demonic spirit to manifest, beginning on the first day of the new year. *A new year was coming, and I was expecting a new anointing and a fresh touch of the Lord.*

Shortly after midnight, I lay down to rest in peace for the first time in weeks. I was abruptly awakened by a hand, almost violently jerking my right leg as if attempting to pull me out of the bed! I assumed my brother, Phillip, was pulling a prank on me. As I sat up, I could see the nightlight and the digital clock, which read 3:00 a.m. Turning to the right, I saw the outline of my brother lying in his bed.

Then something happened that is difficult to explain. Within three feet from my face I saw the face of a handsome man. His features were perfect, and his eyes were full of compassion. I thought an angel of the Lord had entered the room. Suddenly, the face became contorted, twisted with an evil stare followed by hollow demonic laughter. This angel of light was no angel of God! It was the visible face of a fierce evil spirit that was literally laughing at me.

> And no wonder! For Satan himself transforms himself into an angel of light.
> —2 CORINTHIANS 11:14

At that moment something broke forth inside of me. Instead of panicking or wanting to hide under the covers, I began to scream out of my spirit (not with my mind this time, but deep within my inner-most being): *"No! You will no longer torment me. I have had enough! No more!"* My inner man was rising up against this force. I realized later that it was the Holy Spirit within me rising up. As the Bible says, "Let God arise, let His enemies be scattered" (Ps. 68:1).

At that instant I heard a voice. The voice was from within but yet was audible to my spiritual ears. The Holy Spirit spoke to my spirit, saying, *"Son, as long as you live, Satan will use what you see and what you hear against you. It is time that you stand on the only thing that can never be shaken or changed; stand upon My Word!"* Instantly the shaking ceased, and the image of this face of wickedness evaporated into thin air. A surge of peace and fresh anointing filled my spirit. I felt as though a huge weight had been lifted. The atmosphere cleared, and peace flooded the room. That was on January 1, 1979, and according to my clock, it was exactly three o'clock in the morning! Those particular series of attacks have never repeated themselves. Other spiritual battles would arise on my journey, but those demonic manifestations ceased following the revelation from the Holy Spirit instructing me to depend solely on the Word of God and not lean upon my emotions and feelings to fight my battles.

The Lessons I Learned

When the Holy Spirit said, "Satan will use what you see and what you hear against you," I was reminded of Peter, who stepped out of the boat and walked on the water toward Jesus. What held Peter up? The answer: the Word. Jesus said one word to Peter: "Come" (Matt. 14:29).

That one word held up a possibly two-hundred-pound Hebrew! Peter began observing the strong winds and noticed the waves were getting higher. When he lost confidence in the Word, he began to sink.

After this word from the Lord, I realized I had been moved by what I felt and saw. If the attendance in my revivals was good, I expected a great revival; but if the crowds were small, I anticipated little. If I felt physically good, I could minister effectively; but if I felt depressed or tired, then I was hindered. In short, I was being moved by what I felt, saw, and heard. It would be months later that a statement by Smith Wigglesworth would sum up the lesson the Holy Spirit taught me. Smith once said, *"I am not moved by what I see. I am not moved by what I feel. I am moved by what I believe!"* The Lord knew I could never experience the level of growth He desired for me, both personally and in ministry, if I was always being moved by what I felt or didn't feel, or by what I saw or didn't see. God wanted me to rely upon the power of His Word! This is why I would often spend four to ten or fifteen hours a day studying the Word.

In the Bible Jesus was moved with compassion but never by circumstances (Matt. 9:36). If there was a lack of food, He multiplied a boy's lunch and fed a multitude (Matt. 15:34–38). Death did not intimidate him; Christ ruined funerals by raising the corpse from the dead (Luke 7:11–15).

The second great lesson I learned is that God will be faithful to deliver you if you will be faithful to believe Him. It may not come in the manner or time you are expecting, but faith and patience will birth the blessings.

> That you do not become sluggish, but imitate those who through faith and patience inherit the promises.
>
> —HEBREWS 6:12

Through the experience I discovered:

1. *God is not moved by your feelings but by your faith.*

> But without faith it is impossible to please Him, for he who comes
> to God must believe that He is, and that He is a rewarder of those
> who diligently seek Him.
> —HEBREWS 11:6

Christ is touched by the feelings of our infirmities, but He responds to
our prayers of faith. He is moved by compassion when we are suffering
or in need because He also suffered in the flesh. Yet in every miracle
of the New Testament, it was faith that released the power of God to
minister to those in need.

2. *God is not moved by your circumstances but by His Word.*

> Then the LORD said to me, "You have seen well, for I am ready to
> perform My word."
> —JEREMIAH 1:12

We often believe God must come on the scene and help us because the
circumstances are killing us! God is only obligated to His covenant (His
Word), and He is attracted to anyone who knows, quotes, and believes
the words of the covenant! In the Old Testament, men like Moses would
remind God of His covenant with Abraham, Isaac, and Jacob, thus
causing God to turn around difficult situations because of His covenant
with the Hebrew nation through Abraham.

3. *God will deliver you from the attack if you will remain steadfast.*

> No temptation has overtaken you except such as is common to man;
> but God is faithful, who will not allow you to be tempted beyond
> what you are able, but with the temptation will also make the way
> of escape, that you may be able to bear it.
> —1 CORINTHIANS 10:13

The apostle Paul spoke of being delivered from the mouth of the lion:

> But the Lord stood with me and strengthened me, so that the message
> might be preached fully through me, and that all the Gentiles might

hear. And I was delivered out of the mouth of the lion. And the Lord will deliver me from every evil work and preserve me for His heavenly kingdom. To Him be glory forever and ever. Amen!

—2 TIMOTHY 4:17–18

God may make a way of escape by bringing a person into your life who can assist you. God can also change the situation abruptly, thus bringing you out of your difficulty. Angels can assist in your deliverance. Many examples can be given of how God will make a way where there is no way.

This experience and others that would follow gave me valuable understanding of how the adversary operates. This experience would become a teaching tool I would share across the nation in order to help believers through their own supernatural conflicts.

There have been several occasions when I was in seasons of prayer, fasting, and intercession, or engaged in some form of spiritual battle, that I would also experience demonic presence or, on rare occasions, see and hear demonic apparitions very close to the time of three in the morning.

Three O'Clock to Six O'Clock in the Morning—at the Temple

In the days of the temple in Jerusalem, there was much activity that would occur at night. An admonition is written:

> To declare Your lovingkindness in the morning,
> And Your faithfulness every night,
> On an instrument of ten strings,
> On the lute,
> And on the harp,
> With harmonious sound.

—PSALM 92:2–3

Later in Psalms we read of an admonition to those who by night stand in the house of the Lord to lift up their hands and bless the Lord (Ps. 134:1–2). In Solomon's temple, special priests (Levites) were appointed as singers during the night services (1 Chron. 9:33; 23:30).

The night watches were very important in the days of temple. One priest was in charge, called, in the New Testament, the *captain of the temple* (Acts 4:1) and identified in Judaism as the *man of the Temple Mount*. The night guards were positioned in twenty-four stations about the courts and gates of the temple. Out of these twenty-four guard positions, twenty-one were required to be filled only by Levites.[3] Throughout the night the captain of the house would make his rounds to see that all watchmen were at their stations and fully awake. Each priest was to give a special greeting, and any priest caught sleeping had his clothes removed and burned, a process that is also alluded to in Revelation 16:15 in a warning to believers who would be caught sleeping.

There were certain rituals that were very important that priests performed in the temple prior to the arrival of the multitudes and before sunrise. The first assignment before the break of day was the need for the priests to remove the ashes from the brass altar, the remains of the previous day's sacrifices. These ashes were collected, removed in a special container, and dumped outside the East Gate into the Kidron Valley, where it was believed the water of the Kidron washed the ashes away and eventually into the Dead Sea. At the same time, the brass laver was filled with fresh water, and following the removal of the ashes, new wood was laid on the altar to prepare a new fire for the day.

Included in this early morning procedure was the need to refill the seven-branched menorah with fresh olive oil and to replace the wicks in each candle. Each of the seven golden branches held up to six eggs (a way of measuring in that time) of pure, first pressing olive oil. The priest would keep the western branch, which faced the holy of holies, burning while replacing the five wicks and refilling the five golden lamps with oil. After the five were cleaned and refilled, the western branch was later cleaned and refilled, giving the menorah enough light for about twelve hours.

The next important process was the offering of the prayers on the golden altar. This altar was situated in front of the veil that separated the sacred inner court from the holy of holies. According to the Temple Institute in Jerusalem, there were eleven different types of spices that were compounded together to form the holy incense used on the golden altar. One of the first rituals was for the high priest to conduct a lottery with other priests and select the one priest who would bring the hot coals from the brass altar into the inner chamber and lay two fistfuls of incense on the burning coals, thus offering the incense and the prayers of the people up before God (Ps. 141:2). Luke 1 records how Zacharias, the father of John the Baptist, was selected to offer the incense, and Gabriel appeared beside the golden altar to announce that Zacharias's wife would have a son named John (Luke 1:8–13).

The first lamb offered in the morning was prepared right at the time that the red glow of the sunrise could be seen over the mountains in Hebron. As a priest announced the rising of the sun, the morning sacrifice of the lamb would begin.

The process of removing the ashes, relighting the menorah, offering the incense, and placing the lamb's blood on the altar, all have a unique spiritual application for us. First, these procedures began before sunrise, which would be during the fourth watch—the same time that Christ was praying on the mountains in Galilee—and continued until the third hour, which was nine o'clock in the morning. These rituals reveal the need for a believer to spiritually prepare for each day.

Removing the ashes—get the clutter out of your mind

Each day there is clutter that enters our minds. We are bombarded with news, information, and darts from the enemy that leave unclean thoughts or attitudes within us. This negative dust must be removed in the morning by the washing of the water of the Word and the renewing of the mind. If the Lord is the first thing on your mind in the morning, your day will go far better. These ashes are removed by prayer and asking the Lord to cleanse the mind. I have always used good gospel music, including praise and worship, to create a clean atmosphere in and around me each day.

Relighting the menorah—receive a fresh anointing

Oil is symbolic for the Holy Spirit, and the seven-branched golden candlestick is the imagery of the seven manifestations of the Holy Spirit Himself, recorded in Isaiah 11:1–3:

1. The Spirit of the Lord
2. The Spirit of wisdom
3. The Spirit of knowledge
4. The Spirit of understanding
5. The Spirit of counsel
6. The Spirit of might
7. The Spirit of the fear of the Lord

The anointing of the Holy Spirit is a manifestation of the divine presence of God, which is given to a Spirit-filled believer for the purpose of intercession, bringing prayer and deliverance to others, and bringing inspiration in a believer's life. The anointing breaks bondages (Isa. 10:27), ministers healing (Acts 10:38), and brings understanding in spiritual truth (1 John 2:27).

As a teenager, David was anointed on three occasions:

1. As the king to replace Saul (1 Sam. 16:13)
2. To be king of Judah (2 Sam. 2:4)
3. As king of Israel (2 Sam. 5:3)

Yet David was continually at war and confessed, "And I am weak today, though anointed king" (2 Sam. 3:39). Christ was anointed, yet He encountered Satan for forty days of testing (Matt. 3:16–17; 4:1–10). The anointing does not exempt a person from weakness, attack, or even discouragement. A person must receive a renewal and refreshing of the Spirit in his or her life to maintain strength and determination.

The disciples were all filed with the Holy Spirit at the Feast of Pentecost (Acts 2:1–4). In Acts 3, a lame man was healed, and the disciples were called on the carpet before the temple leaders and told not to preach in

Jesus's name. Following a great conflict with the Jewish religious leaders in Jerusalem, the believers conducted a massive prayer meeting and were all filled with the Holy Spirit (Acts 4:31). That occasion included some of the same disciples who earlier received the Spirit at Pentecost many weeks earlier. Yet they all needed a refilling of the Spirit.

This concept of a continual refilling is seen in the need to relight and refill the menorah each morning. The infilling of the Spirit is an experience that each believer recognizes when it occurs (Acts 2:1–4; 10:45; 19:1–8), but it is also a continual process, as revealed in Paul's words:

> And do not get drunk with wine, for that is debauchery; but ever be filled and stimulated with the [Holy] Spirit.
>
> —EPHESIANS 5:18, AMP

Offering the incense—praying every morning to begin your day

Many believers pray only over a meal, when lying in the bed before snoozing off, or at Sunday services when the minister leads the congregation in prayer. Many Orthodox Jews in Israel pray at the Western Wall daily, and Muslims are required to pray five times each day. Dedicated Muslims will stop their activities, even in business, pull out a prayer rug, and face Mecca in Saudi Arabia. The sad fact is that many Christians are not as dedicated to prayer as are those in other religions.

The golden altar in the tabernacle and temple was used for one purpose: to offer special incense before God. The tradition was that as the incense mixed with the coals of fire, the words of God's people would mingle with the holy smoke. As the smoke ascended, the words were rising up into the heavenly temple where the Almighty dwelt. This points out the necessity for every believer to begin his or her day with prayer.

In the days of the temple the most difficult watch was often the fourth watch. Priests served in twelve-hour shifts. We work an average of eight hours a day, from 8:00 a.m. to 5:00 p.m., with a lunch break. The priests, however, served in a morning or evening shift—twelve hours per shift. If a priest came to the temple at six in the evening, he concluded his shift at six in the morning. The most difficult time to remain awake was at the fourth watch, from three to six in the morning. Christ warned us to watch and pray.

- Watch and pray to keep from entering into temptation (Matt. 26:41).
- Watch and pray so as to not be surprised at His coming (Mark 13:33).
- Watch and stay awake and alert (Mark 13:37).

When Christ was entering the Garden of Gethsemane to intercede for three hours, He invited His inner circle—Peter, James, and John—to join Him, instructing them to watch and pray. Although the Romans had four watches, the Jews divided the night into three watches—from six to ten, eleven to two, and three to six in the morning. Christ's common prayer time was at night or early morning. In the same garden, Nicodemus, a member of the Jewish Sanhedrin, came by night to meet Jesus (John 3:1–2).

There may be numerous reasons, some known and others unknown, as to why early-morning prayer is the pattern we see in Christ's life and ministry. The simple reason may be that there is little human activity during this time. This solace and quiet of early-morning meditation in the Word and prayer are apparent for those who have arisen a great while before day to spend time before the Lord. While it may be dark in one part of the world, it is light in another. The fact is that while others sleep and you are praying, you have the full attention of the spiritual powers assigned to bring answers to your prayers!

Conclusion

BUILDING A GODLY LEGACY

THE GREATEST TRUTH I have discovered after more than thirty-four years of ministry is that God uses people—not just certain types of people, but *just plain folks*, common people. Noah was a father before he was a shipbuilder. Abraham was a businessman before he became the father of a nation. David was a shepherd before becoming king. Nehemiah was a cupbearer before he became the construction manager for the temple.

The Legacy of Billy Graham

The influence of a common person can be seen when we trace back the men who have influenced great men in the past. The world recognizes the name *Billy Graham*. Graham attended one year of Bible school in Cleveland, Tennessee, in 1936, at Bob Jones College. Graham was converted to Christ in 1934 after attending a revival where a minister named Mordecai Ham was preaching a twelve-week revival.

Ham was converted to Christ at age eight and was influenced to follow the Lord in ministry during a 1924 gospel meeting occurring in Charlotte, North Carolina. The famous former-baseball-player-turned-preacher, Billy Sunday, had a Laymen's Evangelistic Club that Ham participated in. Billy Sunday influenced Ham, but who was instrumental in influencing Billy Sunday?

Billy Sunday was a well-known baseball player and was won to Christ during a gospel street meeting. After his conversion, Sunday began to work with the Pacific Garden Mission in Chicago and assisted in setting up meetings and working alongside of a great minister named J. W. Chapman. Through organizing the meetings and with Chapman's influence, Billy himself was called into the ministry and became a great soulwinner.

J. W. Chapman has his own testimony. In the late 1870s Chapman was attending Lake Forest College and eventually attended a gospel crusade in Chicago being conducted by the famous Dwight (D. L.) Moody. One day after Moody spoke, Chapman asked for a meeting with Moody, where he sought certainty of salvation and received it as Moody was speaking with him.

Now we come to D. L. Moody. Who won D. L. Moody to the Lord? It was a man named Edward Kimball. Edward was a Sunday school teacher who was quite timid. He was teaching Sunday school with students from Harvard. There was one young man who attended the class for one year. He was eighteen years of age and just off the farm. His name was Dwight. At that time Dwight worked in a shoe store. One day Kimball felt impressed to go into the store and witness directly to Dwight while he was wrapping shoes. This led to a solid conversion experience for Dwight, who later went to Chicago to become a salesman. Later he taught Sunday school and eventually entered full-time ministry. Moody was recognized as the greatest evangelist of the nineteenth century.

Thus we can trace the responsibility for the ministry of Billy Graham back to a common, rather timid man named Edward Kimball. Kimball never saw or met Billy Graham, but when all men stand before the judgment seat of Christ to receive rewards, a special crown will be placed upon Kimball's head. Without his obedience, Moody may have never been converted, thus preventing Chapman from finding his destiny of influencing Billy Sunday, who would have never impacted Ham, who may have never entered the ministry and preached the night Billy Graham was saved!

Your battles are not always about you; often they are about the future of your seed or of someone you may influence for the kingdom.

When we think of noted ministers such as D. L. Moody, Billy Sunday, or Billy Graham, we are seldom informed that the *root* of this ministry tree began with a sincere, unrecognized Sunday school teacher named

Edward Kimball. From his one act of obedience came several generations of preachers and millions of souls into the kingdom of God.

You may not feel fortunate or as *blessed* as someone who has a generational lineage of godly believers, and at times you may feel as though you were left out of the *generation favor club*, as you may have a family tree that is a combination of a weeping willow, a bramble, and a few dead branches. In reviewing your past and looking at the old photos in your home albums, you see the family at the clubs and the drinking parties, and you happen to be one of the first on your tree and in your house to have entered into a redemptive covenant through Christ. Don't feel left out! YOU can initiate a new beginning and purge the old and initiate the new—removing the weights and sins from the past and running a race, passing on your faith to your children and grandchildren!

When I was a child, about age four, I took one small apple seed and planted it near our tiny home in Big Stone Gap, Virginia. Years passed, and a tree grew and produced apples. We moved from there in the late 1960s, and I never saw that tree again—until the late 1990s. I went back to check out where we lived and discovered that the old red brick church where Dad pastored had burnt to the ground, along with the white cinder-block parsonage we grew up in. It was rather disappointing. However, there was that large tree I had planted more than thirty-six years prior that was still producing fruit. I was amazed.

Here is the lesson. The good seed of God's Word that dwells in you and that you are continually planting into the hearts and minds of your own family will outlive you, long after your physical house (your body) has ceased from the earth and has returned to the dust. If you are blessed with a Christian family, continue to produce good fruit in your lives. If you are beginning a family, plant the good seed and expect a good harvest. You can initiate the beginning of a family tree that will one day be marked with a generational legacy in the same manner that the wonderful Billy Graham family has been blessed. The soil is your heart, the seed is the Word of God, and the water is the Holy Spirit. The sunlight is the illumination you receive in God's presence. Plant well, my friend. The fruit of your produce may one day change the world!

Notes

Introduction

1. The information about the family of Jonathan Edwards is adapted from A. E. Winship, *Jukes-Edwards: A Study in Education and Heredity* (Harrisburg, PA: R. L. Myers & Co., 1900), now available through Project Gutenberg, E-Book #15623, released April 14, 2005, http://infomotions.com/etexts/gutenberg/dirs/1/5/6/2/15623/15623.htm (accessed April 12, 2010).

2. Bob Proctor, *You Were Born Rich* (n.p.: Life Success Pacific Rim, 2002), excerpt viewed at Self-Improvement-eBooks.com, "Me and Money," http://self-improvement-ebooks.com/books/YouWereBornRich.php (accessed August 23, 2010).

Chapter 2
Don't Bring Accursed Things Into Your Home

1. This story was told to me verbally by my personal friend and missionary Kelvin McDaniel.

2. National Right to Life, "Abortion in the United States: Statistics and Trends," http://www.nrlc.org/abortion/facts/abortionstats.html (accessed April 15, 2010).

3. W. E. Vine, *Vine's Expository Dictionary of New Testament Words* (Grand Rapids, MI: Fleming H. Revell, 1962).

4. Richard Evans Schultes and Albert Hoffman, "The Nectar of Delight," in *Plants of the Gods* (Vermont: Healing Arts Press, 1992), viewed at http://www.marijauna.org/thc/index.html (accessed April 15, 2010).

5. CADCA.org, "Emergency Room Visits Climb for Misuse of Prescription and Over-the-Counter Drugs," March 22, 2007, http://www.cadca.org/resources/detail/emergency-room-visits-climb-misuse-prescription-and-over-counter-drugs (accessed April 15, 2010).

6. Charles T. Tart, "Marijuana Intoxication: Common Experiences," http://www.paradigm-sys.com/ctt_articles2.cfm?id=44 (accessed April 15, 2010).

7. National Institute on Alcohol Abuse and Alcoholism, "Surgeon General Calls on Americans to Face Facts About Drinking," *NIH News*, April 1, 2004, http://www.niaaa.nih.gov/NewsEvents/NewsReleases/Screenday04.htm (accessed April 15, 2010).

8. Ibid.

9. National Institute on Alcohol Abuse and Alcoholism, "Young Adult Drinking," *Alcohol Alert*, April 2006, http://pubs.niaaa.nih.gov/publications/aa68/aa68.htm (accessed April 15, 2010).

10. National Drug and Alcohol Abuse Hotline, "Alcohol Statistics," http://www.drug-rehabs.org/alcohol-statistics.php (accessed April 15, 2010).

11. Ibid.

12. This information was given verbally to the author from an anonymous man in Union, South Carolina, where the author was ministering in a three-week revival. This gentleman, who will remain nameless, was a computer technician in a major computer firm.

13. Perry Stone, *Breaking the Jewish Code* (Lake Mary, FL: Charisma House, 2009), 146–147. Information about the Jewish traditions of the tefillin is adapted from "Getting Ready for the Bar-Mitzvah—The Tefillin (Phylacteries)," Jewish Celebrations, http://www.mazornet.com/jewishcl/Celebrations/mitzvah/Orthodox/Tefi llin.htm (accessed September 10, 2008).

Chapter 3
Stop the Plagues in Your Home

1. For more information about the excavations of Jericho, see BiblePlaces.com, "Jericho," http://www.bibleplaces.com/jericho.htm (accessed April 13, 2010).

2. Flavius Josephus, *Antiquities of the Jews*, book 5, chapter 2, http://www.biblestudytools.com/history/flavius-josephus/antiquities-jews/book-5/chapter-2.html (accessed August 26, 2010).

3. Vine, *Vine's Expository Dictionary of New Testament Words*, 702–704.

4. Ibid., 1171–1172.

Chapter 5
The Authority of the Blood of Christ

1. Harold L. Wilmington, *Wilmington's Guide to the Bible* (Wheaton, IL: Tyndale, 1981).

2. The Temple Institute, "Yom Kipper: The Miracle of the Crimson Wool," http://www.templeinstitute.org/yom_kippur/crimson_miracle.htm (accessed April 14, 2010).

Chapter 6
Prune Your Family Tree

1. Hugh Sidey, "The *Time* 100: The Kennedys," *Time*, June 14, 1999, http://205.188.238.181/time/time100/heroes/profile/kennedys01.html (accessed April 19, 2010).

2. Digital image from Sirhan Sirhan's diary, dated May 18, can be viewed at http://en.wikisource.org/wiki/Sirhan_Sirhan%27s_notebook (accessed April 19, 2010). Also, Frank Reynolds, "Sirhan Sirhan's Diary Contents Made Known, Despite Protest," *ABC Evening News*, February 25, 1969, referenced at Vanderbilt Television News Archive, http://tvnews.vanderbilt.edu/program.pl?ID=3982 (accessed August 27, 2010).

3. Edward Klein, *The Kennedy Curse* (New York: St. Martin's Press, 2004), 11.

4. This information on the children of the Kennedy sons can be found at "The Kennedys: A Family Tree," *St. Petersburg Times Online*, http://www.sptimes.com/News/111199/JFK/family-tree.shtml (accessed April 19, 2010).

5. Ronald Kessler, *The Sins of the Father* (New York: Warner Books, 1997).

6. Sidey, "The *Time* 100: The Kennedys."

7. Kessler, *The Sins of the Father*, 33.

8. Ibid., 34.

9. Ibid., 99.

10. Ibid., 104.

11. Ibid., 93.

12. Ibid., 149.

13. Josephus, *Antiquities of the Jews*, book 18, chapter 5, http://www.biblestudytools.com/history/flavius-josephus/antiquities-jews/book-18/chapter-5.html (accessed August 30, 2010).

14. Josephus, *Josephus: The Essential Writings*, Paul L. Meier, trans. (Grand Rapids, MI: Kregel Academic, 1990), 268.

15. Ibid., 272.

16. Pollinator Partnership, "What Is Pollination?" http://pollinator.org/pollination.htm (accessed April 22, 2010).

17. ToBuildAGarden.com, "How to Prune Grape Vines," http://www.tobuildagarden.com/growing-vines-groundcovers/how-to-prune-grape-vines.php (accessed April 22, 2010).

Chapter 8
Stand Against the Roaring Lion

1. *Barnes' Notes*, electronic database, PC Study Bible, version 3, copyright © 1997 by Biblesoft. All rights reserved.

Chapter 10
Evict the Enemy From Your House

1. Vine, *Vine's Expository Dictionary of New Testament Words*, 950.

2. Rollin McCraty, Bob Barrios-Choplin, Mike Atkinson, and Dana Tomasino, "The Effects of Different Types of Music on Mood, Tension, and Mental Clarity," *Alternative Therapies in Health and Medicine* 4, no. 1 (January 1998): 75–84, abstracted viewed at http://www.ncbi.nlm.nih.gov/pubmed/9439023 (accessed September 14, 2010).

3. Sara Kirkweg, "The Effects of Music on Memory," Department of Psychology, Missouri Western, http://clearinghouse.missouriwestern.edu/manuscripts/230.php (accessed April 27, 2010).

4. Jeremy Hsu, "Music-Memory Connection Found in Brain," LiveScience.com, http://www.livescience.com/health/090224-music-memory.html (accessed April 27, 2010).

5. T. C. N. Singh, "On the Effect of Music and Dance on Plants," *Bihar Agricultural College Magazine*, vol. 13, no. 1, 1962–1963, as referenced in http://maharishi-programmes.globalgoodnews.com/vedic-music/research.html (accessed August 10, 2010).

6. Robert Sylwester, "Massage And Music: A Brain Connection: Reader's Intriguing Commentary," BrainConnection.com, October 2006, http://brainconnection.positscience.com/content/240_1 (accessed August 10, 2010).

7. TempleInstitute.org, "The Festival of Sukkot," http://www.templeinstitute.org/tabernacles.htm (accessed April 27, 2010).

Chapter 13
Atmospheric Warfare—Full Moons and New Moons

1. Robert Roy Britt, "Full Moon Sends More Dogs and Cats to Emergency Room," LiveScience.com, July 15, 2007, http://www.livescience.com/animals/070715_moon_pets.html (accessed April 19, 2010).

2. David Rose, "The Moon's Effect on Natural Childbirth," ArticleAlley.com, September 15, 2005, http://www.articlealley.com/article_9078_28_html (accessed April 19, 2010).

3. The effect of the full moon on the human body is discussed in one University of Miami study done by Arnold Lieber and is discussed in John Townley, "Can the Full Moon Affect Human Behavior," InnerSelf.com, http://www.innerself.com/Astrology/full_moon.htm (accessed April 19, 2010).

4. "Moon Phases," http://home.hiwaay.net/~krcool/Astro/moon/moonphase/ (accessed April 19, 2010).

5. *Barnes' Notes*, electronic database, PC Study Bible, version 3, copyright © 1997 by Biblesoft. All rights reserved.

Chapter 14
Tapping Into the Spirit World

1. Karen Clickner, "Understanding the Horary Cycle of Healing," TheHerbalAdvisor.com, April 4, 2007, http://www.theherbaladvisor.com/The_Philosophy_of_Healing_29/Understanding_the_Horary_Cycle_of_Healing.shtml (accessed April 16, 2010).

2. Search results for "Morning Offerings," TempleInstitute.org, http://www.templeinstitute.org/search/index.php?query=morning+offerings&type=simple (accessed April 16, 2010).

3. Alfred Edersheim, *The Temple: Its Ministry and Services* (Peabody, MA: Hendrickson Publishers, 2005), 119.

MORE INSPIRING BOOKS FROM
PERRY STONE

Perry Stone brings his unique blend of Bible knowledge, prophecy, and spiritual insight to every topic he covers. If you were challenged and encouraged by *Purging Your House, Pruning Your Family Tree,* you will love his other releases:

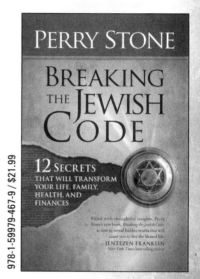

978-1-61638-157-8 / $15.99

978-1-59979-467-9 / $21.99

Exploring the unseen world of departed souls, Perry Stone covers heaven, hell, and eternity in this comprehensive look at the afterlife.

You can discover the hidden secrets that have molded Jewish thinking and lifestyles, making the Jews a blessed ethnic group and a nation that survives against all odds. Transform your life, family, health, and finances!

Available where fine
Christian books are sold

Charisma
HOUSE